PENGUIN PLAYS

# CHIPS WITH EVERYTHING

## THE FRIENDS

## THE OLD ONES

## LOVE LETTERS ON BLUE PAPER

Arnold Wesker, FRSL, Litt. D., was born in Stepney in 1932 and educated at Upton House School in Hackney. From 1948 to 1958 he pursued many trades from furniture maker to pastry cook. His career as a playwright began when Lindsay Anderson, who had read *The Kitchen* and *Chicken Soup with Barley*, brought Wesker to the attention of George Devine at the Royal Court Theatre; Devine sent *Chicken Soup with Barley* to the Belgrade Theatre in Coventry, where it was first produced in 1958, under the direction of John Dexter. A year later, having been turned down by the Royal Court, *Roots* was directed by Dexter, again at the Belgrade, Coventry, and in the following months he directed *The Kitchen* at the Court for two Sunday Night experimental performances 'without décor'. Later in 1959 *I'm Talking about Jerusalem* was added to make up *The Wesker Trilogy*, which created an enormous impact when produced in its entirety at the Royal Court in 1960 and again at the Shaw Theatre in 1978. In 1979 the National Film Development Board commissioned a film script of the three plays which, because Wesker made many cuts and additions, is a new work – *The Trilogy* twenty years on! Over 350,000 copies of the Penguin edition have been sold.

His other plays include *Their Very Own and Golden City* (1965; winner of the Italian Premio Matzotto Drama Award in 1964), *The Four Seasons* (1965), *The Journalists* (1972), *The Wedding Feast* (1974), *Shylock* (1975, previously entitled *The Merchant*), *One More Ride on the Merry-go-Round* (1978), *Caritas* (1980), *Annie Wobbler* (1981), *Four Portraits – of Mothers* (1982), *Bluey* (1984), *Yardsale* (1985), *Sullied Hand* (1985), *Whatever Happened to Betty Lemon?* (1986), *When God Wanted a Son* (1986), *Badenheim 1939* (1987), *Lady Othello* (1987), *Beorhtel's Hill* (1988, Community play commissioned for the 40th anniversary of Basildon) and *The Mistress* (1988). In addition to plays, Arnold Wesker has written poems, short stories and numerous articles. Among these are a collection of articles and fragments, *Fears of Fragmentation* (1970); *Six Sundays in January* (1971), including two stories; a diary; the libretto for a documentary, *The Nottingham Captain*; a TV play, *Menace*; a volume of short stories, *Love Letters on Blue Paper* (1974), the title story of which he adapted for his play of the same name; and a text for a book of primitive paintings by John Allin, *Say Goodbye You May Never See Them Again* (1974). He has also written an essay on education, *Words as Definitions of Experience* (1977); a personal account of a brief stay in *The Sun/ney into Journalism* (1977); a further

collection of short stories, *Said the Old Man to the Young Man* (1978); a book for children, *Fatlips* (1978); and a collection of essays, *Distinctions* (1984). Penguin has published five other volumes of his plays and his first collection of short stories, *Love Letters on Blue Paper*.

Arnold Wesker was artistic director of Centre 42, a cultural movement for popularizing the arts, primarily through trade-union support and participation, from 1961 to 1970. He lives with his wife and one of his three children in North London.

*Arnold Wesker*

# CHIPS WITH EVERYTHING

# THE FRIENDS

# THE OLD ONES

# LOVE LETTERS ON BLUE PAPER

## VOLUME 3

PENGUIN BOOKS

PENGUIN BOOKS

Published by the Penguin Group
27 Wrights Lane, London W8 5TZ, England
Viking Penguin Inc., 40 West 23rd Street, New York, New York 10010, USA
Penguin Books Australia Ltd, Ringwood, Victoria, Australia
Penguin Books Canada Ltd, 2801 John Street, Markham, Ontario, Canada L3R 1B4
Penguin Books (NZ) Ltd, 182–190 Wairau Road, Auckland 10, New Zealand

Penguin Books Ltd, Registered Offices: Harmondsworth, Middlesex, England

Chips With Everything first published by Jonathan Cape Ltd 1962
Copyright © Arnold Wesker, 1962
The Friends first published by Jonathan Cape Ltd 1970
Copyright © Arnold Wesker, 1970
The Old Ones first published in Plays and Players 1972
Published by Jonathan Cape Ltd 1973
Revised edition first published by Blackie & Sons Ltd 1974
Copyright © Arnold Wesker, 1972, 1974
Love Letters on Blue Paper first published by T. Q. Publications with the
Writers and Readers Publishing Cooperative 1978
Reprinted with minor revisions 1990
Copyright © Arnold Wesker, 1978, 1990

—

This collection first published in Penguin Books 1980
3 5 7 9 10 8 6 4 2
All rights reserved

—

The song 'The Cutty Wren', which appears on page 37, is reprinted from If I had a
song, a collection of children's songs published by the Workers' Music Association,
136A Westbourne Terrace, London W.2
The song that appears on page 104 was written by the author and set to music
(copyright © Wilfred Josephs, 1969) by Wilfred Josephs. Permission to use the music
must be obtained from London Management, 235 Regent Street, London, W.1.
The song 'Babylon', which appears on page 227, is reprinted by permission of
United Artists Music. It is recorded by Don McLean on United Artists label
UAS 292851.

—

Set, printed and bound in Great Britain by
Cox & Wyman Ltd, Reading
Set in Monotype Bembo

# CONTENTS

# CHIPS WITH EVERYTHING

First performed at the Royal Court Theatre 27 April 1962, directed by John Dexter, designed by Jocelyn Herbert, with the following cast:

| | |
|---|---|
| CORPORAL HILL | Frank Finlay |
| 239 CANNIBAL | George Innes |
| 252 WINGATE | Colin Campbell |
| 276 THOMPSON | John Kelland |
| 247 SEAFORD | Laurie Asprey |
| 284 MCCLURE | Alexander Balfour |
| 272 RICHARDSON | Colin Farrell |
| 277 COHEN | Hugh Futcher |
| 266 SMITH | John Bull |
| 279 WASHINGTON | Ronald Lacey |
| WING COMMANDER | Martin Boddey |
| SQUADRON LEADER | Robert Bruce |
| PILOT OFFICER | Corin Redgrave |
| P.T. INSTRUCTOR FLT SGT | Michael Goldie |
| RECRUIT | Peter Kelly |
| NIGHT GUARD | Bruce Heighley |
| FIRST CORPORAL | Roger Heathcott |
| SECOND CORPORAL | Michael Blackham |
| FIRST AIRMAN | Michael Craze |
| SECOND AIRMAN | Alan Stevens |

(This production contained more cast than was scripted for.)

# CHARACTERS

*Conscripts*

ARCHIE CANNIBAL 239
WINGATE (CHAS) 252
THOMPSON (PIP) 276
SEAFORD (WILFE) 247
ANDREW MCCLURE 284
RICHARDSON (GINGER) 272
COHEN (DODGER) 277
SMITH (DICKEY) 266
WASHINGTON (SMILER) 279

*Officers*

CORPORAL HILL
WING COMMANDER
SQUADRON LEADER
PILOT OFFICER
P.T. INSTRUCTOR, FLT SGT
GUARD

NIGHT CORPORAL
FIRST CORPORAL
SECOND CORPORAL
AIRMAN

# ACT ONE

## SCENE ONE

*An R.A.F. hut.*

[*Nine new conscripts enter. They are subdued, uncertain, mumbling.* CORPORAL HILL *appears at door, stocky, Northern, collarless man. He waits till they notice him, which they gradually do till mumbling ceases, utterly – they rise to attention. After a long pause*]

HILL: That's better. In future, whenever an N.C.O. comes into the hut, no matter who he is, the first person to see him will call out 'N.C.O.! N.C.O.!' like that. And whatever you're doing, even if you're stark bollock naked, you'll all spring to attention as fast as the wind from a duck's arse, and by Christ that's fast. Is that understood? [*No reply.*] Well is it? [*A few murmurs.*] When I ask a question I expect an answer. [*Emphatically*] Is that understood!

ALL [*shouting*]: Yes, Corporal!

HILL: Anyone been in the Air Cadets? Any of the cadets? Anyone twenty-one or more then? Nineteen? [*Two boys,* ANDREW *and* DICKEY, *raise their hands. To one*] Month you were born?

ANDREW: July, Corporal.

DICKEY: May, Corporal.

HILL [*to* DICKEY]: You're senior man. [*To* ANDREW] You're assistant. Shift your kit to top of hut. Not now – later.

[HILL *scrutinizes the rest. He lays his hand on the two smallest –* DODGER *and* GINGER.]

These small boys, these two, they're my boys. They'll do the jobs I ask them when I ask them; not much, my fires each day, perhaps my bunk – my boys. But they won't do my polishing – I do that myself. No one is to start on them, no one is to bully them, if they do, then they answer to me. [*Pause.*] You can sit now.

[*Reads out list of names, each recruit rises and sits as called. Boys sit on their beds, waiting;* HILL *paces up and down, waiting his time. Then*]

Right, you're in the R.A.F. now, you're not at home. This hut, this place here, this is going to be your home for the next eight scorching weeks. This billet here, you see it? This? It's in a state now, no one's been in it for the last four days so it's in a state now. [*Pause.*] But usually it's like a scorching palace! [*Pause.*] That's the way I want it to be cos that's the way it's always been. Now you've got to get to know me. My name is Corporal Hill. I'm not a very happy man, I don't know why. I never smile and I never joke – you'll soon see that. Perhaps it's my nature, perhaps it's the way I've been brought up – I don't know. The R.A.F. brought me up. You're going to go through hell while you're here, through scorching hell. Some of you will take it and some of you will break down. I'm warning you – some of you shall end up crying. And when that happens I don't want to see anyone laughing at him. Leave him alone, don't touch him.

But I'll play fair. You do me proud and I'll play fair. The last lot we 'ad 'ere 'ad a good time, a right time, a right good scorching time. We 'ad bags o' fun, bags o' it. But I will tear and mercilessly scratch the scorching daylights out of anyone who smarts the alec with me – and we've got some 'ere. I can see them, you can tell them. I count three already, you can tell them, by their faces, who know it all, the boys who think they're GOOD. [*Whispered*] It'll be unmerciful and scorching murder for them – all. Now, you see this wireless here, this thing with knobs and a pretty light that goes on and off? Well that's ours, our wireless for this hut, and for this hut only because this hut has always been the best hut. No other hut has a wireless. I want to keep that. I like music and I want to keep that wireless. Some people, when they get up in the morning, first thing all they want to do is smoke, or drink tea – not me, I've got to have music, the noise of instruments.

Everyone's got a fad, that's mine, music, and I want to be spoilt, you see to it that I'm spoilt. Right, if there's anyone here who wants to leave my hut and go into another because he doesn't like this 'un, then do it now, please. Go on, pick up your kit and move. I'll let 'im. [*No movement.*] You can go to the Naafi now. But be back by ten thirty, cos that's bleedin' lights out. [*Moves to door, pauses.*] Anyone object to swearing? [*No reply. Exit.*]

[*Stunned. A boy rushes in from another hut.*]

BOY: What's your'n say?

SMILER [*imitating*]: My name is Corporal Hill, I'm not a happy man.

BOY [*imitating a Scotsman*]: My name is Corporal Bridle – and I'm a bastard!


## SCENE TWO

*The Naafi.*

　　[*One boy strumming a guitar*]

WILFE:　　　Dear mother come and fetch me
　　　　　　Dear mother take me home
　　　　　　I'm drunk and unhappy
　　　　　　And my virginity's gone.

　　　　　　My feet are sore and I'm weary
　　　　　　The sergeant looks like dad
　　　　　　Oh, a two bob bit would buy me a nip
　　　　　　And a Naafi girl in my bed.
　　　　　　Now Eskimo Nell has gone back to the land
　　　　　　Where they know how to – Eight weeks!
　　　　　　EIGHT STUPID WEEKS, MOTHER!

CHAS: I've left two girls at home, two of them, and I've declared passionate love to them both – both. Poor girls, promised I'd marry them when it was all over. They'll miss me.

WILFE: Wouldn't be so bad if my mother could hear me, but she's as deaf as a bat.

PIP: Bats are blind.

WILFE: Oh dear me, bats are blind, deary, deary me fellows.

PIP: Look old son, you're going to have me for eight painful weeks in the same hut, so spend the next five minutes taking the mickey out of my accent, get it off your chest and then put your working-class halo away because no one's going to care – O.K.?

CHAS: Where are you from then?

PIP: My father is a banker, we idolize each other. I was born in a large country house and I'm scorching rich.

CHAS: You're going to do officer training then?

PIP: No! My father was also a general!

WILFE: Oh my father was a general
  And I'm a general's son
  But I got wise to the old man's lies
  And kicked him up his you know, you
  know, you know, you know what I mean.
  Now Eskimo Nell has gone back to the land –
  EIGHT STUPID WEEKS, MOTHER!

SMILER: Give over, Wilfe, give over.

GINGER: Well roll on Christmas, roll on I say.

DODGER: So what then? You'll be back after four days, and then four more weeks of this –

GINGER: But I'll be married.

DODGER: You'll be what?

GINGER: I'm getting married two weeks from tomorrow –

CHAS: Bleedin' daft to get married. I got two girls back home, one's blonde and one's dark – it's the Jekyll and Hyde in me. Married? Bleedin' daft!

PIP: You mean you can actually think of better things to do than produce babies?

CHAS: You shut your classical mouth you, go away, 'oppit! 'Oppit or I'll lay you down. I haven't liked you from the start.

PIP: Oh sit down, there's a good boy, I wouldn't dream of fighting you.

SMILER: You don't mind being a snob, do you?

PIP: One day, when I was driving to my father's office, the car broke down. I could have got a taxi I suppose, but I didn't. I walked. The office was in the City, so I had to walk through the East End, strange – I don't know why I should have been surprised. I'd seen photographs of this Mecca before – I even used to glance at the *Daily Mirror* now and then, so God knows why I should have been surprised. Strange. I went into a café and drank a cup of tea from a thick, white, cracked cup and I ate a piece of tasteless currant cake. On the walls I remember they had photographs of boxers, auto-graphed, and they were curling at the edges from the heat. Every so often a woman used to come to the table and wipe it with a rag that left dark streaks behind which dried up into weird patterns. Then a man came and sat next to me – WHY should I have been surprised? I'd seen his face before, a hundred times on the front pages of papers reporting a strike. A market man, a porter, or a docker. No, he was too old to be a docker. His eyes kept watering, and each time they did that he'd take out a neatly folded handkerchief, unfold it and, with one corner, he'd wipe away the moisture, and then he'd neatly fold it up again and replace it in his pocket. Four times he did that, and each time he did it he looked at me and smiled. I could see grains of dirt in the lines of his face, and he wore an old waistcoat with pearl buttons. He wasn't untidy, the cloth even seemed a good cloth, and though his hair was thick with oil it was clean. I can even remember the colour of the walls, a pastel pink on the top half and turquoise blue on the bottom, peeling. Peeling in fifteen different places; actually, I counted them. But what I couldn't understand was why I should have been so surprised. It wasn't as though I had been cradled in my childhood. And then I saw the menu, stained with tea and beautifully written by a foreign hand, and on top it said – God I hated that old man – it said 'Chips with everything'. Chips with every damn thing. You breed babies and you eat chips with everything.

[*Enter* HILL.]

HILL: I said ten thirty lights out, didn't I? Ten thirty I said. I want to see you move to that hut like wind from a duck's behind –

WILFE: And O Jesus mother, that's fast mother, that's eight weeks and that's fast!

HILL: That's fast, that's fast, into the hut and move that fast. Into the hut, into the hut, in, in, into the hut. [*Looks at watch. Pause.*] Out! I'll give you . . .


## SCENE THREE

*Parade Ground: morning.*

HILL: Out! I'll give you sixty seconds or you'll be on a charge, one, two, three, four – come on out of that hut, twenty-five, twenty-six, twenty-seven, twenty-eight. AT THE DOUBLE! Now get into a line and stop that talking, get into a line. A straight line you heaving nig-nogs, a straight line.

This is the square. We call it a square-bashing square. I want to see you bash that square. Right, now the first thing you've got to know, you've got to know how to come to attention, how to stand at ease and easy, how to make a right turn and how to step off.

Now to come to attention you move smartly, very smartly, to this position: heels together. STOP THAT! When I was born I was very fortunate, I was born with eyes in the back of my neck and don't be cheeky. Legs apart and wait till I give the command SHUN. When I give the command SHUN, you will move sharply, very sharply, to this position. Heels together and in a line, feet turned out to angle of thirty degrees, knees braced, body erect and with the weight balanced evenly between the balls of the feet and the heels.

Shoulders down and back level and square to the front.

Arms hanging straight from the shoulders.

Elbows close to the sides.

Wrists straight.

Hands closed – not clenched.

Back of the fingers close to the thighs.

Thumbs straight and to the front, close to the forefinger and just behind the seam of the trousers. Head up, chin in, eyes open, steady and looking just above their own height. Come on now, heels together, body erect and evenly balanced between the balls of the feet and the heels – you didn't know you had balls on your feet did you – well you have, use them.

Stand up straight there – keep your mouth shut and your eyes open and to the front. Right, well, you are now standing – somewhat vaguely – in the position of the attention.

To stand at ease you keep the right foot still and carry the left foot to the left so that the feet are about – do it with me – so that the feet are about twelve inches apart. At the same time force the arms behind the back, keeping them straight, and place the back of the right hand in the palm of the left, thumbs crossed, fingers and hands straight and pointing towards the ground. At the same time transfer the weight of the body slightly to the left so as to be evenly balanced. Keep your arms straight and don't bend at the waist. [*Inspects them.*] Right hand inside your left, *your* left not his. Try to make your elbows meet.

When you hear me give the command SQUAD, I want you to jump to that position, smarten up, as if you were going somewhere. We'll try it – stand easy, relax, just relax, but keep your hands behind your back, don't slouch, don't move your feet and don't talk – just relax, let your head look down, RELAX! IF YOU DON'T RELAX I'LL PUT YOU ON A CHARGE!

Squad, squad – SHUN! As you were, I want you to do it together. Squad – SHUN! As you were. Squad – SHUN! STAND AT EASE!

To make a Right Turn: keeping both knees straight, turn through ninety degrees to the right swivelling on the heel of the right foot and the toe of the left raising the toe of the right and the heel of the left in doing so. Keeping the weight of the body on the right foot on completion of this movement the right foot is flat on the ground, the left leg to the rear and the heel raised – both knees braced back and the body in the position of attention. Bring the left foot into the right, good and hard, and for the time being I want that left knee good and high, slam your foot in good and hard and keep still.

Squad, squad – SHUN.

Turning to the right – RIGHT TURN.

All right you creepy-crawly nig-nogs, moon men that's what you are, moon men. I want it done together. As you were.

Squad, turning to the right – RIGHT TURN.

Now, to Step Off. When I say by the front – quick march, I don't want your pretty left foot forward anyways, like this, no, it's got to be scorching smart, like a flash of greased lightning. ONE! Like this [*Petrified stance of a man about to step off.*] ONE! Like that, and I want that left hand up as high as you can get it and your right level with your breast pocket.

Now, on the word – MARCH – I want you only to take a step forward, *not* to march. I want you only to take a step forward, just pretend, got that? Some dimwitted piece of merchandise is sure to carry on. Now then, watch it. SQUAD – by the front – quick MARCH!

[*Sure enough two boys march off and collide with those standing still, and one in the front marches off out of sight.*]

Stop that laughing. I'll charge the next man I see smile.

[*Stands, watching the other one disappear.*]

All right, Horace, come back home. [*Airman returns, sheepishly.*] You nit, you nit, you creepy-crawly nit. Don't you hear, don't you listen, can't you follow simple orders, CAN'T YOU? Shut up! Don't answer back! A young man like you, first thing in the morning, don't be rude, don't be rude. No one's being rude to you.

Stop that laughing. I'll charge the next man I see smile. [*To Smiler*] You, I said wipe off that smile. I said wipe it off.

SMILER: I'm not smiling, Corporal, it's natural, I was born with it.

HILL: Right then, don't ever let me see that face frown or I'll haul you over the highest wall we've got. [*Approaching one of the two marching ones*] You. If you'd been paying attention you might 'ave done it correctly, eh? But you weren't, you were watching the little aeroplanes, weren't you? You want to fly? Do you want to reach the thundering heavens, my little lad, at an earlier age than you imagined, with Technicolor wings? KEEP YOUR EYES ON ME. [*To all*] You better know from the start, you can have it the hard way or you can have it the easy way, I don't mind which way it is. Perhaps you like it the hard way, suits me. Just let me know. At ease everyone. Now, we'll try and make it easier for you. We'll count our way along. We'll count together, and then maybe we'll all act together. I want everything to be done together. We're going to be the happiest family in Christendom and we're going to move together, as one, as one solitary man. So, when I say 'attention' you'll slam your feet down hard and cry 'one'. Like this. And when I say 'right turn' you'll move and bang your foot down and cry 'one-pause-two'. Like this. Is that clear? Is that beyond the intellectual comprehensibilities of any of you? Good! SQUAD – wait for it – atten-SHUN!

SQUAD: ONE!

HILL: As you were, at ease. Did I say slam? Didn't I say slam? Don't worry about the noise, it's a large square, no one will mind. Squad – atten-SHUN.

SQUAD: ONE!

HILL: As you were. Let's hear that 'one'. Let's have some energy from you. I want GOD to hear you crying 'ONE, ONE, ONE – pause TWO!' Squad – atten-SHUN!

SQUAD: ONE!

HILL: Right TURN!

SQUAD: ONE – pause – TWO!

HILL: By the left – quick – MARCH!

[*The boys march off round the stage, sound of marching and the chanting of* 'One, One, One – pause – Two! One, One, One – pause – Two!']

## SCENE FOUR

*Sound of marching feet. Marching stops. The lecture hall.*
[*Boys enter and sit on seats. Enter the* WING COMMANDER, *boys rise.*]

WING COMMANDER: Sit down, please. I'm your Wing Commander. You think we are at peace. Not true. We are never at peace. The human being is in a constant state of war and we must be prepared, each against the other. History has taught us this and we must learn. The reasons why and wherefore are not our concern. We are simply the men who must be prepared. You, why do you look at me like that?

PIP: I'm paying attention, sir.

WING COMMANDER: There's insolence in those eyes, lad – I recognize insolence in a man; take that glint out of your eyes, your posh tones don't fool me. We are simply the men who must be prepared. Already the aggressors have a force far superior to ours. Our efforts must be intensified. We need a fighting force and it is for this reason you are being trained here, according to the best traditions of the R.A.F. We want you to be proud of your part, unashamed of the uniform you wear. But you must not grumble too much if you find that government facilities for you, personally, are not up to standard. We haven't the money to spare. A Meteor, fully armed, is more important than a library. The C.O. of this camp is called Group Captain Watson. His task is to check any tendency in his officers to practical jokes, to discountenance any disposition in his officers to gamble or to indulge in extravagant expenditure; to endeavour, by example and timely intervention, to promote a good understanding and prevent disputes. Group Captain Watson is a busy man, you will rarely see him. You, why are you smiling?

SMILER: I'm not, sir, it's natural. I was born like it.

WING COMMANDER: Because I want this taken seriously, you know, from all of you. Any questions?

WILFE: Sir, if the aggressors are better off than us, what are they waiting for?

WING COMMANDER: What's your name?

WILFE: 247 Seaford, sir.

WING COMMANDER: Any other questions?

[*Exit. Enter* SQUADRON LEADER. *The boys rise.*]

SQUADRON LEADER: Sit down, please. I'm your squadron leader. My task is not only to ensure respect for authority, but also to foster the feelings of self-respect and personal honour which are essential to efficiency. It is also my task to bring to notice those who, from incapacity or apathy, are deficient in knowledge of their duties, or who do not afford an officer that support which he has a right to expect or who conduct themselves in a manner injurious to the efficiency or credit of the R.A.F. You are here to learn discipline. Discipline is necessary if we are to train you to the maximum state of efficiency, discipline and obedience. You will obey your instructors because they are well trained, you will obey them because they can train you efficiently, you will obey them because it's necessary for you to be trained efficiently. That is what you are here to learn: obedience and discipline. Any questions? Thank you.

[*Exit. Enter* PILOT OFFICER. *The boys rise.*]

PILOT OFFICER: Sit down please. I'm your pilot officer. You'll find that I'm amenable and that I do not stick rigidly to authority. All I shall require is cleanliness. It's not that I want rigid men, I want clean men. It so happens, however, that you cannot have clean men without rigid men, and cleanliness requires smartness and ceremony. Ceremony means your webbing must be blancoed, and smartness means that your brass – all of it – must shine like silver paper, and your huts must be spick and span without a trace of dust, because dust carries germs, and germs are unclean. I want a man clean from toe nail to hair root. I want him so clean that he looks unreal. In fact I don't want real men, real men are dirty and nasty, they pick their noses – and scratch their skin. I want unreal, super-real men. Those men win wars, the others die of disease before they reach the battlefields. Any questions? You, what are you smiling at?

SMILER: I'm not, sir, it's natural. I was born like that.

PILOT OFFICER: In between the lines of that grin are formed battalions of microbes. Get rid of it.

SMILER: I can't, sir.

PILOT OFFICER: Then never let me hear of you going sick.

[*Exit. Enter* P.T. INSTRUCTOR, FLIGHT SERGEANT.]

P.T.I.: As you were. I'm in charge of physical training on this camp. It's my duty to see that every minute muscle in your body is awake. Awake and ringing. Do you hear that? That's poetry! I want your body awake and ringing. I want you so light on your feet that the smoke from a cigarette could blow you away, and yet so strong that you stand firm before hurricanes. I hate thin men and detest fat ones. I want you like Greek gods. You heard of the Greeks? You ignorant troupe of anaemics, you were brought up on tinned beans and television sets, weren't you? You haven't had any exercise since you played knock-a-down-ginger, have you? Greek gods, you hear me? Till the sweat pours out of you like Niagara Falls. Did you hear that poetry? Sweat like Niagara Falls! I don't want your stupid questions!

[*Exit.*]

PIP: You have babies, you eat chips and you take orders.

CHAS: Well, look at you then, I don't see you doing different.

[*They march off. Sound of marching feet.*]

23

## SCENE FIVE

*Sound of marching feet and the men counting. The hut. Billet inspection.*
  [ANDREW, *the hut orderly, tidying up. Enter the* PILOT OFFICER]

ANDREW [*saluting*]: Good morning, sir.
PILOT OFFICER: Haven't you been told the proper way to address an
  officer?
ANDREW: Sorry sir, no sir, not yet sir.
  [PILOT OFFICER *walks around.* ANDREW *follows awkwardly.*]
PILOT OFFICER: There's dust under that bed.
ANDREW: Is there, sir?
PILOT OFFICER: I said so.
ANDREW: Yes, you did, sir.
PILOT OFFICER: Then why ask me again?
ANDREW: Again, sir?
PILOT OFFICER: Didn't you?
ANDREW: Didn't I what, sir?
PILOT OFFICER: Ask me to repeat what I'd already said. Are you
  playing me up, Airman? Are you taking the mickey out of me?
  I can charge you, man. I can see your game and I can charge you.
ANDREW: Yes, you can, sir.
PILOT OFFICER: Don't tell me what I already know.
ANDREW: Oh, I wouldn't, sir – you know what you already know.
  I know that, sir.
PILOT OFFICER: I think you're a fool, Airman. God knows why the
  Air Ministry sends us fools. They never select, select is the answer,
  select and pick those out from the others.
ANDREW: What others, sir?
PILOT OFFICER: Don't question me!
ANDREW: But I was only thinking of –
PILOT OFFICER: You aren't paid to think, Airman, don't you know
  that? You aren't paid to think. [*Long pause.*] No, it's no good trying
  that line. [*Sits.*] Why pretend? I don't really frighten you, do I?
  I don't really frighten you, but you obey my orders, nevertheless.

24

It's a funny thing. We have always ruled, but I suspect we've never frightened you. I know that as soon as I turn my back you'll merely give me a V sign and make a joke of me to the others, won't you? And they'll laugh. Especially Thompson. He knows you're not frightened, that's why he's in the ranks. But I'll break him. Slumming, that's all he's doing, slumming. What's your name?

ANDREW: Andrew McClure, sir.

PILOT OFFICER: I don't suppose Thompson's really slumming. There *is* something about you boys, confidence, I suppose, or cockiness, something trustworthy anyway. I can remember enjoying the Naafi more than I do the Officers' Mess. What was your job?

ANDREW: Electrician, sir.

PILOT OFFICER: My father was an electrician. He used to play the piano. He really played beautifully. Tragic – my God – it was tragic.

ANDREW: Had an accident, sir?

PILOT OFFICER: That would be your idea of tragedy, wouldn't it? My father never had that sort of accident; he couldn't, he owned the factory he worked for. It's the other things that happen to people like him. The intangible accidents. No, his fingers remained subtle till he died, and he touched the keys with love whenever he could, but no one heard him. That was the tragedy, Andrew. No one heard him except – four uncaring children and a stupid wife who saw no sense in it. God, Andrew, how I envied that man. I could have bought so much love with that talent. People don't give love away that easily, only if we have magic in our hands or in our words or in our brush then they pay attention, then they love us. You can forget your own troubles in an artist's love, Andrew; you can melt away from what you were and grow into a new man. Haven't you ever wanted to be a new man? [*Places hand on* MCCLURE's *knee in a friendly gesture.*]

ANDREW: Don't do that, please, sir.

PILOT OFFICER [*contemptuous that his friendly gesture was misread*]: Don't ever rely on th is conversation, don't ever trust me to be your friend. I shall no t merely frighten you, there are other ways – and you will need all yo ur pity for yourself. I warn you not to be fooled by good nature, we slum for our own convenience.

[*Enter a* FLIGHT SERGEANT.]

FLIGHT SERGEANT: When is – I beg your pardon, sir.

PILOT OFFICER: You can take over now, Flight. [*Exit.*]

FLIGHT SERGEANT: When is this place going to be straight?

ANDREW: Pardon, Sergeant?

FLIGHT SERGEANT: *Flight* Sergeant!

ANDREW: Sorry, FLIGHT Sergeant.

FLIGHT SERGEANT: When is this place going to be straight, I asked?

ANDREW: I've just straightened it, Serg – er Flight – er Flight Sergeant.

FLIGHT SERGEANT: You what? If I come in here tomorrow and I can't eat my dinner off that floor I'll have you all outside on fatigues till midnight. Have you got that?

ANDREW: Yes, Flight Sergeant.

FLIGHT SERGEANT: Well, keep it. Tight! Tight! Tight, tight –

['Tight, tight, tight', *mixes to sounds of marching feet, men counting.*]


## SCENE SIX

*The billet at night. The boys are tired. Beds are being made, brasses, shoes, webbing attended to.*

ANDREW: And then he says: 'I shall not merely frighten you, there are other ways, and you will need all your pity for yourself.' Man, I tell you it was him was frightened. A tall meek thing he is, trying to impress me.

HILL: It's not him you want to be frightened of, it's royalty. Royalty! I hate royalty more than anything else in the world. Parasites! What do they do, eh? I'm not in this outfit for them, no bloody fear, it's the people back 'ome I'm here for, like you lot. Royalty –

PIP: Good old Corporal Hill, they've made you chase red herrings, haven't they?

ANDREW: And he had something to say about you too, Pip Thompson. He said you were slumming, laddie, slumming; he said: 'Thompson knows you're not frightened, that's why he's in the ranks – but he's slumming.'

PIP: So he thinks you're not frightened? He's right – you're not, are you? But there *are* other ways – he's right about that too.

DODGER: You know, I've been looking at this hut, sizing it up. Make a good warehouse.

GINGER: A good what?

DODGER: Warehouse. It's my mania. My family owns a pram shop, see, and our one big problem is storage. Prams take up room, you know. Always on the look-out for storage space. Every place I look at I work out the cubic feet, and I say it will make a good warehouse or it won't. Can't help myself. One of the best warehouses I ever see was the Vatican in Rome. What you laughing at? You take a carpenter – what does he do when he enters – what does he do when he enters a room, eh? Ever thought about that? He feels how the door swings open, looks straight across to the window to see if the frame is sitting straight and then sits in the chair to see if it's made good – then he can settle down to enjoy the evening. With me it's pregnant women. Every time I see pregnant women I get all maternal. You can have your women's breasts all you want and her legs. *Me*, only one spot interests me – one big belly and we've made a sale. Can't help it – warehouses and pregnant women.

DICKEY: Hey, Cannibal my dear associate, what are you so engrossed in?

CANNIBAL: It's a book about ideal marriage, now leave me be.

DICKEY: Why you dirty-minded adolescent you – put it away.

DODGER: Here, let's have a read.

[*He and some others crowd round to read on.*]

PIP: 252 WINGATE! – give me a hand with this bed, will you, please.

CHAS: Why I bloody help you I don't know, not at all I don't.

PIP: Because you like me, that's why.

CHAS: *Like* you? Like *you*? You're the lousiest rotten snob I know.

PIP: And you like snobs.

CHAS: Boy, I hate you so much it hurts. You can't even make a bed properly.

PIP: It was always made for me.

CHAS: There you go. See what I mean. Boasting of your bleedin' wealth and comfort. Well, I don't want to know about your stinking comforts, don't tell me, I don't want to hear.

PIP: Oh, yes you do. You love to hear me talk about my home. We have a beautiful home, Charles, twenty-four rooms, and they're all large and thick with carpets.

CHAS: Modern?

PIP: No, built in the time of George III.

CHAS: I don't want to know.

PIP: They started to build it in 1776 when George Washington was made commander-in-chief of the American colonists and the great-grandfathers of the Yanks were issuing the Declaration of Independence. A jubilant period, Charles – exciting. Did you know that while my great-great-grandfather was trading with the East India Company in the land of the strange chocolate people, bringing home the oriental spoils, the American grandfathers were still struggling to control a vast land at a time when there was no communication? But they didn't struggle long. Each time my great-grandfather came home he heard more bad news about those traitorous Americans. Returning from India in 1830, with a cargo of indigo, he heard, twenty-three years after everyone else, that the steamboat had been invented. Terrible news. Returning in 1835 with a cargo of teak they told him about the strange iron horse that ran on wheels. Terrible, terrible, news. Returning in 1840 with a cargo of coriander he was so enraged that he refused to believe it possible to send messages through the air, and so he died without ever believing in the magic of telegraph. What do you think of that, Charles boy? Still, my favourite relative was his father, a beautiful boy, the kind of boy that every aunt wanted to mother and every cousin wanted to marry. The only thing was he was incredibly stupid, much more than you, Charles, and strangely enough he was called Charles also. My family talk about him to this very day. You see, the fact was that very few people ever realized he was so stupid because he was such a handsome boy and very rarely spoke. And because of his silence everyone thought he was very wise, and this was so effective that he increased our family fortune by double. [*Nearly everyone is listening to him by now.*] You want to know how? Well it was like this. Shortly after the shock of losing America, the English were disturbed by another event – another shock that rocked the whole of Europe and set my family and all their friends shaking. One day, the French kings and princes found themselves bankrupt – the royalty and the clergy never used to pay any taxes, you see they left that on the shoulders of the middle class and the commoners, and yet they still managed to become bankrupt. So what did they do? They called a meeting of all the representatives of all the classes to see what could be done – there hadn't been such a meeting for over a century, what a party! What a mistake! because, for the first time in a long while, the commoners not only found a means of voicing their discontent over the paying of taxes, but they suddenly looked at themselves and realized that there were more of them than they ever imagined – and they weren't fools. Now, they voiced themselves well, and so loudly that they won a victory, and not simply over the tax problem, but over a dozen and one other injustices as well. Big excitement, jubilation, victory! In fact, they found themselves so victorious and so powerful that they were able to cut off the heads of poor Louis XVI and Marie Antoinette and start what we all know as the French Revolution.

CHAS: What about Charlie, the silly one?

PIP: Patience, my handsome boy, don't hurry me. Now, my family had a lot of interest in France and its royalty, so they decided to send this beautiful boy out to see what was happening to their estates and fortunes. And do you think he did? Poor soul, he couldn't understand what the hell was happening. The royalty of all Europe was trembling because of what the French did to Louis and Marie, and he just thought he was being sent on a holiday. To this day we none of us know how he escaped with his life – but, not only did he escape with his life, he also came back with somebody else's life. A French princess! And would you believe it, she was also a simpleton, a sort of prototype deb with a dimple on her left cheek. Her family had given her all their jewels, thinking that no one would touch her, since she was so helpless, and indeed no one did. No one, that is, except our Charles. He met her on his way to Paris in a Franciscan monastery and asked her to teach him French. There were her relatives being beheaded one by one and there was she, chanting out the past tense of the verb 'to be'. You can guess the rest, within four weeks he was back in England with a lovely bride and four hundred thousand pounds'-worth of jewellery. They built a new wing to the house and had seven children. The rooms glitter with her chandeliers, Charlie boy – and – well, just look at the way your mouth is gaping – you'll get lockjaw.

HILL: Don't you tell stories, eh? Don't you just. I bet you made that one up as you went along.

PIP: That's right, Corporal, the French Revolution was a myth.

CHAS: Tell us more, Pip, tell us more stories.

PIP: They're not stories, Charlie boy, they're history.

CHAS: Well, tell us more then.

PIP: What's the use?

CHAS: I'm asking you, that's what's the use. *I'm asking you.*

[PIP *picks up his webbing to blanco. The others withdraw and pick up what they were doing.* CHARLIE *is left annoyed and frustrated.* HILL *takes a seat next to the fire and plays a mouth-organ. In between sounds he talks.*]

HILL: I was pleased with you lads today. You're coming on. When you did those last about turns I felt proud. You might even be better than the last lot we had. Know that? And by Christ that last lot were good. But there's one of you needs to buck up his ideas, shan't mention names.

SMILER: I try, Corporal.

HILL: Well, you want to try harder, my son. Look at you.

SMILER: I look at myself every day, Corporal.

HILL: That stupid smile of yours, if only you didn't smile so much. Can't you have an operation or something? I'll go bleedin' mad looking at that for another five weeks.

DODGER: Oh, my gawd, listen to this! Listen what it says here. 'Between two hundred and three hundred million spermatozoa are released at one time of which only one succeeds in fertilizing the female ovum.' Jesus! All them prams!

GINGER: Give us a good tune, Corp, go on.

HILL: You're my treasure, aren't you, eh, Ginger lad? Don't know what I'd do without you. What shall I play for you, you name it, I'll play it.

GINGER: Play us the 'Rose of Tralee'.

HILL: You want the 'Rose of Tralee', my beauty? You shall have it then.

[CORPORAL HILL *plays, the boys rest, work, write letters, and listen.*]

GINGER: When's the Christmas Eve party?

DODGER: Tomorrow a week, isn't it?

HILL: Uh-huh.

[*Continue sound of mouth-organ – change to*]


## SCENE SEVEN

*The Naafi. Christmas Eve Party.*

[*The rock-'n-'roll group play vigorously. The boys jiving, drinking, and singing. Officers are present.*]


WING COMMANDER: Look at them. Conscripts! They bring nothing and they take nothing. Look at them. Their wild dancing and their silly words – I could order them at this moment to stand up and be shot and they'd do it.

SQUADRON LEADER: You're drinking too much, Sid.

WING COMMANDER: Civilians! How I hate civilians. They don't know – what do they know? How to make money, how to chase girls and kill old women. No order, no purpose. Conscripts! They bring their muddled lives and they poison us, Jack; they poison me with their indifference, and all we do is guard their fat bellies. I'd sacrifice a million of them for the grace of a Javelin Fighter, you know that?

SQUADRON LEADER: Don't let them see you scowl. Smile, man, smile. It's a Christmas Eve party. We're guests here.

SMILER [*to* WILFE]: Go and offer the Wing Commander a drink, then, go on.

WILFE: Leave off, will you, man? All evening you have been pestering me. What do I want to go giving officers drinks for?

SMILER: Go up to him and say 'with the compliments of our hut, sir', go on.

WILFE: I'll pour a bottle on you soon if you don't leave off.

SMILER: Your fly button's undone.

WILFE: Where? Smiler, I'll bash you – you tantalize me any more this evening and I'll bash that grin right down to your arse, so help me, I will.

SMILER: Listen to him. Wilfe the warrior. Do you talk like this at home? Does your mummy let you?

WILFE: Now why do you talk to me like that? Why do you go on and on and on? Do I start on you like that? Take this away, will you boys, take him away and drown him.

SMILER: Go after one of them Naafi girls, go on, Wilfe. Go and find out if they're willing.

CANNIBAL: Naafi girls! Camp bloody whores, that's all they are.

DICKEY: Well, he's woken up. Cannibal has spoken, come on, me ole cocker, say more.

CANNIBAL: Who's for more drinks?

DICKEY: Good old Cannibal! He uttered a syllable of many dimensions. The circumlocircle of his mouth has moved. Direct yourself to the bar, old son, and purchase for us some brown liquid. We shall make merry with your generosity.

CANNIBAL: I don't know where he gets the words from. He lies in his bed next to me and he talks and he talks and he sounds like an adding-machine.

DICKEY: You're under-educated, my old son – you're devoid of knowledgeable grey matter. You should've gone to a technical school like me; we sat in study there and ate up books for our diluted pleasure. We developed voluble minds in that technical college and we came away equipped with data. Data! That's the ticket – the sum total of everything. Direct your attention to the bar I say, and deliver us of that inebriating liquid, my hearty.

CANNIBAL: Ask him what he means. Go on, someone! I don't know. He lies on his bed next to me and he talks and he mumbles and talks and he mumbles. One night he woke up and he shouted: 'Kiss me, Mother, kiss your dying son.'

DICKEY: You lie in your teeth, O dumb one. Buy the drinks.

CANNIBAL: And another night he crept up to me and he was crying. 'Let me in your bed,' he moaned, 'let me get near you, you're big and warm.'

DICKEY: You're lying, Cannibal. Don't let me hear more of your lies.

CANNIBAL: Shall I tell them how you pray at night?

[DICKEY *throws his beer over* CANNIBAL *and they fight.*]

WING COMMANDER: Separate those men! Hold them! Stop that, you two, you hear me, an order, stop that! [*They are separated.*] Undisciplined hooligans! I won't have fighting in my camp. Is this the only way you can behave with drink in you? Is it? Show your upbringing in your own home where it grew but not here, you hear me? Not here! This is Christmas Eve. A party, a celebration for the birth of our Lord, a time of joy and good will. Show me good will then. I will not, will not, will not tolerate your slum methods here. This is a clean force, a clean blue force. Go to your huts, stay there, stay there for the rest of the evening and don't wander beyond ten feet of your door. Disobey that order and I shall let out the hell of my temper so hard that you'll do jankers the rest of your National Service.

[DICKEY *and* CANNIBAL *leave. On the way,* DICKEY *trips over, and* CANNIBAL *helps him to his feet.*]

WING COMMANDER: They don't even fight seriously – a few loud words, and then they kiss each other's wounds. God give us automation soon.

SQUADRON LEADER: You suffer too much, Sid.

WING COMMANDER: Nonsense! And forget your theories about my unhappy childhood. Mine is a healthy and natural hatred.

SQUADRON LEADER: I haven't time to hate – it takes me all my time to organize them.

WING COMMANDER: Look at them. What are they? The good old working class of England. Am I supposed to bless them all the time for being the salt of the earth?

SQUADRON LEADER: They provide your food, they make your clothes, dig coal, mend roads for you.

WING COMMANDER: Given half the chance you think they would? For me? Look at them, touching the heights of ecstasy.

PIP: They're talking about us – the officers.

CHAS: What are they saying?

PIP: They're saying we're despicable, mean, and useless. That fight disturbed the Wing Commander – we upset him.

ANDREW: Don't say 'we' and imagine that makes you one of us, Pip.

PIP: Don't start on me, Andy, fhere's a good man.

ANDREW: Don't do us any favours.

PIP: I don't have to drop my aitches in order to prove friendship, do I?

ANDREW: No. No, you don't. Only I've known a lot of people like you, Pip. They come drinking in the pub and talk to us as though we were the salt of the earth, and then, one day, for no reason any of us can see, they go off, drop us as though that was another game they was tired of. I'd give a pension to know why we attract you.

WING COMMANDER: What do you know about that one, Jack, the one with the smart-alec eyes and the posh tones?

SQUADRON LEADER: Thompson? Remember General Thompson, Tobruk, a banker now?

WING COMMANDER: So that's the son. Thompson! Come here, Airman.

PIP: Sir?

WING COMMANDER: Enjoying yourself?

PIP: Thank you, sir.

WING COMMANDER: Gay crowd, eh?

PIP: I imagined you would dislike conscripts, sir.

WING COMMANDER: I haven't met you before, Thompson; your father impressed me but you don't.

PIP: Is that all, sir?

WING COMMANDER: I can have you, boy. I can really have you – remember that.

CHAS: What'd he want, Pip, what'd he say?

PIP: He wouldn't dare. Yes, he would. He's going to test you all. The old fool is really going to play the old game. I wonder what method he'll choose.

WILFE: What d'you mean, old game, what old game?

PIP: How he hates you; he's going to make an announcement. Listen how patronizing he'll be. Whatever happens, do as I tell you – don't question me, just do as I tell you.

ANDREW: If you have a war with that man, Pip, don't use me as fodder, I'm warning you.

PIP: Help, Andy, I'm helping, or do you want to be made fools of?

WING COMMANDER: Silence everybody, your attention please, gentlemen – Thank you. As you all know we hoped, when we organized this gay gathering for you, that we'd have a spot in the evening when everyone would get up and do a turn himself. A dirty recitation, or a pop song. I'm sure that there's a wealth of native talent among you, and now is the chance for you to display it in all its glory, while the rest of us sit back and watch and listen. My officers are always complaining of the dull crowds we get in this camp, but I've always said no, it's not true, they're not dull, just a little inhibited – you – er know what inhibited means, of course? So now's the time to prove them wrong and me right. You won't let me down, will you, lads? Who's to be first? Eh? Who'll start?

PIP: Very subtle, eh, Andy?

WILFE: Will someone tell me what's going on here? What's so sinister about a talent show?

WING COMMANDER: The first, now.

PIP: Burns, Andrew –

ANDREW: Burns?

PIP: Your bloody saint, the poet –

ANDREW: I know he's a poet but –

PIP: Recite him, man, go on, get up there and recite.

ANDREW: Recite what? I –

PIP: In your best Scottish accent now.

ANDREW: Hell, man [*once there*] I – er – Burns. A poem.
[*Recites it all, at first hesitantly, amid jeers, then with growing confidence, amid silence.*]

> This ae nighte, this ae nighte,
> *Every nighte and alle,*
> Fire and fleet and candle-lighte,
> *And Christe receive thy saule.*

> When thou from hence away art past,
> *Every nighte and alle,*
> To Whinny-muir thou com'st at last;
> *And Christe receive thy saule.*

If ever thou gavest hosen and shoon,
  *Every nighte and alle,*
Sit thee down and put them on;
  *And Christe receive thy saule.*

If hosen and shoon thou ne'er gav'st nane
  *Every nighte and alle,*
The whinnes sall prick thee to the bare bane;
  *And Christe receive thy saule.*

From Whinny-muir when thou art past,
  *Every nighte and alle,*
To Purgatory fire thou com'st at last;
  *And Christe receive thy saule.*

If ever thou gavest meat or drink,
  *Every nighte and alle,*
The fire sall never make thee shrink;
  *And Christe receive thy saule.*

If meat and drink you ne'er gav'st nane,
  *Every nighte and alle,*
The fire will burn thee to the bare bane
  *And Christe receive thy saule.*

This ae nighte, this ae nighte,
  *Every nighte and alle,*
Fire and fleet and candle-lighte,
  *And Christe receive thy saule.*

[*Ovation.*]

WING COMMANDER: Come now, something more cheerful than that. How about a song – something from Elvis Presley.

[*Band and boys begin pop song.*]

PIP: Not that, not now.

WING COMMANDER: Lovely, yes, that's it, let's see you enjoying yourselves.

PIP: Don't join in, boys – believe me and don't join in.

WILFE: What *is* this – what's going on here?

WING COMMANDER: Look at them – that's them in their element.

PIP: Can't you see what's happening, what he's thinking?

WING COMMANDER: The beer is high, they're having a good time.

PIP: Look at that smug smile.

WING COMMANDER: Aren't they living it up, just, eh? Aren't they in their glory?

PIP: He could lead you into a swamp and you'd go.

WING COMMANDER: Bravo! Bravo! That's the spirit! Make merry —it's a festive occasion and I want to see you laughing. I want my men laughing.

[*Loud pop song.* PIP *moves to guitarist and whispers in his ear. Boy protests, finally agrees to sing* 'The Cutty Wren', *an old peasant revolt song. Boys join in gradually, menacing the officers*]

ALL:

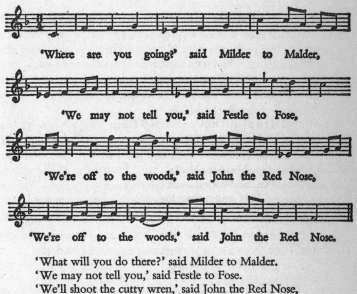

'Where are you going?' said Milder to Malder,

'We may not tell you,' said Festle to Fose,

'We're off to the woods,' said John the Red Nose,

'We're off to the woods,' said John the Red Nose.

'What will you do there?' said Milder to Malder.
'We may not tell you,' said Festle to Fose.
'We'll shoot the cutty wren,' said John the Red Nose,
'We'll shoot the cutty wren,' said John the Red Nose,

'How will you shoot him?' said Milder to Malder.
'We may not tell you,' said Festle to Fose.
'We've guns and we've cannons,' said John the Red Nose,
'We've guns and we've cannons,' said John the Red Nose.

'How will you cut her up?' said Milder to Malder.
'We may not tell you,' said Festle to Fose.

'Big hatchets and cleavers,' said John the Red Nose,
'Big hatchets and cleavers,' said John the Red Nose.

'How will you cook her?' said Milder to Malder.
'We may not tell you,' said Festle to Fose.
'Bloody great brass cauldrons,' said John the Red Nose,
'Bloody great brass cauldrons,' said John the Red Nose.

'Who'll get the spare ribs?' said Milder to Malder.
'We may not tell you,' said Festle to Fose.
'Give them all to the poor,' said John the Red Nose,
'Give them all to the poor,' said John the Red Nose.

WING COMMANDER: Quite the little leader, aren't you, Thompson?
Come over here, I want a word with you in private. Stand to
attention, do your button up, raise your chin – at ease. Why are
you fighting me, Thompson? We come from the same side, don't
we? I don't understand your reasons, boy – and what's more you're
insolent. I have every intention of writing to your father.

PIP: Please do.

WING COMMANDER: Oh, come now. Listen, lad, perhaps you've
got a fight on with your father or something, well that's all right
by me, we all fight our fathers, and when we fight them we also
fight what they stand for. Am I right? Of course I'm right. I understand you, boy, and you mustn't think I'm unsympathetic. But it's
not often we get your mettle among conscripts – we need you.
Let your time here be a truce, eh? Answer me, boy, my guns are
lowered and I'm waiting for an answer.

PIP: Lowered, sir?

WING COMMANDER: You know very well what I mean.

[WING COMMANDER and OFFICERS leave.]

HILL: Well, a right mess you made of that interview. If there's any
repercussions in our Flight, if we get victimized cos of you, boy,
I'll see you –

PIP: Don't worry, Corp, there won't be any repercussions.

CHAS: Well, what in hell's name happened – what was it all about?

SMILER: This party's lost its flavour – let's go back to the hut, eh?
I've got a pack of cards – let's go back and play cards.

CHAS [of PIP]: Talk to him is like talking to a brick wall. PIP!

## SCENE EIGHT

*The Naafi.*

PIP: You've got enemies, Charles boy. Learn to know them.
[*The others have gone.*]

CHAS: Enemies? I know about enemies. People you like is enemies.

PIP: What do *you* mean when you say that, Charles?

CHAS: Oh, nothing as clever as you could mean, I'm sure.

PIP: Come on, dear boy, we're not fighting all the time, are we? You mustn't take too much notice of the way I talk.

CHAS: You talk sometimes, Pip, and I don't think you know that you hurt people.

PIP: Do I? I don't mean to.

CHAS: And sometimes there's something about your voice, the way you talk – that – well, it makes me want to tell you things.

PIP: You were telling me about enemies you like.

CHAS: You're embarrassed.

PIP: You were telling me –

CHAS: Now why should I embarrass you?

PIP: – enemies you like.

CHAS: No, about people you liked who were enemies. There's a difference. I'm surprised you didn't see the difference.

PIP: Go on.

CHAS: Go on what?

PIP: What do you mean?

CHAS: Mean?

PIP: What you just said.

CHAS: Well, I said it. That's what it means.

PIP: Oh, I see.

CHAS: I do embarrass you, don't I?

PIP: A bit. Are you an only child, Charles?

CHAS: I got six brothers. You?

PIP: Four brothers.

CHAS: What I meant was people say things meaning to help but it works out all wrong.

PIP: You could have meant a number of things, I suppose.

CHAS: Words do mean a number of things.

PIP: Yes, Charles.

CHAS: Well, they do.

PIP: Mm. I'm not sure why we started this.

CHAS: Well, you said we got enemies, and I was saying –

PIP: Oh, yes.

CHAS: There, now you've lost interest. Just as we were getting into conversation you go all bored.

PIP: Don't nag at me, Charles.

CHAS: Charlie.

PIP: Oh, I can't call you Charlie – it's a stupid name.

CHAS: Now why did you have to say that? Making a rudeness about my name. Why couldn't you leave it alone. I want to be called Charlie. Why couldn't you just call me Charlie? No, you had to criticize.

PIP: All right, Charlie then! Charlie! If you don't mind being called Charlie you won't ever mind anything much.

CHAS: You're such a prig – I don't know how you can be such a barefaced prig and not mind.

PIP: I'm not a prig, Charles, that's so suburban – a snob perhaps but nothing as common as prig, please. Tell you what, I'm a liar.

CHAS: A liar?

PIP: Yes – I haven't got four brothers – I'm an only son.

CHAS: So am I.

PIP: You? Yes – I might've guessed. Poor old Charlie. Terrible, isn't it? Do you always try to hide it?

CHAS: Yes.

PIP: Not possible though, is it?

CHAS: No. Funny that – how we both lied. What you gonna do when they let us out of camp?

PIP: When is it?

CHAS: Next Friday.

PIP: Oh, go into the town, the pictures perhaps.

CHAS: Can I come?

PIP: Yes, I suppose so.

CHAS: Suppose so! You'd grudge your grandmother a coffin.

PIP: But I've just said you could come.

CHAS: Yes, dead keen you sounded.

PIP: Well, what do you want?

CHAS: Don't you know?

PIP: Oh, go to hell!

CHAS: I'm sorry, I take it back, don't shout. I'll come – thanks. [*Pause.*] If I was more educated you think it'd be easier, wouldn't it, between us?

PIP: What do you mean 'us'?

CHAS: Let me finish –

PIP: For God's sake don't start wedding me to you –

CHAS: Just let me –

PIP: And don't whine –

CHAS: You won't let me –

PIP: You are what you are – don't whine.

CHAS: Let me bloody finish what I was going to say, will you! You don't listen. You don't bloody listen.

PIP: I'm sorry –

CHAS: Yes, I know.

PIP: I'm listening.

CHAS: Oh, go to hell – you–

PIP: I'm sorry, I take it back, don't shout, I'm listening.

CHAS: I didn't say *I* thought it'd be easier if I was more educated – I said *you'd* think it'd be easier, I thought *you'd* think it. And I was just going to say I disagreed – then you jumped.

PIP: Yes, well, I thought – yes, well, you're right Charles, quite right. It's no good wanting to go to university –

CHAS: Facts, that's all it is.

PIP: Like me and work – manual labour. The number of intellectuals and artists who are fascinated by manual labour. Not me though, Charles. I haven't the slightest desire to use my brawn, prove myself a man, dirty my nails.

CHAS: And facts don't mean much to me either.

PIP: It's dull, repetitive, degrading.

CHAS: Intelligence counts, not facts. Stick your education, your university. Who cares why Rome was built.

PIP: Van Gogh with the miners; Hemingway, hunting.

41

CHAS: Even if I knew all about that it wouldn't make it any easier.

PIP: God, how I despise this yearning to be one of the toilers.

CHAS: I knew someone who used to wear a bowler cos he thought it made him look educated.

PIP: The dignity of labour!

CHAS: But it wouldn't make it any easier –

PIP: The beauty of movement!

CHAS: Not between us –

[*They smile.*]

## SCENE NINE

*The hut.*

SMILER: What shall it be – poker, pontoon?

WILFE: I'm for bed.

SMILER: 'I'm for bed', little boy is tired.

WILFE: You can go on man – nothing seems to affect you.

CANNIBAL: What happened? They kick you out too?

SMILER: We got sick – you game for poker?

DICKEY: The squalor overcame you, eh? Ah, well, welcome back to the delinquents.

[*Enter* HILL.]

HILL: Well, I've got a right bunch, haven't I, a real good crowd, that's a fact.

GINGER: Come off it, Corp – you know we're O.K. on the square.

DODGER: That's all that counts, isn't it, Corp?

HILL: My boys – even them, my own little boys let me down.

SMILER: It's poker, Corp, you playing?

HILL: I shan't say anything now because you're away home in two days – but when you come back it's rifle drill and bayonet practice – and that's tough, and if you slack – I'm warning you – no more easy life, it'll be back to normal for you all.

DODGER: Play us a tune, Corp.

HILL: You don't deserve no tunes – a kick up the arse you deserve, the lot, where it hurts, waken you up.

[CHARLES, SMILER, PIP, *and* DICKEY *sit down to play. The others lie in their beds, and* HILL *plays the mouth-organ.*]

GINGER: There's a bloody great moon outside. Dodge, you seen it? With a whopping great halo.

DODGER: Nippy, too. Who wants some chocolate? My uncle has a sweet shop. [*Produces dozens of bars.*]

DODGER: Ginge, what trade you going to apply for?

GINGER: Driver – I'm going to get something our of this mob – it's going to cost them something keeping me from civvy street. Driving! I've always wanted to drive – since I don't know how long. A six BHP engine, behind the wheel controlling it – nyaaaaaaarr. I dream about it. I dream I'm always in a car and I'm driving it, but I got no licence. I always know I've never driven a car, but somehow it comes easy to me and I've never got a ruddy licence. I'm always being chased by cops – and I keep dreaming it, the same dream. I got no licence, but I'm driving a car and the police are after me. What'll I dream about when I can drive a car, I wonder.

DODGER: You won't. Stands to reason you won't need to; when you got the real thing you don't pretend. How about some tea? Ginger, my cock, make some tea on the stove and we'll eat up these biscuits also.

CANNIBAL: Dreams is real you know, they may be pretending in your sleep, but they're real. I dreamt my girl was a prostitute once and when I see her next day she looked like one and I give her up.

DODGER: What's wrong with prostitutes? We need them, let's keep them I say. Nationalize them. Stuck in clubs like poor bleedin' ferrets.

WILFE: Don't it make you sick, eh? Don't it make you sick just – these eight weeks, these two years, the factory – all of it? Don't it make you just bleedin' sick? I SAID SICK, MOTHER, SICK! Poor dear, she can't hear a word.

[*Pause. Mouth-organ. Warm hut.*]

CANNIBAL: I'm going to get in that Radar-Plotting lark. All them buttons, them screens and knobs. You have to learn about the stars and space for that.

DICKEY: That's astronomy, my fine fellow. The code of the heavens.

Radar! Radar is the mystic digits of sound-waves; you have to have an enlightened degree of knowledge for that. Cannibal, my son, you're not arrogant enough, not standard enough for that. But I could – oh yes, I could rise to the heights of radar. I've put in for that.

SMILER: I think I'll go into Ops. Bring the planes in. Operations calling D17, are you receiving me, are you receiving me – over! D17 calling flight-control, I'm receiving you – left jet gone, I said gone, think I'll have to make a forced landing, stand by for emergency. Nyaaaaaaah passssssssss, brrrrrrrrrr – we'll all learn a trade and then 'oppit – nyaaaaaaaaaa. . .

[*Pause.*]

ANDREW: I like us. All of us, here now. I like us all being together here. In a way you know I don't mind it, anything. Old Corp and his mouth-organ – all of us, just as we are, I like us.

[*Pause. Mouth-organ. Warm hut.*]

GINGER: We've run out of coke you know – water won't ever boil.

PIP: Then we'll pinch some.

DICKEY: What?

PIP: That's all right with you isn't it, Corp? You don't mind a little raiding expedition?

HILL: You think you'll get in the coke yard? You won't, you know, mate; there's a wire netting and a patrol on that.

PIP: We'll work out a plan.

CHAS: Oh, knock it off, Pip, we're all in bed soon.

PIP: Think we can't outwit them?

DODGER: You won't outwit them, mate, they've got it all tied up neat, not them, me old *lobus*.

PIP: If you can't outwit them for a lump of coke, then they deserve to have you in here for a couple of years.

HILL: I know what you are, Thompson – you're an agent provocative.

WILFE: I'm game, how do we do it?

GINGER: We could snip the wire and crawl through.

PIP: No. We want to raid and leave no sign.

ANDREW: What do we put it in?

DICKEY: Buckets.

DODGER: Too noisy.

PIP: Buckets with sacking at the bottom. How high is the netting?

HILL: About six feet. You'll need a ladder.

WILFE: Take it from the fire hut near by.

CANNIBAL: What if there's a fire?

WILFE: Let it burn.

PIP: No, no risks. Efficient, precise, but humane. They happen to be the only qualities for absolute power. That's what we want – absolute success but without a price. Coke in ten minutes, with no one caught and no one but us the wiser. Trust me?

## SCENE TEN

*A large square of wire netting.*

[*A* GUARD *walks round it. Boys are in the shadows.*]

PIP: Now watch him – he walks round slowly – we can make three moves for each round except the last one and that requires speed. I want the first three stages started and finished between the time he disappears round the first corner and before he turns the third. If he changes his course or hurries his step or does anything that means one of us is caught, then we all, all of us make an appearance. He can't cop the lot. Right? [*All exeunt.*]

[GINGER *dashes to wire, and places chair – dashes to other side of stage.* PIP *runs to chair, jumps up and over.* DODGER *runs to take chair away and joins* GINGER. *The* GUARD *appears and carries on round.* DODGER *runs back, places chair.* WILFE *runs to chair with another, jumps on it, and drops chair into* PIP's *hands, runs off.* DODGER *runs on, and withdraws chair. The* GUARD *appears, and continues.* DODGER *runs on with chair again.* ANDREW *runs with buckets to chair, jumps up and passes them to* PIP. GINGER *runs to take chair away.* GUARD *appears, and continues. In like process, two buckets are returned 'full' of coke. In the last stage,* PIP *jumps back over netting, leaving chair.* GINGER *and* DODGER *appear with two stools.* DICKEY *dashes on to top of two stools, leans over wire and reaches down for chair, which he throws to* ANDREW. DODGER *and*

GINGER *run off with the two stools.* GUARD *appears and continues. This scene can be, and has to be, silent, precise, breathtaking, and finally very funny.*]

## SCENE ELEVEN

*The hut again.*
    [*Mouth-organ.* DODGER *pouring out tea, drinking, eating. Silence.*]

DICKEY: Yes. Yes – very satisfactory. Very pleasing. I wouldn't've thought we could do it.

CHAS: No more you wouldn't have done it without Pip.

DICKEY: Do I detect in young Charles the ineffable signs of hero worship?

CHAS: You'll detect black and blue marks, that's what you'll detect.

DICKEY: I think we've got a love affair in our midst.

CHAS: Just because I respect a man for his nerve? You gone daft?

DICKEY: No, I think my mental balance is equilibralized, it's you I fear for my Charlie boy. First you start off baiting young Thompson here and now you can't take your eyes off him.

PIP: Don't act the goat, Dickey.

DICKEY: I'm correct in my observations though aren't I, Lord Thompson?

PIP: No observation you make is correct, Dickey, you just remember other people's.

DICKEY: But you have a marvellous mind, don't you?

CHAS: He has.

DICKEY: Now there's a question. Would we have pinched the coke without Pip's mind?

HILL: You always need leaders.

PIP [*ironically*]: Always!

HILL: Well, don't you always need leaders?

PIP: Always, always!

HILL: Yes, always, always?

PIP: Always, always, always! Your great-great-grandfather said there'll always be horses, your great-grandfather said there'll always be slaves, your grandfather said there'll always be poverty and your father said there'll always be wars. Each time you say 'always'the world takes two steps backwards and stops bothering. And so it should, my God, so it should –

WILFE: Easy, Airman, easy.

GINGER: Hey, Dodge – come and look outside now. Have you ever seen a halo as big as that! – look at it.

DODGER: Means frost.

ANDREW:      This ae nighte, this ae nighte,
                *Every nighte and alle,*
             Fire and fleet and candle-lighte,
                *And Christe receive thy saule.*

**SLOW CURTAIN**

# ACT TWO

## SCENE ONE

*The hut, dark early morning.*
    [*Enter night* GUARD.]

GUARD: Hands off your cocks and pull up your socks, it's wake to
the sun and a glorious day. [*Pulls off blankets of one near by.*] Rise,
rise, rise and shine – Christmas is over. CHRISTMAS IS OVER.
[*Exit.*]
    [*There have been moans and movements. Return to silence. Enter*
    HILL. *Pause.*]
HILL: CHRISTMAS IS OVER, he said.
    [*Moans and movements.*]
It's over, done, finished. You're 'ome. You're 'ome again and it's
rifles today. Rifles and a stricter routine. You've been slacking. I've
warned you and told you and today is judgement day, especially
for you, Smiler – today is especially judgement day for you. You
too, Airmen Wilfe Seaford, and Archie Cannibal, you shan't be
passed. I intend making you the smartest squad in the glorious
history of flying – and I will. But you – A/C2 Thompson – you're
too good for me, too smart. The Wing Commander and all the
officers in charge of this camp have got their guns on you and
they're aiming to throw the book at you – the whole, heavy
scorching book, so you beware and guard your mouth. I've heard,
I know – so guard your mouth. CHRISTMAS IS OVER. [*Exits.*]
WILFE: Christmas is over and don't we know it. Rouse, yourself,
Smiler, or you'll get us all in the cart.
SMILER: Leave off.
WILFE: Rouse yourself, I say – I aren't suffering cos of you. Get up or
I'll turn you under your bed.

[*No reply.* WILFE *does so.* SMILER *rises from under the rubble and angrily fights with* WILFE *till separated by others.*]

ANDREW: Cut it out or I'll lay you both.

DICKEY: It's the basic animal rising to undiluted heights in them. A nasty morning, my boys, a nasty morning, nasty tempers, and a nasty undiluted life.

CANNIBAL: And you can shut your undiluted mouth for a start, too. I'm not stomaching you the rest of the time.

DICKEY: What side of the bed did you rise from?

CANNIBAL: I'm fit for you, so don't worry.

[*Enter* HILL *with rifles.*]

HILL: Come and get them. Don't grab them, don't drop them, and don't lose them. We start with them first thing after breakfast and I intend to train you so hard that you'll not be happy unless they're in bed with you.

[*Exit. Immediately, half the boys start playing cowboys and Indians, dropping behind beds and crawling on the floor, firing them at each other,* 'BANG. BANG.' *Enter* HILL.]

HILL: The next man to pull that trigger, his feet won't touch the ground.

[SMILER *clicks one unintentionally.*]

You – I've wanted to pounce on you, Smiler.

SMILER: It slipped, Corp – an accident.

HILL: You say accident, I say luck. I'm charging you, Smiler, just a little charge, a few days' jankers to start with – that's all.

PIP: Why don't you charge us all, Corporal?

HILL: YOU SHUT UP. You, I've warned. All of you, I've warned. The joke's over, the laughing's done. Now get ready. [*Exit.*]

DODGER. We used to have a master who'd crack a joke, and then look at his watch to see we didn't laugh too long.

HILL: All right, get fell in, the lot of you.

## SCENE TWO

*The parade ground.*
  [*The men in threes.*]

HILL: The first thing is – not to be afraid of it. It won't hurt you and if you handle it correctly you can't hurt it. [*Only one boy laughs.*] I know you think they're nice toys. With one of them in your hand you feel different, don't you, you feel a man, a conquering bloody hero? You want to run home and show your girl, don't you? Well, they're not toys – you can kill a man wi' one o' them. Kill 'im! Your napkins are still wet – you don't really understand that word 'kill', do you? Well, *you* can be killed. There! Does that bring it home to you? A bullet can whip through your flesh and knock breath out of *you*. Imagine yourself dying, knowing you're dying, you can feel the hole in your body, you can feel yourself going dizzy, you can feel the hot blood, and you can't breathe. You want to breathe but you can't, the body you've relied on all these years doesn't do what you want it to do, and you can't understand it. You're surprised, you're helpless, like those dreams where you're falling – only dying isn't a dream because you know, you know, you know that you're looking at everything for the last time and you can't do a bloody thing about it, that's dying. And that's a rifle. So don't let me catch anybody aiming it at anybody – loaded or not. Now, you hold it here, just below the barrel, pushing it out slightly to the right and forward, with the butt tucked well in at the side of your feet – so – well in firm, straight, at ease – and at the command to 'shun' I want that rifle brought smartly in at the precisely same moment. So. Atten-shun! Together, and your hand holding firmly on to that rifle. I don't want that rifle dropped – drop that rifle and I want to see you follow it to the ground. Right. Squad – atten-shun!

SQUAD: One!

  [SMILER *drops gun.*]

HILL: Leave it! Smiler, you nasty squirming imbecile! Can't you hear me? Can't you hear anything? Don't anything go through your thick skull? Look at you. Slob! Your buttons, your blanco, your shoes – look at them. They're dull. You're dull! You're like putty. What keeps you together, man? You're like an old Jew – you know what happens to Jews? They go to gas chambers. Now pick it up. Squad – atten-shun!

SQUAD: One!

HILL: Now to slope and shoulder arms, you make three movements. Watch me, follow me and you won't make a mess of it. I'll do it slowly and I'll exaggerate the movements. Shoulder ARMS! One pause, two pause, three. Slope ARMS! One pause, two pause, three. Again [*Repeats.*] Now – you do it. Squad! Shoulder ARMS!

SQUAD: One pause, two pause, three.

HILL: Slope ARMS!

SQUAD: One pause, two pause, three.

[*Repeats order.*]

HILL: You're no good, Smiler, you're no good. Shoulder ARMS! Smiler, one pace forward march. The rest, about turn. By the left, quick march.

[*The squad march off, all except* SMILER. *The wall of the guardroom drops into place as scene changes to*]


## SCENE THREE

*The guardroom.*

[SMILER *at the slope. Enter* HILL *and two other corporals.*]


FIRST CORPORAL: This him?

HILL: That's him.

SECOND CORPORAL: What's your name, lad?

SMILER: Smiler.

SECOND CORPORAL: I said your name, lad.

SMILER: 279 A/C2 Washington, Corporal.

FIRST CORPORAL: Washington, is it? You mustn't lie then, ha-ha! If you mustn't lie, then tell us, is your mother pretty? Is she? Answer me, lad. Do you know it's dumb insolence not to answer an N.C.O.? We'll make that six day's jankers, I think. Answer me, lad.

SMILER: Yes. She was.

FIRST CORPORAL: Have you ever seen her undressed? Eh? Have you, lad? Have you seen her naked?

SECOND CORPORAL: Wipe that smile off your face, lad.

SMILER: I'm not smiling, Corporal, it's natural, I was born like it.

FIRST CORPORAL: Arguing with an N.C.O. We'll make that nine days' jankers.

HILL: All right Smiler, order arms, slope arms, order arms, slope arms, slope arms, slope arms.

[*The two corporals walk round him.*]

FIRST CORPORAL: You're a slob, Smiler.

SECOND CORPORAL: A nasty piece of work.

FIRST CORPORAL: You're no good, lad.

SECOND CORPORAL: No good at all. You're an insult.

FIRST CORPORAL: Your mother wasted her labour.

SECOND CORPORAL: Your father made a mistake.

FIRST CORPORAL: You're a mistake, Smiler.

SECOND CORPORAL: A stupid mistake.

FIRST CORPORAL: The Queen doesn't like mistakes in her Air Force.

SECOND CORPORAL: She wants good men, Smiler, men she can trust.

FIRST CORPORAL: Stand still, boy. Don't move. Silent, boy. Still and silent, boy.

HILL: That'll do for a taster, Smiler. That'll do for the first lesson. Tomorrow we'll have some more. We'll break you, Smiler, we'll break you, because that's our job. Remember that, just remember now – remember – About TURN! By the left – quick march, eft – ite, eft – ite. Remember, Smiler, remember.

[*Exit.*]

## SCENE FOUR

WING COMMANDER's *office*.
  [*With him at a table are* SQUADRON LEADER *and* PILOT OFFICER.]

WING COMMANDER: Just remember who we're dealing with – remember that. I don't want a legal foot put wrong – I just want him broken in.

PILOT OFFICER: Not broken in, sir, but loved – he's only lost temporarily, for a short, natural time, that's all.

WING COMMANDER: Bloody little fool – sowing seeds of discontent to semi-educated louts; what do they understand of what he tells them?

SQUADRON LEADER: Gently, Sid, anger'll only make it easier for him to be stubborn.

PILOT OFFICER: Leave it to me, sir. I think I know how to do it, I think I know the boy very well.

WING COMMANDER: I know the boy, by Christ I know him, I've known them all and I've broken them all.

  [HILL *marches* PIP *into the room and goes.*]

PIP: You called me to see you, sir.

WING COMMANDER: Take your hat off, blast you, Thompson, take it off, lad, in front of an officer.

SQUADRON LEADER: Please sit down, won't you, Thompson, sit down and be at ease for a little while; we'd simply like a chat with you.

WING COMMANDER: Your square bashing is coming to an end. We're concerned about you. We have to find you something to do. It has to be decided now.

SQUADRON LEADER: I think, Wing Commander, if you'll excuse me, it would be more correct to say that Personnel must decide that in London, but we can recommend from here, isn't that the case? We are on the spot, so we can recommend.

PILOT OFFICER: We see, Thompson, that you've put down administration orderly as your first and only choice. A very strange choice.

WING COMMANDER: A damn fool choice, boy, your brains, your carriage and background, damn perversity!

SQUADRON LEADER: You know what administration orderly implies, don't you, son?

WING COMMANDER: Anything and everything – waste, absolute waste.

SQUADRON LEADER: Anything from dishwashing to salvage, from spud-bashing to coal-heaving.

[*Pause.*]

PILOT OFFICER: Listen Pip, excuse me, sir?

WING COMMANDER: Yes, yes, carry on.

PILOT OFFICER: Let's drop the pretence. We're the same age and class, let's drop this formal nonsense. The Air Force is no place to carry on a family war, Pip. This is not a public school, it's a place where old boys grow into young men, believe me. Don't force me to start listing all your virtues and attributes. We're not flatterers, but don't let's be falsely modest either – that's understood between us, I'm sure. God, when I think of what I did to try and get out of coming into this outfit – two years wasted I thought. But waste is what you yourself do with time – come on man, if people like us aren't officers, then imagine the bastards they'll get. This is a silly game, Pip – why look, you're even sulking. Admin orderly! Can you see yourself washing dishes?

PIP: It might be a pretence to avoid responsibility.

PILOT OFFICER: You, Pip? Come now! It may be that you want to prove something to yourself. I don't know, why don't you tell us?

PIP: Your tactics are obvious, please don't insult my intelligence. I do not feel obliged to explain my reasons to you.

WING COMMANDER: You'll do what you're told.

PILOT OFFICER: It's not a question of obligation, no one's forcing –

PIP: I have no wish to –

PILOT OFFICER: But there's no one forcing you –

PIP: I said I have no wish to –

PILOT OFFICER: But–no-one-is-forcing-you –

PIP: I have no wish to explain anything to you I say.

[*Pause.*]

WING COMMANDER: Corporal Hill!

  [*Enter* HILL.]

HILL: Sir?

WING COMMANDER: The men in your squad are slobs. Their standard is low and I'm not satisfied. No man passes out of my camp unless he's perfect – you know that. Pull them together, Corporal Hill, fatigues, Corporal Hill. They're a wretched bunch, wretched, not good enough.

HILL: Yes, sir [*Exit from room.*]

  All right, fall in, the lot of you.

  [*Boys enter.*]

  You're slobs, all of you. Your standard is low and I'm not satisfied. No man passes out of my hut unless he's perfect, I've told you that before. You're a wretched bunch – a miserable, wretched bunch, and since you're not good enough, it's fatigues for you all. Squad will double mark time.

  [*They do so for one minute. Exeunt at the double. The Inquisition resumes.*]

WING COMMANDER: Carry on, P.O.

PILOT OFFICER: Right, Thompson, I have some questions to ask you. I don't want clever answers. You wish to be an administration orderly?

PIP: That is correct, sir.

PILOT OFFICER: Doesn't it occur to you that that very act, considering who you are, is a little – revealing? It's a rather ostentatious choice, isn't it?

PIP: It could be viewed like that.

PILOT OFFICER: You enjoy mixing with men from another class. Why is this? Do you find them stimulating, a new experience, a novelty, do you enjoy your slumming?

PIP: It's not *I* who slum, sir.

PILOT OFFICER: I suppose you feel guilty in some way for your comfortable and easy upbringing; you feel you must do a sort of penance for it.

PIP: A rather outdated cause to be a martyr for, don't you think, sir?

PILOT OFFICER: Possibly, Thompson, possibly. You enjoy their company, though, don't you?

PIP: I enjoy most people's company.

PILOT OFFICER: Not ours, though.

PIP: Certain standards are necessary, sir.

PILOT OFFICER: A very offensive reply, Thompson – it's almost a hysterical reply – a little too desperately spoken, I would say. But look, we haven't stiffened, we aren't offended, no one is going to charge you or strike you. In fact we haven't really taken any notice. We listen to you, we let other people listen to you but we show no offence. Rather – we applaud you, flatter you for your courage and idealism but – it goes right through us. We listen but we do not hear, we befriend but do not touch you, we applaud but we do not act. To tolerate is to ignore, Thompson. You will not really become an administration orderly, will you?

PIP: What I have written, stays.

PILOT OFFICER: You will not be a foolish, stiff, Empire-thumping officer – no one believes in those any more. You will be more subtle and you will learn how to deal with all the Pip Thompsons who follow you. I even think you would like that.

PIP: What I have written stays. You may recommend as you please.

PILOT OFFICER: Yes, we shall put you up for officer training.

[OFFICERS *exeunt. Scene changes to*]

## SCENE FIVE

*The Square. A dummy is hanging. It is bayonet practice for the squad.*

HILL: Even officers must go through this. Everyone, but everyone must know how to stick a man with a bayonet. The occasion may not arise to use the scorching thing but no man passes through this outfit till he's had practice. It's a horrible thing, this. A nasty weapon and a nasty way to kill a man. But it is you or him. A nasty choice, but you must choose. We had a bloke called Hamlet with us once and he had awful trouble in deciding. He got stuck! I don't want that to be your fate. So! Again, hold the butt and drop the muzzle – so. Lean forward, crouch, and let me see the horriblest leer your face can make. Then, when I call 'attack' I want to see you rush towards that old straw dummy, pause, lunge, and twist your knife with all the hate you can. And one last thing – the scream. I want to hear you shout your lungs out, cos it helps. A horde of screaming men put terror in the enemy and courage in themselves. It helps. Get fell in, two ranks. Front rank will assume the on-guard position – ON GUARD! Run, scream, lunge.

[HILL *demonstrates it himself. One by one, the men rush forward at the dummy, until it comes to* PIP. *He stands still.*]

I said attack. Thompson, you, that's you. Are you gone daft? I've given you an order – run, scream, you. Are you refusing to obey? A/C Thompson I have ordered you to use your bayonet. You scorching, trouble-making, long-haired, posh-tongued, lump of aristocracy – I'll high jump you, court-martial you. I'll see you rot in every dungeon in the force. Oh, thank your lucky stars this ain't the war, my lad; I'd take the greatest pleasure in shooting you. You still refuse? Right – you men, form up a line behind this man; I'll need you all for witnesses. A/C2 Thompson, I am about to issue you with a legitimate order according to Her Majesty's rules and regulations, Section ten paragraph five, and I must warn you that failing to carry out this order will result in you being charged under Section ten paragraph sixteen of the same book. Now, when I say attack, I want to see you lower your gun in the attack position and race forward to lunge that dummy which now faces you. Is that order understood?

PIP: Yes, Corporal.

HILL: Good. I am now about to give the command. Wait for it and think carefully – this is only practice and no one can be hurt. Within ten seconds it will all be over, that's advice. Attack.

[*Silence. No movement.*]

Squad – slope ARMS! A/C2 Thompson – I'm charging you with failure to obey a legitimate order issued by an N.C.O. in command under Her Majesty's Air Force, and may God help you, lad.

[*All march off except* THOMPSON.]

## SCENE SIX

[*Enter* ANDREW.]

ANDREW: Idiot.

PIP: You?

ANDREW: Who the hell is going to be impressed?

PIP: You, Andrew?

ANDREW: Yes, Andrew! I'm asking you – who the hell do you think is going to be impressed? Not me. The boys? Not them either. I've been watching you, Pip – I'm not impressed and neither are they.

PIP: You don't really think I'm interested in the public spectacle, Andy, you can't? No, no I can see you don't. Go off now. Leave me with it – I've got problems.

ANDREW: No one's asking you to make gestures on our behalf.

PIP: Go off now.

ANDREW: Don't go making heroic gestures and then expect gratitude.

PIP: Don't lean on me, Andy – I've got problems.

ANDREW: I don't think I can bear your martyrdom – that's what it is; I don't think I can bear your look of suffering.

PIP: I'm not suffering.

ANDREW: I don't know why but your always-acting-right drives me round the bend.

PIP: I'm not a martyr.

ANDREW: It's your confident cockiness – I can't stand your confident cockiness. How do you know you're right? How can you act all the time as though you know all right from wrong, for God's sake.

PIP: Don't be a bastard Jock.

ANDREW: I'm trying to help you, idiot. The boys will hate any heroic gesture you make.

PIP: Andy, you're a good, well-meaning, intelligent person. I will die of good, well-meaning, and intelligent people who have never made a decision in their life. Now go off and leave me and stop crippling me with your own guilt. If you're ineffectual in this world that's your look-out – just stay calm and no one will know, but stop tampering with my decisions. Let *them* do the sabotaging, they don't need help from you as well. Now get the hell out – they wouldn't want you to see the way they work.

[*Exit* ANDREW.]

## SCENE SEVEN

PILOT OFFICER: It goes right through us, Thompson. Nothing you can do will change that. We listen but we do not hear, we befriend but do not touch you, we applaud but do not act – to tolerate is to ignore. What did you expect, praise from the boys? Devotion from your mates? Your mates are morons, Thompson, morons. At the slightest hint from us they will disown you. Or perhaps you wanted a court martial? Too expensive, boy. Jankers? That's for the yobs. You, we shall make an officer, as we promised. I have studied politics as well, you know, and let me just remind you of a tactic the best of revolutionaries have employed. That is to penetrate the enemy and spread rebellion there. You can't fight us from the outside. Relent boy, at least we understand long sentences.

PIP: You won't impress me with cynicism, you know.

PILOT OFFICER: Not cynicism – just honesty. I might say we are being unusually honest – most of the time it is unnecessary to admit all this, and you of all people should have known it.

PIP: I WILL NOT BE AN OFFICER.

PILOT OFFICER: Ah. A touch of anger, what do you reveal now, Thompson? We know, you and I, don't we? Comradeship? Not that, not because of the affinity of one human being to another, not that. Guilt? Shame because of your fellow beings' suffering? You don't feel that either. Not guilt. An inferiority complex, a feeling of modesty? My God. Not that either. There's nothing humble about you, is there? Thompson, you wanted to do more than simply share the joy of imparting knowledge to your friends; no, not modesty. Not that. What then? What if not those things, my lad? Shall I say it? Shall I? Power. Power, isn't it?

Among your own people there were too many who were powerful, the competition was too great, but here, among lesser men –
here among the yobs, among the good-natured yobs, you could be
king. KING. Supreme and all powerful, eh? Well? Not true? Deny
it – deny it, then. We know – you and I – we know, Thompson.

PIP: Oh, God –

PILOT OFFICER: God? God? Why do you call upon God? Are you
his son? Better still, then. You are found out even more, illusions
of grandeur, Thompson. We know that also, that's what we know,
that's what we have, the picture you have of yourself, and now that
we know that, you're really finished, destroyed. You're destroyed,
Thompson. No man survives whose motive is discovered, no man.
Messiah to the masses! Corporal Hill! [*Exit.*]

HILL [*off stage*]. Sir?


## SCENE EIGHT

[*Enter* HILL.]

HILL: I have instructions to repeat the order, Thompson. The powers
have decided to give you another chance. I don't know why, but
they know what they're doing, I suppose. When I give the order
'attack' I want you to lean forward, run, thrust, and twist that blade
in the dummy. Have you understood?

PIP: Yes, Corporal.

HILL: Run, thrust and twist that blade – good. ATTACK.

[PIP *pauses for a long while, then with a terrifying scream he rushes at
the dummy, sticking it three times, with three screams.*]

## SCENE NINE

*The hut.*
　　[CHARLES *and* PIP.]

CHAS: What they say, Pip? What they want you for, what did they
　　say? Hell, look at your face, did they beat you? Did they make you
　　use the bayonet? They did, didn't they? I can tell it from your face.
　　You're crying – are you crying? Want a cigarette? Here, have a
　　cigarette. The others have all gone to the Naafi, it's New Year's
　　Eve, gone for a big booze-up. Bloody fools – all they do is drink. I
　　think I'll give it up, me. Well, what did they say, man – talk to
　　me? You know why I didn't go to the Naafi – I – I was waiting for
　　you. It seemed fishy them calling you in the evening, so I waited to
　　see. Pip? I'm telling you I waited for you. I wanted to tell you some-
　　thing, I want to ask you a favour; I've been meaning all these last
　　days to ask you this favour. You see – you know me, don't you,
　　you know the sort of bloke . . . I'm – I'm, I'm not dumb, I'm not a
　　fool, I'm not a real fool, not a bloody moron and I thought, well,
　　I thought maybe you could, could teach me – something, anything.
　　Eh? Well, not anything but something proper, real.
PIP: Ask someone else – books, read books.
CHAS: Not books! I can't read books, but I can listen to you. Maybe
　　we'll get posted to the same place, and then every evening, or
　　every other evening, or once a week, even, you could talk to me a
　　bit, for half an hour say. Remember how you talked that night
　　about your grandfathers, about all those inventions and things.
　　Well, I liked that, I listened to that, I could listen all night to that.
　　Only I want to know about something else, I want to know about
　　– I don't even know how to put it, about – you know, you know
　　the word, about business and raw materials and people working
　　and selling things – you know, there's a word for it –
PIP: Economics.
CHAS: Enocomics – that's it.
PIP: Economics not enocomics.

CHAS: Ee-mon-omics.

PIP: No, Ee –

CHAS: Ee

PIP: Con

CHAS: Con

PIP: Om

CHAS: Om

PIP: Ics.

CHAS: Ics.

PIP: Economics.

CHAS: Economics. There, about that, could you? I'd listen, you could draw diagrams and graphs; I wasn't bad at maths.

PIP: Someone else, Charles, not me, someone else.

CHAS: There you go. You're a hypocrite – a hypocrite you are. You take people to the edge. Don't you know what I'm asking you, don't you know what I'm really asking you?

PIP: Ask someone else.

CHAS: But I want to be with you – I want to. Ah, you give me a pain in the neck, you do, you're a coward. You lead and then you run away. I could grow with you, don't you understand that? We could do things together. You've got to be with someone, there's got to be someone you can trust, everyone finds some-one and I found you – I've never asked anyone before, Jesus, never –

PIP: Ask someone else.

CHAS: Someone else. Someone else. It's always someone else, you half-bake you, you lousy word-user you. Your bleedin' stuffed grandfathers kept us stupid all this time, and now you come along with your pretty words and tell us to fend for ourselves. You clever useless leftover you. Oh, you're cocky, aren't you – Ask someone else. The truth is – you're scared, aren't you? You call us mate, but you're a scared old schoolboy. The pilot officer was right, you're slumming. You're a bleedin' slummer –

PIP: And he also said 'we will listen to you but we will not hear you, we will befriend you but not touch you, we will tolerate and ig-nore you'.

CHAS: Well, what did that mean?

PIP: We'll do anything they want just because they know how to smile at us.

CHAS: You mean *I'll* do what they want, not you, boy. You're one of them – you're just playing games with 'em, and us mugs is in the middle – I've cottoned on now. [*Long pause.*] I'll do what *you* want, Pip.

PIP: Swop masters? You're a fool, Charles, the kind of fool my parents fed on, you're a fool, a fool –

[*Fade in the sound of marching feet and the Corporals repeating the insults they heaped upon* SMILER *and change to*]

## SCENE TEN

*A roadway.*

[SMILER *has run away from camp. He is desperate, haggard and tired. Mix:* 'You're a fool, Charles' *to* 'You're a slob, Smiler' 'A nasty piece of work' 'You're no good lad', *etc., rising to crescendo* –]

SMILER: LEAVE ME ALONE! Damn your mouths and hell on your stripes – leave me alone. Mad they are, they're mad they are, they're raving lunatics they are. CUT IT! STUFF IT! Shoot your load on someone else, take it out on someone else, why do you want to pick on me, you lunatics, you bloody apes, you're nothing more than bloody apes, so damn your mouths and hell on your stripes! Ahhhhh – they'd kill me if they had the chance. They think they own you, think that anyone who's dressed in blue is theirs to muck about, degrade. YOU BLOODY APES, YOU WON'T DEGRADE ME! Oh my legs – I'm going home. I'll get a lift and scarper home. I'll go to France, I'll get away. I'LL GET AWAY FROM YOU, YOU APES! They think they own you – Oh my back. I don't give tuppence what you say, you don't mean anything to me, your bloody orders nor your stripes not your jankers nor your wars. Stick your jankers on the wall, stuff yourselves, go away and stuff yourselves, stuff your rotten stupid selves – Ohh – Ohhh. Look at the sky, look at the moon, Jesus look at that moon and the frost in the air. I'll wait. I'll get a lift in a second or two, it's quiet now, their noise is gone. I'll stand and wait and look at that moon. What are you made of, tell me? I don't know what you're made of, you go on and on. What grouses you? What makes you scream? You're blood and wind like all of us, what grouses you? You poor duff bastards, where are your mothers? Where were you born – I don't know what grouses you, your voices sound like dying hens – I don't know. That bloody lovely moon is cold, I can't stay here. I'll freeze to death. That's a laugh, now that'd fool them. Listen! A bike, a motor-bike, a roaring bloody motor-bike. [*Starts thumbing.*] London, London, London, London, LONDON! [*The roar comes and dies.*] You stupid ghet, I want a lift, can't you see I want a lift, an airman wants a life back home. Home, you bastard, take me ho'ooooome. [*Long pause.*] Now they'll catch me, now they'll come, not much point in going on – Smiler boy, they'll surely come, they're bound to miss you back at camp – eyes like hawks they've got – God! Who cares. 'Stop your silly smiling, Airman' – 'It's not a smile, Corp, it's natural, honest, Corp. I'm born that way. Honest Corp, it's not a smile . . .'

[*Enters hut.*]


# SCENE ELEVEN

*The hut.*

[CHARLES *and* PIP *as we left them.* SMILER *is now with them.*]

SMILER: The bastards won't believe it's natural. Look at me, me!

[*A very broken* SMILER *stands there.* SMILER *turns to* PIP *for help.* PIP *approaches him and takes him gently in his arms. They sway a moment.*]

SMILER: Wash my feet for me.

[SMILER *collapses.* PIP *lays him on the ground. He is about to remove his shoes –*]

CHAS: Leave him. I'll do it.

[CHARLES *doesn't know what to do to begin with. Surveys* SMILER. *Then – picks him up and lays him on his bed, looks at him; thinks; takes off his shoes and socks.*]

CHAS: His feet are bleeding.

[*Takes a towel and pours water from pot on it; washes* SMILER'S *feet; a long unconscious moan from* SMILER; *clock strikes midnight; sound of boys singing 'Auld Lang Syne'.* CORPORAL HILL'S *voice, loud.*]

HILL [*off stage*]: You pass out with the band tomorrow – rifles, buttons, belts, shining, and I want you as one man, you hear me? You'll have the band and it'll be marvellous; only you Smiler, you won't be in it, you'll stay behind a little longer, my lad – HAPPY NEW YEAR.

[*Silence. One by one the rest of the men come in, returning from the Naafi. They make no sound, but their movements are wild and drunk. No sound at all – like a T.V. with sound turned off, till they see* SMILER.]

DODGER: Look at his feet. The rotten bastards, look at his feet.

ANDREW: What'd he do?

CHAS: Tried to hop it.

ANDREW: Couldn't make it?

CHAS: Walked for miles and then came back.

CANNIBAL: They had it in for him, you've got no chance when they got it in for you.

GINGER: He's staying behind, you know? I reckon they'll make him do another two weeks of this.

DICKEY: Give me the chance, just give me one chance and I'd have them. Five minutes in civvy street and I'd have them chasing their own tails.

WILFE: Ah, you wouldn't, man – you talk like this now but you wouldn't, and you know why? Cos you'd be just as helpless there, you'd be just as much wind and nothing there, man. 'Just gimme the boss,' you'd say, 'just gimme him for one hour in uniform and I'd teach him what a man is.' That's all you'd say, civvy street, the forces – it's the same, don't give me that.

GINGER: What about Smiler's stuff?

CANNIBAL: I'll do it.

CHAS: No, you won't, I'm doing it.

CANNIBAL: All right, all right, then. Blimey, what's gotten into you? Jumping at me like that – I don't much want to do my own buggers, let alone his. Takes all the guts out of you, don't it. Look at him, lying there like a bloody corpse. His feet are cold.

DODGER: He's like a baby. Sweet as a sleeping baby. Have you ever watched a baby sleep? It always looks as though it's waiting for something to happen, a grown-up seems to be hiding away but a nipper seems to trust you, anyone. He's done it, ain'tee, eh? He's really had it –

CHAS: For Christ's sake, give over – you talk like he was dead or something. Come on, help cover him.

[*As many as possible manoeuvre* SMILER *so that his jacket and trousers come off, with the least disturbance. This action is done lovingly and with a sort of ritual.* DODGER *takes a comb to* SMILER's *hair and* CHARLES *gently wipes a towel over his face. Then they tuck him in bed and stand looking at him. Unknown to them the* PILOT OFFICER *has been watching them.*]

PILOT OFFICER: Beautiful. Tender and beautiful. But I'm sorry, gentlemen, this man is needed in the guardroom.

[*Enter* HILL.]

HILL: Squad – shun!

[*The men slowly come to attention, except* CHARLES, *who, after a pause, moves to his bed and sits on it. One by one the other boys, except* PIP, *also sit on their beds in defiance.*]

PILOT OFFICER: Corporal – take that smiling airman to the guard-room.

CHAS: YOU'LL LEAVE HIM BE!

PILOT OFFICER: And take that man, too.

GINGER: You won't, Corporal Hill, will you?

PILOT OFFICER: And that man, take the lot of them, I'll see them all in the guardroom.

PIP: You won't touch any of them, Corporal Hill, you won't touch a single one of them.

PILOT OFFICER: Do you hear me, Corporal, this whole hut is under arrest.

PIP: I suggest, sir, that you don't touch one of them. [PIP *and the*

PILOT OFFICER *smile at each other, knowingly, and* PIP *now begins to change his uniform, from an airman's to an officer's.*] We won't let him will we Charles – because you're right. Smiler has been badly treated and you are right to protect him. It's a good virtue that, loyalty. You are to be commended, Charles, all of you; it was a brave thing to do, protect a friend. We lack this virtue all too often, don't you agree, sir? These are good men, sometimes we are a little hasty in judging them – don't you agree, sir, a little too hasty? These are the salt of the earth, the men who make the country, really. Don't worry, Charles, nor you, Ginger, nor you, Andrew – none of you, don't worry, you shan't be harmed – it was a good act. We like you for it, we're proud of you, happy with you – you do agree, don't you, sir? These are men we need and these are the men we must keep. We are not hard men, Charles – don't think ill of us, the stories you read, the tales you hear. We are good, honest, hard-working like yourselves and understanding; above all we are understanding, aren't we, sir? There, that's a good fit, I think. [*The* PILOT OFFICER *hands a list over to* PIP. PIP *reads out the list.*]

PIP: 239 A/C2 Cannibal – [CANNIBAL *rises to attention*] administration orderly, posted to Hull. [*Stands at ease. Same procedure for others.*]

252 A/C2 Wingate – administration orderly, posted to Oxford.

247 A/C2 Seaford – administration orderly, Cyprus.

284 A/C2 McClure – typing pool, Malta.

272 A/C2 Richardson – administration orderly, Aden.

277 A/C2 Cohen – administration orderly, Halton.

266 A/C2 Smith – administration orderly, Lincoln.

279 A/C2 Washington – put back three weeks to flight 212 – decision of employ will be made at a later date.

Squad – Squad, SHUN.

[*Sudden loud sound of brass band playing the R.A.F. March Past.*]

## SCENE TWELVE

*Music of March Past. The Parade Ground. Passout Parade. The men march into position. A flagpole is moved in.*

HILL: Squad atten-shun! Shoulder arms! Right turn! By the left quick march! Lift your heads, raise them, raise them high, raise them bravely, my boys. Eft-ite, eft-ite, eft-ite, eft. Slope that rifle, stiffen that arm – I want to see them all pointing one way, together – unity, unity. Slam those feet, slam, slam, you're men of the Queen, her own darlings. SLAM, SLAM! SLAM! Let her be proud. Lovely, that's lovely, that's poetry. No one'll be shot today my boys. Forget the sweat, forget the cold, together in time. I want you to look beautiful, I want you to move as one man, as one ship, as one solid gliding ship. Proud! Proud! Parade, by centre, quick march, saluting to the front.

[*Men salute to audience, return back to face* WING COMMANDER. *Music stops.* WING COMMANDER *on a rostrum. Officers around him.*]

WING COMMANDER [*a long, broad, embracing smile*]: I am satisfied. Good. Good men. One of the best bunch I've had through my gates. Smart, alert, keen. Two years of service in Her Majesty's Air Force lie ahead of you, I am confident of the service you will give, you have turned out well, as we expected, nothing else would have done, just as we expected. God speed you.

[GINGER *comes to attention. Lays rifle on ground. Steps forward to flagpole and takes ropes in his hands.*]

HILL: Parade about turn.

[*Men now facing audience again.*]

SQUADRON LEADER: Parade, for colour hoisting. PRESENT ARMS! [GINGER *very very slowly hoists the R.A.F. colours. Let it be a tall pole. 'The Queen' is played, and there is a*

SLOW CURTAIN

# THE FRIENDS

'If the root be in confusion, nothing will be well governed'

> CONFUCIUS: 'The Great Digest'
> Translated by Ezra Pound

Now let us sleep until the world becomes morning'

ALI MIRDREKVANDI: *About General Burke and his men on the milky way*

# AUTHOR'S NOTE

Confronted for the first time with directing the première of my own play, I discovered myself in a position of being able to shape the internal rhythms as I had written them. These rhythms are here indicated by the spaces or asterisks in the printed text.

FOR CHARLOTTE

First performed by Stockholm's Stadsteater at the Lilla Teatern, on 24 January 1970, directed by Arnold Wesker, designed by Teresa Gogulska, with the following cast:

| | |
|---|---|
| ESTHER | Jane Friedmann |
| MANFRED | Hakan Serner |
| CRISPIN | Per Myrberg |
| TESSA | Gurie Nordwall |
| SIMONE | Gun Arvidsson |
| MACEY | Olof Bergstrom |
| ROLAND | Gosta Ekman |

First performed in Great Britain at the Roundhouse, on 19 May 1970, directed by Arnold Wesker, designed by Nicholas Georgiadis, with the following cast:

| | |
|---|---|
| ESTHER | Susan Engel |
| MANFRED | Ian Holm |
| CRISPIN | Roy Marsden |
| TESSA | Anna Cropper |
| SIMONE | Lynn Farleigh |
| MACEY | John Bluthal |
| ROLAND | Victor Henry |

# CHARACTERS

ESTHER
MANFRED
CRISPIN
TESSA
SIMONE
MACEY
ROLAND

# ACT ONE

---

## SCENE ONE

*In a large bed, richly covered and coloured maroon, lies* ESTHER. *Though ill and tired from her illness, yet she is at work slowly cutting with a pair of scissors round the shape of an enlargement of an old sepia photograph of her mother – date about 1911. This to be added to a mosaic of old photographs – some enlarged, some their original size – which she is building up on an old screen to the left of her bed. Each photograph is of a member of her family: aunts, uncles, cousins, grandparents. It is an area of the set rich in brown, black and white tones and nostalgia. Helping her is her lover* ROLAND.

MANFRED, *her brother, sits reading and writing notes by a large old carved desk.*

CRISPIN, *a friend and partner, sits restlessly at the foot of her bed, constructing his own invented toy.*

*Hanging behind the bed, jarring yet touching, is a portrait of Lenin. Near the desk is a re-creation of the Crick-Watson model of the structure of the D.N.A. molecule of heredity, two-thirds done.*

*All the 'Friends' are between the ages of 40 and 45.*


ESTHER: Only children's faces are really beautiful. Little girls with bows and broderie anglaise; spontaneous, cruel, full of uninhibited love, like tigers. The rest is stupid and vulgar, brutal and pompous. You're not listening, Manfred.

MANFRED: I am, Ketzel, I am. Just a few more lines.

ESTHER: Except the sound of French, that's beautiful; and Russian icons and pre-Raphaelites and Venetian chandeliers.

ROLAND: Last night I slept very soundly. Long and deep.

MANFRED [*reading*]: 'The electron is a completely universal fundamental particle ...'

75

ROLAND: I can't remember the last time I slept so soundly.

MANFRED: '... It is stable and long-lived. For all practical purposes it is indestructible and is at present in the universe in inexhaustible numbers ...'

ESTHER: And Baroque churches and houses, fountains and market-places and the music of organs and Norman arches and wine and the cooking of friends and the sound of friends.

ROLAND: And because of that long sleep everything about me is sharp and alive.

MANFRED: 'Electron devices and electronic techniques can therefore be used as effectively in any terrestrial environment as in the near-vacuum of outer space with unrivalled speed of response and sensitivity and ...'

ESTHER: Stop it, Manfred.

MANFRED: '... can convey information more efficiently than any other kind ...'

ESTHER: It's lunacy.

MANFRED: '... and lend themselves to the control and regulation of small or large amounts of power.'

ESTHER: You surround yourself with books which you start and never finish.

ROLAND: I can't explain how beautiful that sleep was.

ESTHER: A book of essays brings you to study architecture; the book on architecture brings you to a history of cities.

ROLAND: I can isolate sounds and tastes and smells.

ESTHER: The impact of cities brings you to sociology; sociology leads you to science and electronics; and electronics involves you in trying to understand theories totally incomprehensible to you.

CRISPIN: Look at that model.

ROLAND: It was a sleep that unclogged the pores of my skin.

CRISPIN: It grows, without him touching it, it grows.

ESTHER: Then he starts on another essay – and he's off again.

CRISPIN: What *is* an essay?

ESTHER: An essay on Marxist theories of art brings him to a study of the history of revolutions, which introduced him to Voltaire, who is insufficient, so he goes on to the Paris Commune which brings him back to Marx again.

CRISPIN: One man's digest of another man's thoughts. That's all an essay is.

ESTHER: And we have to listen each time he makes a leap forward to start another circle, and the room becomes cluttered with books that he buys and he buys and he buys in a great fever. That's what you've got, Manfred, a great fever.

ROLAND: Esther, lovely, don't, you'll tire yourself out.

CRISPIN: Come and sit with your sister, you callous bastard.

MANFRED [*book in hand*]: Well I ask you, listen to this: ' . . . we are moving into phases of creative disorder; everywhere the lines are blurred. Physics and biology have reached outside their classic bounds; the important work is being done within the shifting, undogmatic contours of 'middle fields' such as biochemistry, molecular biology or physical chemistry . . .'

CRISPIN: That model, just look at it.

MANFRED: Well, news like that terrifies me.

CRISPIN: And that model terrifies me.

ESTHER: And he grows bald and he has headaches and he refuses to wear glasses.

MANFRED: Well, doesn't it terrify you?

CRISPIN: Everything terrifies me. Babies, dogs, flies, lightning.

ESTHER: And English lawns with cats, and Italian renaissance music and fragile, lily-like, art-nouveau girls. Beautiful!

MANFRED: ' . . . we are moving into phases of creative disorder; everywhere the lines are blurred . . .' Good God!

ESTHER: Manfred, please. Can't you see I want as much of you as I can get?

MANFRED: All my life you'll have me, Kitten.

ESTHER: Will I, Manfred? In the grave, too?

MANFRED [*coming to her*]: I'm a pig. I'm sorry, Ketzel. [MANFRED *and* ROLAND *straighten the crumpled sheets; she smiles and enjoys their fussing. They step back and regard her.*] Good God, how exquisite you look, like a doll.

ESTHER: Fragile you mean, and pale – like a sick child. Oh, I get tired so quickly.

MANFRED: That wasn't quickly. You've been talking for the last two hours – a steady drone while I was reading.

CRISPIN: She used to be so silent and shy.

ESTHER: She used to have nothing to say; now she'd give long speeches if she could, in public.

CRISPIN: What would your speeches be, Ketzel?

ESTHER: Long lists of all the things I really care about, and why. Who do I hate, who do I love; what do I value, what do I despise; what pleases, what offends me? And when I knew, I'd nail the list to the door of the Commons – no, that's common – the doors of St Paul's.

MANFRED: Sleep, Ketzel, and by the time you wake you'll smell hot toast and thick coffee.

ESTHER: It's such a funny thing, sleep. A body curls itself up, closes its eyes and waits. It does absolutely nothing else, a few turns perhaps, but just lies, passively, waiting for something to happen to it.

MANFRED: Sleep. [*Kissing her*] Lovely eyes, lovely lips. No one's leaving, sleep. [*Pause. Looks at photo montage.*] Our grandfather and grandmother from Odessa. Our mother, aged nineteen. Her brothers, Theo, Nachum, Abraham. Their children, their children's children . . . the cousins we've never seen . . .

[*They move away from the bed.* CRISPIN *hugs himself into a red velvet wing-backed armchair.* ROLAND *sits on the floor at the foot of the bed in a simple Yoga position.* MANFRED *returns to his model.*]

CRISPIN [*to* ROLAND]: Well that's cruel. I say that's cruel. She, your sweetheart, so ill, and you – you sit, contemplating, peacefully.

MANFRED: She's not *so* ill, Crispin. The blood-count was better yesterday.

CRISPIN: She's dying, Manfred, face it, she is.

MANFRED: We don't know that.

CRISPIN: Say it to yourself: my sister's dying.

MANFRED: We don't know –

CRISPIN: Say it to me and to Roland.

MANFRED: We don't know for certain.

ROLAND: That lunch –

– I tasted each part of it, my throat separated each part, sharply. And those smells, you know? – how meals smell just of food or a particular spice? Well this lunchtime I smelt each part. Crisply, like a sting. And sounds. It's as though I'm hearing the sound of velvet for the first time, and the movement of wood where the joints in the furniture are, and Crispin's breathing. Listen. Can't you hear the tiniest shifting of everything in the room? [*Pause*] I think I'm turning into an aesthete.

[CRISPIN *rises suddenly, and moves to draw the curtains across the window.*]

MANFRED: But it's still daylight, you're shutting out the light.

CRISPIN: Candles. Light candles.

MANFRED: Candles? Now?

CRISPIN: There's candles, isn't there? Well, light them.

ROLAND: Pull those curtains back, Crispin, there's nothing to be frightened of.

CRISPIN: You're also frightened, you. But you won't admit it, will you?

MANFRED: Crispin!

CRISPIN: Well he is, and you – playing around with your molecules of heredity. Who the hell wants to know how the mess happened anyway?

MANFRED: Crispin, hush.

CRISPIN: Light candles, light them!

MANFRED [*hugging him*]: Crispin, hush. [CRISPIN *rejects him and returns to chair alone.*] We'll light them.

[MANFRED *lights four candles sitting in candelabra. He cannot work, so they all sit in the flickering glow.*]

ROLAND: And I'm going to stop eating from now – except foods with primary tastes, like fruit and meat, very uncooked, and nuts.

CRISPIN: I'm cold.

[MANFRED *goes to the bedside and takes the cover, which he lovingly wraps around* CRISPIN.]

[*Reaching to record-player*] And music, let's have music.

MANFRED: Esther!

CRISPIN: Esther won't mind. She likes waking up to music.

[*It is the second part of Mahler's eighth symphony.*]

\*

MANFRED: Who do I hate, who do I love; what do I value, what do I despise; what pleases, what offends me? Them's thoughts, them is.

ROLAND: And I shall cease to be obese. It's so humiliating to have a body that won't do what you want it to do. I would stop using words if I could.

CRISPIN: Do you know I've stopped reading in the lavatory. I kept feeling it was an insult to the writer.

ROLAND: Funny, it's quite the reverse for me. I'm so disgusted with the act, I need a book to help me rise above it. I sometimes wish we didn't belong to this generation. Talk like that should feel, instinctively – crude.

CRISPIN: It doesn't offend.

ROLAND: Then it should. There were times when to pick our noses and put our feet on chairs and swear in front of girls and find it thrilling when they swore straight back was all delight. Such defiance, so sweet, so full of its own kind of dignity. But it's such a minor kind of dignity I feel, now; such an ephemeral delight, such a tiresome sort of defiance. There's no – no nobility in it. We're such an odious lot, us; not noble at all. No, no – majesty.

CRISPIN: Like this room. No majesty here. Dishonest, that's what it is. We own five shops selling twentieth-century interiors which we've designed, *we've* designed, mind you, and yet look at this room. Bits and pieces from other men's decades.

MANFRED: We've neglected those shops.

ROLAND: I hate them. Everything about them. I hate them.

CRISPIN: You know why? We didn't design what we *knew* was good.

ROLAND: But what the people said they wanted.

CRISPIN: So's not to 'impose'!

ROLAND: So's to give them a sense of 'participation'!

CRISPIN: In the name of 'democracy'!

ROLAND: Couldn't say our tastes were superior to theirs –

CRISPIN: – that would place us in a class we were asking them to overthrow! [*Pause*] What long discussions we had.

ROLAND: I always remember a character in an Eliot novel asking: 'Don't you think men overrate the necessity for humouring everybody's nonsense, till they get despised by the very fools they humour?'

CRISPIN: What lovely, long discussions we had.

ROLAND: Terrible shops!

MANFRED: Esther keeps complaining: 'Why are you here all the time? Who's looking after the shops?'

CRISPIN: Tell her. I keep saying we should tell her.

MANFRED: What good would it do, Crispin?

CRISPIN: We're going to be bankrupt. She should know.

MANFRED: She'll know soon.

CRISPIN: And why haven't the girls come?

ROLAND: Auditors are long-winded.

CRISPIN: You should have gone with them.

ROLAND: We should all have gone. Poor girls. Not even they care any longer. Only they're women, tenacious, heavy with loyalties – like unmilked cows. [*Pause*] I wonder if your eyes change colour when you turn into an aesthete?

CRISPIN: That music. Turn it off. Please!

[CRISPIN *seems to want to vanish into the armchair and blanket.* MANFRED *turns off the music at its most vibrantly passionate passage. Silence*]

ROLAND: Music never could soften pain.

CRISPIN: *You* don't think she's suffering pain, do you?

ROLAND: She aches, that's all.

CRISPIN: She says she aches but we all know –

ROLAND: There's fatigue, weariness, only that.

CRISPIN: You're a fool, Roland, after all her bleeding and that bruising – you don't want to believe it.

ROLAND: When Esther suffers pain so will I, that's how I'll know – it'll come to me also; that's what being an aesthete means.

MANFRED: That's wrong, Roland. Esther wouldn't like that. You mustn't make predictions like that to yourself, not even in a joke. I know you, you make predictions then can't find reasons why you shouldn't fulfil them.

CRISPIN: Listen to his voice. How softly he speaks, still.

MANFRED: Stop talking about me as if I wasn't here.

CRISPIN: Gentle Manfred. How does he do it? Where does he find it? All that gentleness?

MANFRED: And stop pretending cruelty, Crispin. No one believes you.

ROLAND: Do you ever think how strange, but really strange people are? There was once a man I knew, shortly after we'd opened the partnership, who asked me to arrange the inside of a large room like a grand concert hall, with pastel murals showing vistas of people arranged on seats and in boxes listening to music. And into this room he invited his friends every Sunday morning to watch him conduct gramophone records. [Pause] He wasn't an aesthete.

CRISPIN: I remember, when I was working on my own, a woman rang me up, at three in the morning. She'd sat all night looking at her bedroom wall. It had to be red. There and then. It had to be painted red. And I rode to her house five miles away, on a bicycle, hopefully imagining it was a ruse to get me to her bedchamber in a needful hour. But it wasn't. There on the floor, when I arrived, was a brush and a tin of red paint and I had to work, while she watched, for three hours, sitting up in bed. And after it she paid me twenty pounds. One wall. [Pause] Manfred says nothing. He doesn't find the world strange. Only lovely and interesting. Explanations for everybody, no evil for him. Lovely compassions and tender opinions he has.

MANFRED: Stop talking about me as if I wasn't here.

CRISPIN: You still think we love each other, don't you?

MANFRED: And don't shout at me.

CRISPIN: If only he didn't deny the existence of evil. That's what I can't bear.

ROLAND: Stop it, Crispin.

CRISPIN: Evil, evil, Manfred, chant it, lad.

ROLAND: Crispin!

CRISPIN: Evil, Manfred. They took a child from its mother, Manfred, and smashed its head against the wall. Evil!

ROLAND: Stop it or go home.

CRISPIN: A willingness to do a thing which is the opposite of goodness. A *willingness*, a love, an active willingness. Evil! Evil, evil, evil, say it, Manfred.

ROLAND: Crispin!

CRISPIN: Say it!

MANFRED: Our trouble, Crispin, us lot, the once-upon-a-time bright lads from up north, is that we've no scholarship. Bits and pieces of information, a charming earthiness, intelligence and cheek, but – no scholarship. Look at these books here. [*He picks up a pile and throws them round him.*] Renan, Taine, Kirkegaarde, Wittgenstein, Spengler, Plato, Jung, Homer, Vico, Adorno, Lukacs, Heine, Bloch – you've not heard of half of them, have you? And half of them, two-thirds, I'll never read. Do you know, new knowledge disrupts me. Because there's no solid rock of learning in this thin, undernourished brain of mine, so each fresh discovery of a fact or an idea doesn't replace, it undermines the last; it's got no measurement by which to judge itself, no perspective by which to evaluate its truth or its worth; it can take no proper place in that lovely long view of history scalloped out by bloody scholarship, because each new concern renders the last one unimportant. No bloody scholarship, us. And when I sometimes get a feeling that two people in love or one man afraid of death might be a supreme consideration, along comes this man with his 'we are moving into phases of creative disorder' and his 'everywhere the lines are blurred' and I've no defence. He sounds so right, I think, and besides – he's got scholarship. What's 'silly loving' and 'banal dying' in all that? Evil? You want me to confess to the knowledge of evil? I confess it. I say it – evil! So? And what shall I do with *that* bit of knowledge?

CRISPIN: Only a bloody Jew would discover evil with sadness instead of despair.

MANFRED [*moving to* ESTHER's *bed*]: I'll never do anything right for you, Crispin. Look how she sleeps; so sweet. What the hell do I care for the dead knowledge of evil when I'm blessed with a sister as sweet as this?

[*Pause, listening*] The girls are coming.

[TESSA *and* SIMONE, *the last two of the Friends, enter with* MR
MASON, 'MACEY', *aged about fifty-five, Jewish, who has been the
manager of their main shop*.]

TESSA: Yes, the girls *are* coming and what's more they're hot and
mad and full of war. Tell them, Macey.

MACEY: Tessa, I've told you, no alarms.

SIMONE: Not now, Tessa. [*Hangs up coats*.]

TESSA: And what are we in darkness for? Who's drawn the curtains?
[*She rushes to blow out the candles and violently draw aside the
curtains*.]

MACEY: Alarms aren't necessary.

TESSA: Are you going mad! Candles!

MACEY: She doesn't listen.

TESSA: Broad daylight and you light candles.

MACEY: It's like talking to a brick wall.

TESSA: Look at them.

SIMONE: Come on, take off your shoes. Crispin, fetch a bowl of
water. [*Goes to pour drinks*.]

TESSA: They sit fair, square and immovable.

MANFRED: Tessa, lower your voice – Esther.

TESSA: I'll wake her, shall I wake her?

SIMONE: All right now, Tessa.

TESSA: Shall I get her on to you? You'll listen to her, the darling's
dying, you'll listen to her.

SIMONE: You've frightened them enough.

TESSA [*sitting in eighteenth-century chair and taking off her shoes*]:
Twenty years! Out! Like that!

SIMONE: Roland, move off your haunches; it's tantalizing.

TESSA: And I've told them and told them, and they don't listen.

SIMONE: Macey, take a seat.

TESSA [*moving to stool by coffee table*]: I hate that chair.
[SIMONE *joins her and massages her feet*.]
Tell them, Macey.

MACEY: That's not nice, Tessa, to come in straight away to a house
and not say hello or ask about people. No grace, your generation.

ROLAND: Hallelujah!

SIMONE [*to* CRISPIN]: Please!

84

MANFRED: Macey, I've a new thought for you. [*Picking up a book*]

TESSA: Macey's got something to say.

MANFRED: There's a man here says that the coming of print gave man a one-dimensional view of the world and crippled all his other perceptions.

TESSA: Let Macey tell you the news.

MANFRED: Ssh! He says 'the phonetic alphabet makes a break between eye and ear' and man has used this to change from 'the tribal to the civilized sphere' and 'since it's obvious that most civilized people are crude and numb in their perceptions' then it follows that the printing press has held back progress for five centuries and we must start all over again to unify the senses.

TESSA: Crispin, you stop them. Ouch! Gently, Simone, I've got bunions.

MANFRED: Isn't that staggering? Now I find that one thought alone upsets everything, every thing.

TESSA: Manfred, let Macey speak.

MACEY: What's so staggering about it? What staggers me more is that print has been around for the last five hundred years and not only is two-thirds of the world still illiterate, but even those who could read never did and still don't, so where's his proof? How can you be crippled by something you never engaged in? Maybe it's the other way round? Maybe they got crippled because they *didn't* read.

TESSA: I want them to know.

MACEY: Tessa, no alarms.

MANFRED: But words act like dams, he says.

MACEY: Nonsense! I've never heard such nonsense. Lovely things like words? 'Languor' – listen to it. It sounds like what it is – full of lingering and longing: 'languor!' 'Anguish', 'miasmatic', 'crackling', 'surreptitious', 'sonorous', 'asinine'. Lovely words. Dams? Gates more like, to everywhere, to every-possible-where. What else is there? Can you think of something better?

TESSA: He's like an old grandmother. You're like an old grandmother.

ROLAND: He is an old grandmother.

CRISPIN: Leave him alone, he's *my* grandmother.

MACEY: If you're listening to a man talking and you're not sure you like what he says, what helps you to be sure? He sounds right, but something nags at you. To *feel* he's wrong is not enough, you want to locate it, more precisely.

TESSA: Locate it, then; for Christ's sake locate it!

MACEY: He's attacking the world, let's say. He's critical. That's good, very good to be critical. It's a stupid, ignorant, vulgar place, he's saying. And you agree; most of the time it is. And he's saying it sadly; that makes you think he's noble. But still, something's missing, he doesn't sound quite right, if only you can find the right words for it. What are they? What will describe, as near precisely as matters, what's wrong?

TESSA: Have you ever heard a man talk so much?

MACEY: Let me talk! How can I know what I'm thinking if I don't talk? Words, you're looking for the words. If only you can find them you'll understand. Suddenly, you know. He's critical, he's sad, but – but what? 'Dispassionate'! That's it, that's the word. And suddenly all the other words that sounded good – like 'critical' and 'sad' – are pushed just a little aside and a new view of him filters through. *His* sadness has nothing to do with the suffering of the world, it has to do with his image of himself. He wants you to see him being sad. That word 'dispassionate' has enabled you to suspect him of wanting to see the world as full of ignorance because, by comparison, he can then appear clever. And that leads you further; *because* you've discovered that he's dispassionate you then recognize that the details of his criticism are barren. There! another word that's come to you – 'barren', and sterile.

MANFRED: There's something wrong.

TESSA: Will you please let Macey tell you.

MANFRED: You sound right but there's something wrong. I'll think about it.

TESSA: Macey?

MACEY: All right, all right. It's a rotten business, it's my right to procrastinate. There! 'procrastinate', wonderful word –

TESSA: Macey!

MACEY: You're bankrupt! Manfred, Roland, Crispin – I think it's what you all wanted and it's happened. You're bankrupt.

CRISPIN [*moving to get the bowl of water*]. Good!

TESSA: Good?

CRISPIN: Yes, good!

MACEY: Good?

CRISPIN: Good! Good!

MACEY: But I don't understand you any more. Given up, is it? My lovely boys given up?

MANFRED: We're not boys any more, Macey. You've grown old with us so you haven't noticed.

MACEY: But you've gotten unhealthy, closed, incestuous. Is it a holiday you want? Go away then, all of you. I'll look after things, day and night I'll look after things, like always, I'll stay with it. I'll sell things, I'll mortgage my house, we'll all sell things. Macey'll stay. Wouldn't I do that for you? Wouldn't I do anything for you?

ROLAND: Spell it out, Macey.

MACEY: You're not listening, even. Do I deserve that? [*No response, they wait.*] Well, I've cracked each problem as it came up. I've kept my eye on the accounts, daily, there's no mess but there's no money. The sum is simple. You've neglected to order what you once knew would sell, you've not commissioned new designs like you used to, you've not done any yourselves, and so now sales don't equal bills and they've not been equalling bills for a long time. The reserve capital is eaten up; you've not listened to my warnings – except Tessa, and all she's done is design three new lines of wallpaper and matching fabrics and – that's it.

  [CRISPIN *leaves*.]

Tessa wanted me to tell you because she said you wouldn't listen to her, so I've told you and so now I'm going – except I want to see my Esther.

ROLAND: Stay, Macey. It's not so bad. We're not really bankrupt. I wish we were, but unfortunately we've all got large private accounts. At least I have. It's hateful, I've always hated it, this trick of mine, knowing the feel of money, but there we are, we're rich. The business will fold because we want it to, but the bills will be paid and adequate notice given to the staff. So now let's forget the shops, let's not talk about it this evening, or ever more. [*Pause*] I'm becoming an aesthete.

MACEY: A what?

MANFRED: He's turning into an aesthete.

MACEY: He's turning into an aesthete? It's possible? He's had an operation or something?

[ESTHER *wakes up suddenly and irritably.*]

ESTHER: Where's my coffee?

TESSA: Esther!

ESTHER: It's never ready when I want it. You neglect me as well?

TESSA [*going to her*]: Esther, hello, my kitten. The day's over. We're all home, together again. How are you now? You look so rested. Look at her, Simone, she has colour again.

ESTHER: Never mind my colour, where's my coffee and my hot toast? What are you all doing here? Macey, why are you here? Go back to work. I won't have all this idleness. I've never been able to bear idleness.

MACEY: Esther! Such shouting.

ESTHER: And my coffee – where is it?

MANFRED: Hush, Ketzel. I'll get it for you. You've woken up earlier than usual, that's all.

MACEY: What do you mean 'go back to work'? The day's over. And, if it wasn't over, I couldn't come and visit you? What's this?

ESTHER: Look, Macey, bruises. My body, full of bruises, look at me, my arms, my legs, full of pain. I'm racked with pain and you all stand around.

ROLAND: You haven't got pain, Esther.

TESSA: Shut up, Roland.

ROLAND: She hasn't got any pain, she keeps saying she has and you believe her and I know she hasn't got any pain.

[CRISPIN *enters with a bowl, a jug of hot water and a towel.*]

CRISPIN: Tessa, your water.

MANFRED: I'll get your coffee and toast, Ketzel. [*Leaves.*]

MACEY: 'Ketzel'. I had a sister we used to call Ketzel: tiny kitten. She became a mathematician, very rabbinical she was. Esther, I got a story for you. A rabbi died and went to heaven and he managed to get a word in edgeways with God and he said, 'Hey, God, is it true you chose the Jews?' and God said, 'Yes,' and the rabbi said,

'Well, do me a favour and choose someone else.' Isn't that funny? Good, she laughs. It's all right then.

ESTHER [*despite laughing*]: But I'm still so tired.

[ROLAND *rushes from room.*]

TESSA: Lie back then, Kitten. Here, lift a little and I'll re-arrange your pillows. There, they need punching. Better? Do you want more?

SIMONE: Come on, Tessa, your water's here. It'll get cold.

[SIMONE *kisses* ESTHER *who closes her eyes and dozes again. Then she urges* TESSA *back to the chair, places her feet in the hot water and washes them.*]

CRISPIN: Come on, Macey, there's nowt left for thee nor me to do except drink.

MACEY: And why the dialect all of a sudden?

CRISPIN: So's not to see the seriousness of it.

MACEY: I didn't intend to stay. Say my little piece and go, that's what I intended.

CRISPIN: Eat with us, Macey. Tha's not done that in a long while; we're not together much longer.

MACEY: I feel uncomfortable, Crispin, and hurt. I love you all still, but you don't take it like you used to. I'm like a father intruding on his children's privacy. You're all very strange to me in these surroundings. It's so large, this house, and full of other things. Not like the shop at all. Full of light and brightness there, but here – Old Nick lives here. It's too rich.

CRISPIN: Aye, it seems like it right now because we're all living together. Usually, though, it's only Manfred, Esther and Roland. But with Esther's dying –

MACEY: Stop that! Are you mad?

CRISPIN: With Esther being ill – we've all camped down.

MACEY: You don't leave each other alone, you've not been apart for weeks now. Is that what you want?

CRISPIN: We've been brought together, like, an' now noa one of us can bear to lose sight of t'other.

MACEY: I know, I know, that's just it. I've watched it. But it could go on for years. It's not good, Crispin. Tell them that. Tell them that it's not good.

CRISPIN: Nay. It's very good, Macey. We should've always lived like it; shared our property, confronted one another's problems – right! Good! *Wilt* tha stay?

MACEY: I don't know. I'll drink my drink and think about it.

[*Pause*]

TESSA: Crispin, come and brush my hair.

CRISPIN: Not while Simone's washing your feet I won't.

TESSA: All right, Simone, thanks, enough now.

[SIMONE, *hurt, leaves* TESSA *to soak her feet.* CRISPIN *brushes* TESSA's *long hair.*]

SIMONE: Another drink, Macey?

MACEY: Yes, I'll have that, thank you. And you'll make the dinner, won't you?

SIMONE: Yes.

MACEY: Silent Simone, working for everyone.

SIMONE: That's my pleasure, Macey. Besides, even when I do talk they shut me up. My class credentials aren't acceptable, don't you know!

MACEY: Ha! Class! One day will I give them a lesson about class; such nonsense I've had to take from them all these years.

SIMONE: Such nonsense we've both had to take, eh, Macey?

MACEY: Poor Simone, you do no one thing and you do everything.

SIMONE: It's because I can do no *one* thing that I do everything. I'm very useless, Macey. Here, drink, stop questioning me, I'm embarrassed. It's easier doing things. [*She reaches to continue work on a small tapestry on stand.*]

MACEY: Then do something for me, Simone. Sell the business.

SIMONE: Sell it? Me?

MACEY: Don't let them wind it down. Find someone to buy it. You'll get a good price and I can stay with it. I'm too old for change.

SIMONE: You sell it, Macey. If you want to stay there you sell it.

MACEY: But I'm only a manager, you're a director.

SIMONE: Act on our behalf. I give you permission. We don't care.

MACEY: Extremes! Everything you do is an extreme. Megalomaniacs! I've always said that you were megalomaniacs. After one shop was a success you didn't open another *one* but another *five*! Esther never designed small tapestries, they had to be enormous, for cathedrals and boardroom walls and airports. And look at all those books. Manfred doesn't buy one at a time, but whole libraries, from professors who die, desperately hoping their books will give him their cleverness. And Roland. A brilliant man, brilliant! Figures were games for him. And look at him. He wants to become an aesthete! Once he wanted to be a voluptuary. From one extreme to another. Excessive. All of you. It's all mad and wrong. Six of the most talented people in the field and you're all – you're all – well I don't know what you're all doing. I don't understand it. It's not anything I understand at all.

SIMONE: The streets are filled with strange, young people, Macey. Beautiful boys and girls with long hair and colourful bits and pieces they buy from our shop. All styles – Victorian, art-nouveau, military – as though they're attracted by the pomp and circumstance of traditions they hated – like cats playing with mice before devouring them. And they want only one thing, these people. To love. It's as though they're surrounded by so much ugliness and greed that they have to spend all their time convincing themselves that other things exist. And they try to be frightened of nothing. Anyhow, whatever it is – I'm not much good at that kind of analysis – two of them came into the shop today and held out their hands. In one hand was a black handkerchief containing money, in the other hand a packet of plain biscuits. And one of them said, 'Have some money,' like that, 'Have some money,' as though he were offering me a cigarette. And do you know I was embarrassed. But I put my hand into the black handkerchief and took out two pennies, they were all pennies. 'Now have a biscuit,' the other one said. I was mesmerized but I took it, and ate it, and they watched me very closely, smiling and eager, as though waiting to see if I'd learned the lesson. Then they walked out, offering pennies and biscuits to other people. I heard one person say, 'Not today, thank you.'

MACEY: It makes me very angry.

SIMONE: Does it, Macey?

MACEY: They all wear masks, they've all got comfortable poses.

SIMONE: Doesn't it find even a little, little echo in you?

MACEY: And they shift about in personalities that've got nothing to do with them, and they drag around some old cult, and they stick alien feelings on to themselves –

SIMONE: After all, they like our shops.

MACEY: – alien feelings! Like those shabby second-hand clothes. Nothing fits.

SIMONE: Nothing?

MACEY: All right, so they've got a – a sweet-natured grubbiness, but they're still susceptible to loud-mouthed culture and political fraudulence. They'll never produce anything, not this time around. Have to abandon hope this decade. An uncomfortable lot. It irritates me.

SIMONE: What's irritating about the young is that we're not.

MACEY: Possibly, possibly. I'm reaching the age where I employ a desperate charm in order to gain the attentions of all those lovely young girls whose silly little minds I despise. And the price I pay for this flattery is to listen to their flat, dull thoughts which they offer with that shrill immodest modesty, you know? – how they hide their awful conceits by trying to be humble? Terrible age, really; the age where I only want to hurt, give pain, make others suffer. A sour age.

[*Suddenly* MANFRED, *carrying a tray of coffee and toast in one hand, drags in* ROLAND *with the other.* ROLAND *is struggling to put on a shirt through which blood is seeping.* SIMONE *stifles a scream. He has been cutting his body with a razor and rubbing salt into it.*]

MANFRED: Look what I found this bloody fool doing.

[ESTHER *sits up but cannot see what has happened and* MANFRED *immediately goes to distract her. The others move in to* ROLAND.]

ROLAND [*hissing whisper*]: Don't! Leave me.

ESTHER: Did I hear a scream?

ROLAND: And don't tell her anything.

SIMONE: It's nothing, Kitten. I broke a glass, a little cut.

[SIMONE *bends down pretending to pick up something.* TESSA *takes a towel and covers* ROLAND's *shoulders. Then he comes deeper into the room and sits on a stool, tense from his self-inflicted pain.*]

ESTHER: Why is Roland in a towel? Roland – why are you in a towel?

SIMONE: He's just washed his hair.

[ROLAND *pathetically rubs his hair.*]

MANFRED: I'm sorry it took so long, Ketzel.

ESTHER: You know, there was once a doctor who discovered he had leukaemia because one day he bought a new microscope and tested it by looking at a sample of his own blood.

TESSA [*to* ROLAND]: What have you done?

CRISPIN: Razor cuts, they're razor cuts.

MANFRED [*to* ESTHER]: The blood-count was good last week, don't forget, so they must have found the right drug for you, my kitten.

ROLAND: Tell me she's not suffering.

TESSA: What good do you think you're doing, fool, what good?

ESTHER [*to* MANFRED]: You know how *I* knew? Roland was making love to me one night and asked me, 'Where did you get those bruises from?' 'What bruises?' I asked him. 'Those ones,' he said, 'there, and there, and there and there and there.'

CRISPIN: And salt. He's rubbed them in with salt.

ROLAND: Stop staring at me. Go away. She'll see you.

SIMONE: Let me sponge you.

ROLAND: Don't come near me. Please. Perhaps she won't die. Please God make it hurt more. I've never had any pain in my life, make it hurt more, it's not fair to give pain so unevenly, make it, make it.

TESSA: Fool!

[*As he talks,* ROLAND *is rubbing himself, and thus rubbing the salt deeper into his wounds. In the petrified silence* ESTHER *becomes suspicious.*]

ESTHER: What is it? Why is everyone standing around? I know what it is. It's depression time again. I'm dying and you want me to make it easier for you by pretending I'm not, isn't it? Come on now, we're all too clever for dramatic deceits like that. And what's more, your silence and pretending make my misery worse. Much, much worse. MACEY! I want to go on living! ROLAND! I *don't* want to die. MANFRED, SIMONE, TESSA! All of you. I-do-not-want-to-die. [*Pause*] My God, that was cruel of me, wasn't it. Oh, forgive me, everyone, don't take notice. I didn't mean to give you pain.

TESSA [*low and fierce to* ROLAND]: Fool, fool, fool.

ESTHER: Yes, I did. I did want to give pain. I should say I don't mind, make it easier for you, but I do – I do – I just do. [*Long pause*] Manfred I want to walk. Help me.

[*She rises, talking,* MANFRED *helping.*]

Do you know anybody who was prepared to die? Despite all the suffering and the knowledge of suffering and man's inhumanity, everyone wants to go on living – for ever and ever, gloriously.

[*She takes a stick and slowly circles the room, touching, remembering.*]

Some people of course know that when they're old they'll become tired and ready to go; or else they grow to despise themselves so much for not being what they thought they were that they become anxious and eager to fade out. Not me, though. Just not me. I can't tell you how much I cherish everything. I know there's a lot that's obscene and ugly but it's never been too oppressive, I've always had the capacity not to be oppressed. *You* know that, don't you, Roland? In the end there's such sweetness, such joy in hidden places. I want to stay on and not miss anything. I want to stay with you, all of you, close and warm and happy. Why shouldn't I want that? And think – all those things I haven't done. Every year the world finds something new to offer me: another man makes music or carves an impossible shape out of the rocks or sings us a poem. Someone is always rising up, taking wing, and behind him he pulls the rest of us; and I want to be there, for every movement, every sound. Why should I want to die away from all that?

[ESTHER *falters,* CRISPIN *goes to her.*]

That's made me tired again, that has.

[ESTHER *returns to her bed, exhausted.*]

I keep wanting to talk and I keep getting tired. Manfred, take the pillows away.

[ESTHER *slides down into the bed with eyes closed.*

SIMONE *moves to* MANFRED, *who has left the bed and is desolate and cannot contain his anguish. She clasps him in her arms.*]

TESSA [*rushes to* CRISPIN]: Hold me, Crispin, just this once more, I'll not ask thee again.

[*She clasps him but his response betrays reluctance.*

MACEY, *disturbed, moves as though drawn, despite himself, to* ROLAND. *He picks up the sponge, unable to believe he could ever bring himself to do it, and gently sponges* ROLAND's *back.*]

MACEY: You're children, you're all children. Go away from each other. It's not right, you don't know what you're doing, any of you.

## SCENE TWO

*Three hours have passed. Dinner has been eaten.*
ESTHER *sleeps.* MANFRED *lies on top of the blankets close to her.* SIMONE *sews buttons on a shirt.* MACEY *has remained. He is a little drunk.*

MACEY: Why don't I go? [*Pause*] There's a great stillness in you, girl. I've never known anyone to radiate such calm. How can you be still in a house like this? [*Pause*] Why don't I go?

SIMONE: Stay, Macey. There's no shop tomorrow. Help us kill Sunday.

MACEY: Look at him, Manfred, there. He won't leave her alone. He can't hold on *for* her. [*Pause*] I've drunk too much. Everyone's crawled into some corner of the house and no one's said anything to me and I don't know what I'm supposed to do. Why are you so still?

SIMONE: Everyone tells me that. It's not stillness really, it's fear. A protective silence. If I say too much or do too much I'm always afraid someone'll stamp on me. I feel so raw most of the time, such a useless human being.

MACEY: That lot'd miss you for a start. Cuddling their tempers when their arses need kicking.

SIMONE: That's just because I'm so desperate to be wanted. I'd do anything for that.

MACEY: Why don't I go? I feel like I've caught a disease.

SIMONE: They're lucky, the others. The same art college, same warm northern city, same kind of labouring fathers and tight-lipped mothers.

MACEY: Ha! Labouring fathers and tight-lipped mothers. I like that.

SIMONE: And they built the shops for them.

MACEY: Only they never came.

SIMONE: My lot came instead.

MACEY: Not Crispin's driver dad nor Roland's religious floor-scrubbing mum.

SIMONE: But slim young actresses and architects' wives.

MACEY: Not Tessa's bricklaying brothers.

SIMONE: But politicans' daughters.

MACEY [*indicating* MANFRED *and* ESTHER]: Not even their parents: The Leeds Jewish Anarchists' Association – ten hours a day stitching linings; no furniture and all books.

SIMONE: And you know, Macey, it's broken their hearts.

MACEY: I know it.

[MANFRED *comes forward. He seems in a trance.*]

MANFRED: How strange.

MACEY: So you were awake then?

MANFRED: I think I've been dreaming.

MACEY: Oh, so you weren't awake then?

MANFRED: But I wasn't asleep.

MACEY: So you *were* awake then!

MANFRED: I've got a powerful urge to say something. As though I've been instructed, as though I've had a vision.

MACEY: Good. Now I *am* going.

MANFRED: But I can't bring myself to say it. It sounds so banal. And yet lying there, it didn't seem stupid, it seemed profound, and desperately urgent. Even now, I don't feel fully awake, I feel – don't laugh – possessed. But – [*turning to* ESTHER] possessed by her. I want to say – [*He finds it difficult.*] – I've got to say – we must be honest. That's all. Just four words. Isn't that dull? But it was a great need, all of a sudden; we – I must be honest. Who do *I* hate, who do *I* love, what do I value, what do I despise, what pleases *me*, what offends *me*? Esther's questions. And I want to go around asking everybody else. What offends *them*? That's why revolutions happen, isn't it? – something offends. Macey, you, why are you a manager?

MACEY: I should've gone.

MANFRED: You manage other men's affairs, you don't create or invent or produce but you manage what other men produce. Why? A man who loves words. Why? You won't answer, will you.

MACEY: Simone, Manfred – good night to you.

MANFRED: Esther's dying. Macey. We're growing old bit by bit.

Every word is a second, passing. It'll never return, never. That's so
absolute. I shall never be young again. I shall never laugh the same
way again. I shall never love for the first time again, never discover
my first sight of the sea, nor climb my first mountain, nor stumble
across literature, never; I'll reach out to recapture or remember –
but the first ecstasy of all things? Never again. So, it's important. I
*must* know. What do I really love? What do I dare to say I despise?
[*As though trying to remember something he once told himself secretly*]
Englishmen! I despise the Englishman. His beliefs embarrass him.
[*Pause*] Is that all I wanted to say? A bit weak, wasn't it? [*Trying
again*] Belief demands passion and passion exposes him so he believes in nothing. He's not terrified of action. Action, battles, defeats – they're easy for him. No, it's ridicule. Passion invites
ridicule; men wither from that. Listen to an Englishman talk,
there's no real sweetness there, is there? No simplicity, only sneers.
The love sneer, the political sneer, the religious sneer – sad. [*Pause,
suddenly:*] Macey's right. We must sell the shop, not fold it up.
Sell it and start again, something else. I want to talk about it. Simone, call Tessa and Crispin, drag Roland out from wherever he's
crawled – we'll talk, plot. It's so long since we've plotted. [*Long
pause*] Terrible, isn't it? I can't bring myself to believe any of that.
Lying there it sounded so logical and right; but saying it, actually
using the words – nothing. Stale.

[MANFRED *returns to his model, adding to it unenthusiastically.*]

SIMONE: Manfred, can *I* say something to you –?

MANFRED: I don't think so, Simone . . . Thanks, but – forget
it.


SIMONE: Play me a game of chess, Macey. Keep me company.

MACEY: I must go.

SIMONE: I'm not very good, you can beat me.

MACEY: Why don't I go?

SIMONE: Here. [*Indicates eighteenth-century chair.*] This one.

MACEY: Now.

SIMONE: Beautiful chair, isn't it?

MACEY: Before the others return.

SIMONE: I know other people's pain is a net, but stay – I beg you.

97

Look, look at the chessmen. Crispin made them, he's made the king like Don Quixote and Sancho Panza is the Queen trying to protect him.

[*They play. While they are playing,* ROLAND *enters with 'paper' burning in his fingers. He brings it to an ashtray and watches it burn.* MACEY *is incredulous when he realizes what it is.*]

MACEY: That's money!

ROLAND: Watch. [*Takes another pound note and burns it.*] Look at it. What does it make you feel?

[MACEY, *unable to control himself, stamps it out.*]

So? What've you saved? Does it make you feel better now? *You* should do it. Take a pound note from your wallet and burn it. Try. Look, I'll do it again. Watch.

[MACEY *is mesmerized as* ROLAND *burns another*].

The last time I did that was in a restaurant with Esther. She cried.

MACEY: I could never do that, never.

ROLAND: You don't know, try it.

MACEY: I could never bring my hands to strike the match. Physically, I couldn't do it. I know it without even trying.

[SIMONE, *realising she's lost* MACEY, *reaches for the shirt and continues sewing on buttons.*]

SIMONE: You're cheating, aren't you, Roland. Three pound notes? Nothing more?

ROLAND: You're right, of course. Such little gestures for big angers. Aaaah!

SIMONE: Your back?

ROLAND: Hot. Hot and throbbing. Now I feel I want to bathe in ice. If only I didn't have to move. Pain needs contemplation, it's irritating otherwise. So petty – irritation.

[ROLAND *takes up his Yoga position*]

[TESSA *and* CRISPIN *return. He is in a vicious mood, waving a letter at* SIMONE.]

CRISPIN: Another one.

TESSA: Crispin, no!

CRISPIN: I've found another one. Wherever I go I find thy letters and thy notes waiting for me, like an ambush. In t' pockets when I reach for cigarette, under t' pillows, on t' deck – everywhere.

Tha even posts 'em to me. We live in t' same house and tha posts me letters. Tha little mad girl, thee, why dast dae't?

SIMONE: Crispin, please, I beg you.

CRISPIN: I've told thee, again and again. I've told thee but tha dastna listen. An' what in hell is't tha' doing that for? Can't I sew me own buttons? Look at her! Look at that long, ancient, Gothic face. Full of apology for belonging to her class. Do you knoa how she sees us, Macey? As working-class heroes bringing light and beauty to our mums and brothers. Stop looking so sad for me.

SIMONE: All right, I promise, never again, but no more scenes.

CRISPIN: Nay, don't run away, I'm not ower finished yet.

SIMONE: So cruel. You're so cruel and unsubtle.

CRISPIN: Listen to t'words she uses. 'Unsubtle'. What's subtlety got to do wi' anything? She misuses words and emotions like an illiterate office girl.

SIMONE: All right, I'm hurt, you've succeeded. Don't go on.

CRISPIN: Listen to this: [*reading from letter*] 'Oh my darling. Instinctively I sense a crisis in your soul.' A crisis in my soul! That's how subtle she is. 'O God I am sad with you. Do not evade my glances of concern.' How's that for a nice, fat platitude – 'Do not evade my glances of concern.' And I have to read it, every day. Words pour out of her, biliously, each one killing the one before. '. . . the mundane, mediocre, timid, dreary phrases of our heart . . . the dull, safe minds . . . if only we could look outside and raise the level of pleasure to great stimulation and beauty and progress and satisfaction . . .' What does any of it mean? Where dast find time to write all this great nonsense? 'Oh my dearest, what the hell does friendship mean? One feels all the depths of pain and difficulty – and you chose to insult and ignore me as if my natural interest to communicate at such times was wrong and ugly and I feel like an old jar of marmalade left to mildew . . .'

> [*These last words bring* CRISPIN *to a slow halt as the pain of* SIMONE'*s letters reaches him through the last poignant image. He feels ashamed and retreats from her.*
>
> TESSA *goes to* SIMONE *to comfort her.*]

SIMONE: Forgive me, Tessa. I couldn't keep it to myself all the time. I thought I could give him strength – that's not bad, is it?

TESSA: It's all right, don't go on. I don't mind.

SIMONE: You do, I know it. I can feel it in the way you touch me.

  [TESSA *moves to be near* CRISPIN.]

Oh God, I feel so rejected, I can't bear it. There's such pain in this house, such pain.

  [*The Friends are a tableau of misery and silence. They have known each other most of their lives.*]

ROLAND: I always think that while a *good* man sins or acts out some wretched piece of misery or offends his own gentleness, God turns away and doesn't look and leaves him alone to do it in private. That's a good world, that one, with a Good God. It consoles me, that. Doesn't make it easier to bear, but it's kinder.


## SCENE THREE

*Some hours later. About 2 a.m.*

MANFRED *is reading at his desk and making more notes.* ROLAND *is sitting beside* ESTHER's *bed and reading to her from Djuna Barnes's* Nightwood. SIMONE *is by now drunk.* MACEY *sleeps in a chair.* CRISPIN *plays chess with himself.* TESSA *sits at his feet strumming a guitar.*

ROLAND: 'Nora had the face of all people who love the people – a face that would be evil when she found out that to love without criticism is to be betrayed. Nora robbed herself for everyone! incapable of giving herself warning, she was continually turning about to find herself diminished. Wandering people the world over found her profitable in that she could be sold for a price for ever, for she carried her betrayal money in her own pocket. Those who love everything are despised by everything, as those who love a city, in its profoundest sense, become the shame of that city.'

ESTHER: No more, Roland. Manfred, help me, I want to walk out into the room.

MANFRED: No, Ketzel, stay resting. We'll come to you if you want.

ROLAND: Let her walk.

ESTHER: I want to stretch and move.

ROLAND: Let her if she wants to.

ESTHER: You should be glad, shouldn't he, Roland?

ROLAND: She wants to step out and be alive. Come on, Kitten, ignore him.

[*Everyone rises to move things out of her way as* ROLAND *and* MANFRED *guide, like a queen, this pale and dying beauty to a stately chair.*

SIMONE *places a low, soft stool under her feet. They all seem to be play-acting an exaggeration of a relationship they each have with her – she is adored by them.*]

ESTHER: Come on, Manfred, you're dying to tell us what you've been reading about. We're all ready.

[MANFRED *picks up his papers and, with mock seriousness, begins to read from his notes as though recounting a thriller.*]\*

MANFRED: You thought there were only social revolutions, the French, the industrial and the Russian, eh? Well you're wrong, listen to this, I've got others for you just as epoch-making. This book tells that in 1600 a man called Gilbert, who was the personal physician to Queen Elizabeth the First, wrote a 'famous' book called *De Magnete* about an electroscope which turned out to be 'indispensable to the development of physical science' and which enabled a man called Thompson to discover that electricity was made of particles which he called electrons and this discovery had 'the most profound effect on physical science'. 1897! Revolution number one! And then an American physicist called Millikan measured the electric charge of an electron which led to the extraordinary conclusion that its mass was $1/1835$th of a hydrogen atom and thus demonstrated that particles even *smaller* than atoms existed. Revolution number two. Next, a few years later, the Curies! Radium! The nature of radio-activity revealed! And what was its nature? Within it, atoms spontaneously exploded! Out went radiation while behind was left – a new atom! – thus showing that the immutability of the elemental atoms was a myth and so 'twentieth-century science was launched on its fateful journey into the restless world of the atom'. That was the third revolution. Now – it gets even more exciting – a man called Max Planck developed a theory called the quantum theory which said that radiant heat was a discontinuous mass made up of particles

---

\* It is of paramount importance that the actor makes as much sense of this precis as possible while at the same time clowning the story.

and *not* smooth waves, and that was 'so revolutionary' that even its originator didn't believe it! Einstein had to prove him right! Drawing conclusions which were *themselves* revolutionary! – because he applied Planck's ideas with 'devastating results to the photo-electric effect and discovered that light itself also consisted of multitudes of individual parcels of energy and not waves'. 'Physicists were incredulous'! It says so here. [*taps book.*] Numbers four and five. But that was nothing, because he then went on not to the sixth revolution but to a revolutionary concept of the very nature of revolutions. He shook the unshakeable concepts of physics! – with his famous theory of relativity which, as we all know, has the central principle that all natural phenomena are subject to the same laws for an observer moving at one speed as they are for another observer moving at another speed. If you went on a trip in space you'd return to find your twin brother older than yourself. 'Common sense mocked' said the headlines. But man cannot live by theories alone. While the theorists were theorizing, the experimentalists were experimenting. Back to the atom. Beginning in Manchester and ending in Cambridge a man called Rutherford, following in the footsteps of Thompson who, you will remember discovered the electron, pursued experiments into the nature of the atom which, he found, was essentially empty! All that was there was a nucleus of miniscule size and gargantuan density in which all the atom's mass was concentrated with electrons orbiting like planets round the sun. Another revolution is taking shape. Inspired by Rutherford, a Dane called Niels Bohr applied quantum theory to the behaviour of electrons inside atoms in order to understand how light was born. 'And God said "let there be light,"' and all the little atoms spat out light. The revolution shapes on. Not without difficulty however. Bohr was unable to find the spectra for complicated atoms and he couldn't account for the behaviour of extra nuclear electrons in any but the simplest of atoms. Now his failure became another man's challenge, a young German physicist in 1924 called Werner Heisenberg, at the tender age of twenty-three set out to invent a mathematical theory which would account for the spectral lines which could be observed. But – also in 1924 – unknown to Heisenberg who was courageously going forward – Louis de Broglie of Paris was going all the way back. 'Light is waves,' had said everyone. 'No, light is particles' had said Einstein. 'Electrons are grains of matter,' had said Thompson. 'No,' de Broglie now said, 'they're trains of waves'. No revolution is without its problems! The thrilling microscopic world of the atom refused to behave in the same way as the mediocre macroscopic world of man. It was not the same as planets round the sun, and along came an Austrian physicist called Erwin Schrodinger to demonstrate it. Based on de Broglie's conjecture he evolved an entirely new mathematical approach specifically designed to describe the behaviour of this incredible miniature world. Revolutions within revolutions! But – young Heisenberg was not satisfied with merely a mathematical description of the dual nature of the electron and so, in 1927, like Einstein – but in a different context – he revised the fundamental meaning of physical measurement. No less! How does one know anything about atomic particles? To what extent can we measure them? Can you measure their properties? The analysis of the microscopic nature of the atomic world was such that it drove him to introduce an extraordinary pinciple which is called 'the principle of uncertainty' – very wise! – which states this: 'that in the nature of things it is impossible to specify the exact position and the exact velocity of an electron at the same minute; the uncertainty in the position could be decreased only by increasing the uncertainty in the speed or vice-versa;' and guess what – the product of the two uncertainties turned out to be a simple multiple of Planck's constant! 'Of course, Heisenberg's uncertainty doesn't affect the behaviour of the world in the gross but its transformation of the fine detail from an exact and predictable pattern into a blur of probabilities was yet another major revolution in scientific thought!'

ESTHER: Wait a minute, wait a minute. Say that again – 'but its transformation of the fine detail from an exact and predictable pattern into a blur of possibilities was yet another major revolution in scientific thought'?

MANFRED: Precisely.

ESTHER: Oh really now.

MANFRED: The revolution approaches its climax. 1930, a Cambridge mathematician called P. A. M. Dirac. He synthesizes the physical ideas of Planck, Heisenberg, de Broglie and Schrodinger, fits them into the framework of Einstein's theory of relativity and low and behold – a book called Relativistic Quantum Mechanics in which

Music © 1969 Wilfred Josephs

*Freely-like an improvisation*

We've bur-ied the win-ter mar-ried the spring, and now we have a time to pause and think a-gain and sing

We've plant-ed seeds grant-ed birds their songs, now we have a time to rest and right a-gain those wrongs.

**TOGETHER:**

Chorus *(faster)*

If there's a heart in you, a part of you that can re-lent re-live for-get for-give then

*(slower)* *(faster)*

cov-er wounds I've gi-ven you for wounds are wounds and

*(slower)*

words are words and no a-mount of cry-ing cry-ing

*(slower)* *(faster)*

cov-ers them or heals them____ Live with them

*(slowing down)* *(slower)*

Live with them Live____ with them.____

undreamt of phenomena were revealed such as the creation and annihilation of particles and antiparticles. It was, this author says 'an epoch-making book'. Epoch-making! And have we read it? And all those revolutions – have we heard about them? And that was only up to 1930, there's another forty years to go! And my God! What shall we do?

ESTHER: You will grow bald and become blind and I have no patience with you any longer.

TESSA [to a guitar]:

TESSA:      The leaves are turning,
            The earth has turned,
            And now there is a time for burning
            Hates we left
            Unburned.
            The year's beginning,
            Long nights will sow
            Soft seeds for those softer days
            The wrong ways
            Must go.


TOGETHER: If there's a heart in you . . .


ESTHER: Simone, stop drinking.

SIMONE: I'm not drunk. What does it matter?

MACEY [who has slowly woken up during the song]: Jesus! what a head I've got. Why don't you all go to bed? What time is it? Two-thirty in the morning, lunacy! Argh! My mouth's like starch washing day.

ESTHER: Simone, give Macey a long cool drink. Relax, Macey. It's the best time of night. I don't even feel tired.

MACEY: You just don't leave each other alone.

ESTHER: Feel this room, Macey. Quiet, friendly – it's a gentle room, this.

MACEY: Why didn't I go home?

ESTHER: Nothing can touch us here –

MACEY: You think not?

ESTHER: Isn't that so, Manfred? Manfred! What's he doing now?

MANFRED: The appeals, Ketzel – I forgot to sign the cheques.

MACEY: The what?

ESTHER: You didn't know, did you, Macey, that Manfred forced us all to agree that one-third of our profits should go to help the third world?

MACEY: What profits, for God's sake? Am I in a madhouse or something?

ESTHER: Not charities, not cancer research or ex-prisoners, nothing marginal like that. Revolution, Macey: arms for South Africa, medical supplies for North Vietnam, funds for guerrillas in Latin America, books for Cuba.

CRISPIN: It should all be medical supplies.

SIMONE [*savagely*]: Makes you feel more humanitarian, doesn't it?

CRISPIN [*imploring*]: Simone!

ESTHER: The third world, Macey. We're all frightened of it. Our parents left us a heritage of colonial and racial bitterness and the third world hated them and is going to make us pay for it, and so we're all frightened.

MANFRED: Hatred is only an expediency for them, Ketzel.

ESTHER: Such a gentle person, my brother. Other people's need to hate makes such sense to him. *His* reasons for sending arms *now* is because they're oppressed *now*; mine are, the sooner it's done the sooner real men can take over from the rabble-rousers. Rabble-rousers frighten me, they're only rebels, not revolutionaries. My brother's a rebel, Macey, I – am a revolutionary. He talks about leaders of our time, I see a need for men who belong to the end of a long line of all time. He's obsessed with our responsibility to the twentieth century, I'm obsessed with our responsibility to an accumulation of twenty centuries of sensibility. My brother is a rebel because he hates the past, I'm a revolutionary because I see the past as too rich with human suffering and achievement to be dismissed. Women are natural revolutionaries, aren't they, Simone? Men are only ever rebels, their angers are negative, tiny. Like students, a kind of boyish energy. Do you know one of the reasons why I despise a capitalist society? Because it produces men who *enjoy* the violence of opposing it.

MACEY: Strange energies you all have. How can you concern yourselves with so much?

ESTHER: Macey thinks I'm teasing, Manfred; tell him it's only because I'm so wretchedly ill that I sound like teasing. Tell him. [*Closes her eyes.*]

[CRISPIN *begins to wander round the room, touching things, as though drugged.*]

SIMONE: Crispin! You look like a zombie.

CRISPIN: Don't shout at me, Simone. No retaliations now. I feel raw, lass. Harsh words is like burns. Can't take it. Peace, Simone, pax, pace, pace.

SIMONE: You're tender when you like, aren't you?

CRISPIN: Sssh. No little revenges, Simone; pace, pace, pace.

SIMONE [*mocking*]: Pace, pace, pace!

[*Silence; out of which grows a contrapuntal duologue between* MANFRED *and* CRISPIN. MANFRED *whispers to* MACEY *while* CRISPIN *talks to the others.*]

CRISPIN: We've chosen good colours, gentle colours. Does that mean we're gentle, you reckon?

MANFRED [*coming down to confide in* MACEY]: I know what I despise.

CRISPIN: It's that there's so much suffering in the world that I suddenly need other kinds of knowledge, to soothe it all out.

MANFRED: I know but I daren't say it.

CRISPIN: These colours soothe me, the touch of velvet, those paintings.

MANFRED: I've been feeling it for years, but I'd stutter if I tried.

CRISPIN: Is that wrong? To want to be soothed?

MANFRED: Even now, as I'm talking, I'm trying to bring myself to wrap sounds round those feelings. Perhaps, I think, my tongue will trip up, accidentally, in the middle of a sentence about something else. [*Pause*]

CRISPIN: Roland –

MANFRED: Hate them –

CRISPIN: Kiss me.

[ROLAND *and* CRISPIN *kiss each other on the lips and remain clasped during* MANFRED'*s next words.*]

MANFRED [*whispering almost*]: The working class! Hate them! It's coming, Macey. Despise them! I can hear myself, it's coming. Hate them! The working class, my class, offend me. Their cowardly acquiescence, their rotten ordinariness – everything about them – hate them! There!

[CRISPIN *breaks away from* ROLAND *to take* TESSA *in his arms, rocking her, cradling her.* ROLAND *lays his head in* ESTHER'*s lap.*]

CRISPIN: That's what I want to do – I've just realized.

MANFRED [still whispering]: Those endless dreary episodes of 'ordinary life' on television.

CRISPIN: I want to caress everything, touch people, comfort them, make them calm, tell them not to be worried, that it'll be all right.

MANFRED: And there sits the ordinary man, watching himself, pleased and familiar, not even spellbound, just dumbly recognizing.

CRISPIN: Have you listened to a car go round corners? Isn't that a violent noise?

MANFRED: 'Eh,' he says, 'that's me it is. Gladys, come and look, just like you and me and Jack and Gwen and Kate and bloody ordinary Sammy in the pub. No need to change then, is there? We're good enough to make telly about.'

CRISPIN: I can't bear violence any more, or the news about violence: car crashes, accidents by fire, famine, earthquake, war.

MANFRED: And then his children watch; and slowly they begin living a copy, not of their parents' real life, but the watered-down version other people have made of their parents' real life on the telly.

CRISPIN: I can't bear the violence of speech.

MANFRED: Isn't that extraordinary?

CRISPIN: Ugly people with violent voices, violent images on street corners, violent prejudices – it batters me.

MANFRED: But look what happens next, Macey.

CRISPIN: Me nerves – they're all frayed and battered.

MANFRED: Along comes a new generation of writers and they begin writing new episodes about the *children* – whose ordinariness has doubled because all they've had to look up to was the pale reflection of their parents which the last generation of writers put on the screen.

[SIMONE, *isolated, is drawn to sit by* CRISPIN *and* TESSA. CRISPIN *offers the comfort of his arms to her so that his strength is given to both women.*]

CRISPIN: Peace, I need peace.

MANFRED: And soon, Macey – you'll see, there'll be stories about their children and their children's children, and the characters on the screen will become more and more feeble –

CRISPIN: Peace and silence.

MANFRED: – and the more banal their utterances the more like real life it'll seem until one day the screen will just be blank, an electronic fog, and they'll sit there and accept it and say nothing.

CRISPIN: Peace, silence. Blessed peace and silence.

MANFRED: We're all poisoned by this hatred, aren't we?

CRISPIN: It'll be all right. Don't worry.

MANFRED: A real cancer, this one, growing from faint beginnings, little suspicions, all those people we loved –

CRISPIN: I promise you –

MANFRED: Sad, like disappointed lovers, all that love, gangrenous, inside us.

CRISPIN: We must just be calm.

MANFRED: I try to ignore it, start afresh, find the world extraordinary –

CRISPIN: It's true – we must love one another, or die.

MANFRED: – but I've no energy, no appetites for new loves.

CRISPIN: Believe me.

MANFRED: Some men could, some men could stay perplexed and wondering all their life and still survive. All their life –

CRISPIN: It will –

MANFRED: – amazed!

CRISPIN: – everything will be all right.

MANFRED: Each moment – surprised!

CRISPIN: I promise you.

MANFRED: And finally – joyous! Joyous to be witness to it all. Lovely men they were, Macey, not sour and thorny like us, but eager, capable – splendid outrages. [*Pause*] Terrible!

CRISPIN: Peace –

MANFRED: Waste!

CRISPIN: – and silence.

MANFRED: That's what I really wanted to say.

CRISPIN: Blessed peace and silence.

MANFRED: We're too old to pretend.

[*Suddenly* MANFRED *stops speaking, his attention drawn by* ROLAND, *who is slowly rising away from* ESTHER *as though he has just discovered something dreadful. One by one they all turn to look at* ROLAND *and each of them knows –* ESTHER *is dead.*]

# ACT TWO

## SCENE ONE

*The same room. Some hours later.*
*The body of* ESTHER *lies under some blankets.* ROLAND *has gathered a number of garments belonging to her and laid them at the foot of her bed. He sits, gazing at the body, holding a jumper to his face.*

[SIMONE *enters in a dressing-gown.*]

SIMONE: Roland?

ROLAND: She had an odour, a faint delicate odour.

SIMONE: Roland!

ROLAND: When I'd come into a room I'd know she was there. Here, this sheet, this blouse, a pullover – where her breasts were. If I hold it near me I can be reminded.

SIMONE: You ought to leave this room, Roland.

ROLAND: Not a perfume, nothing sweet and sickly, but the smell of movement, skin that had worked hard, to protect vulnerable parts.

SIMONE: Do you want me to sponge you?

ROLAND: Please. I think so.

[SIMONE *undoes his shirt, pulls it down and slowly sponges.*]
[*Referring to his self-immolation*] How crude that was. What a vulgar gesture. [*Pause*] You're not frightened of dying, are you?

SIMONE: No.

ROLAND: What will you do now?

SIMONE: I'd like to do just that: die, go away and die. Creep into the river or the stones on the street. [*Pause*] Give me a reason why not to, Roland. [*Silence*] You know what defeats me? My capacity for nostalgia. I can project myself forward twenty years from now and feel myself regretting what I've not done today. That's what makes the present so oppressive; it's bad enough aching for the years gone by and suffering today's mess, but somehow I manage to suffer tomorrow's reproach also, before it comes. And it all defeats me. [*Pause*] Just walk out, away. Do it now. I'd get such peace. [*Pause*] Give me a reason why not, Roland.

ROLAND: You're drunk, Simone. Go back to bed. You've been drinking all night.

SIMONE: Never mind whether I've been drinking. Give me a reason why I shouldn't do it now, get up and walk away and never come back. You can't, can you?

ROLAND: I'm not the right person to ask.

SIMONE: You can't give me a reason, can you?

ROLAND: No, I can't. Please leave me alone now, Simone.

[*He takes up his simple Yoga sitting position and closes his eyes.*]

SIMONE [*rising*]: You don't know what it's like to talk and not be heard; to offer and not be taken; to be full and not needed. There's not a creature needs me, not one single one. They'll use me, drink with me, tolerate my company, but not need – not really need me. I feel so useless and rejected, so dismissed. You've never known that, have you? God's chosen ones you lot are, but not me. Look at my face. [*Looking into a long 'Gothic' mirror*] Long and Gothic you say, you like telling me that, flirting with the past. And my eyes, full of pleading. Who can look at them? Full of pleas and sighs and expectations – watery, dog-like; and long limbs – drooping over this chair, like a wet doll, awkward, embarrassing, waiting for crumbs; and they all know it, and they retreat. I don't blame them. Who can blame them? And I want to creep away, just pick myself up and go and not come back. I'd love that, I'd so love that.

[SIMONE *now regards* ROLAND *in his sitting position. Then, with great contempt:*]

It's all nonsense, Roland. Lie in green fields if you want peace, climb mountains or walk in forests if you want to meditate. You won't come to terms with death that way.

[*He ignores her; she watches a few seconds longer then leaves him. After she has gone he relaxes, opens his eyes, reaches for a garment into which he buries his face, then crumbles, miserably, into the folds covering the dead woman.*]

## SCENE TWO

*Later.* ROLAND *whimpering.*

ROLAND: Take me with you. I don't really want to go on. I'm so tired, Esther, and empty. Pick me up also, it must be so easy.

[*Silence.*

MACEY *enters. He's just emerged from trying to sleep, and is tucking his shirt into his trousers.*]

MACEY: I can't sleep in this house; you're whimpering all night and the others keep moving about. What the hell good do you think you're doing there, and those cuts all exposed? Put something over you, you bloody child, you.

[*He offers him a black pullover, which* ROLAND *ignores. Leaves him to agitatedly put on his tie in front of the mirror.*]

You're weird, all of you. And unnatural. Esther was the only healthy one of the lot of you. Just let the press get pictures of you all now. That'd be a scoop. 'The Trend-makers'! Huh! The habit of discontent was all your lot ever created. Making the young feel that the world belonged only to them. Real little class terrorists you were, intimidating everyone over the age of twenty-five with your swinging this and your swinging that. You never thought you'd grow old or die. Even the politicians and the poets were frightened of you, you screamed so loudly about your squalid backgrounds. Here, let me help you. Look at you. They'll fester, those cuts. You must be racked with pain. And put a pullover on, it's cold.

[*He helps the pathetically struggling* ROLAND *to put on the black pullover, then wanders miserably round the room.*]

This room is festering. With gloom. Restless bloody house. [*Stops in front of* MANFRED's *model.*] Questions! Suddenly everyone's full of little heavyweight questions. 'Who do you hate? Who do you love?' 'Why are you a manager?' Who asks questions at my age? I know why I'm a manager, what good does it do me? [*Finally the atmosphere drawing an answer from him*] Because each morning I wake up knowing that I don't love the woman at my side, and haven't done so for the last fifteen years – That defeats me that does, that really does defeat me. No love – no appetites, for nothing. Even before the day begins I'm done. [*Pause*] But, I've managed. A good father taught me discipline so I managed. Why, I asked myself, why *exactly* did I resent her? Very important to know. She's not a bad woman, very good in fact, even wise – about simple things – loyal, sense of humour – everyone loves her – except me; so why? You know why? Because *I* had the capacity to grow and *she* didn't. She grew, true, but, one day she stopped and I went on. Simple! Not a reason for resentment, you'd say – such a strong emotion, resentment. True. But what I had to force myself to accept was that she was a reflection of *me*: I chose her. At one time in my life my entire capacity to love had focused on her. And I had to ask myself, 'Could I have been capable of such small needs?' So I resent her because she makes me despise myself. She reminds me, every day, that at one time in my life I'd wanted such small things. But the next discipline was really hard; you listening, Roland? Really hard! It was to avoid building up those little heavyweight philosophies about man and the world out of my own personal disappointments; to avoid confusing self-hatred with hatred of all men; to face the fact that though I'd failed, others hadn't. There! Two disciplines! Two honest confessions! But who's satisfied? No one is – are they? Because they're no good really, those little bits of honest confession. What am I supposed to do with them, tell me what?

[ROLAND *is trying to climb up alongside* ESTHER].

What-are-you-doing-for-God's-sake? Get away from that body. Leave it alone!

[MACEY *in righteous anger pulls* ROLAND *violently to the floor, causing him great pain.*]

I'm sorry, son, I'm sorry.

ROLAND: No, no. It's good.

MACEY: Those cuts, I forgot those cuts.

ROLAND: Leave me, it's good I say.

MACEY: I just forgot them. I'm sorry.

ROLAND: It's good, I say. The pain, it's good, it's good, IT'S GOOD!

MACEY: You disgust me. [*Leaving*] If you imagine you can overcome death by creeping up on it like that you're mistaken. And not all your silly self-inflicted pain will help either. One day you're going to die and that's that.

ROLAND: There's no such thing as death.

MACEY: Idiot!

ROLAND: Death doesn't exist.

MACEY: Mumbo jumbo! Idiot! IDIOT!

[MACEY *leaves.* ROLAND *creeps back to the pile of garments and again smells them, desperately trying to recapture the living* ESTHER.]

## SCENE THREE

*An hour later.*

ROLAND *still at the foot of the bed.* TESSA *is at his side, trying to draw him away.*

TESSA: Roland, come on, sleep, lovely.

ROLAND: I'm really frightened now, Tessa, of everything. I'm panicking. All those years gone and I don't like any of them and I'm panicking.

TESSA: You've given yourself too much pain, lad. Daft pain. And you're tired. Shall I make you a hot cup of tea? Without milk? Some lemon and lots of brandy in it? Will that be nice?

ROLAND: That tight brain I had, all wrapped up with confidence – it's fallen apart. Everything I love I don't feel for now. What do I do?

TESSA: Don't ask, Roland, please don't ask.

ROLAND: Panicking. I'm panicking. I can feel it, Tess. Terror and panic.

TESSA: Come away.

ROLAND: Where will it be? When I die, where will it be? How will it happen? Will I know I'm dying? Will I lie there knowing everything and knowing I can't stop it?

TESSA: You're not fair, Roland. It's not right, all this now.

ROLAND: Not even words. I can't find words; and words I find I don't want to use, and words I use I don't believe in. What do I do?

TESSA: Hush.

ROLAND: Tell me, Tess. I've run down. Look. Stopped. That was my last word.

[*He has said it, but only after he has said it does he realize it must be true, for now he opens his mouth to say something and cannot. Real terror and panic show in his eyes now.*]

TESSA: Roland, stop it. You're forcing yourself. It's not honest. You can't stop talking. It's not possible. Say 'Tessa', say that. 'Tessa, Tessa, Tessa.' Scream then. ROLAND!

[ROLAND *releases a sad and desperate moan and pitches his face into* TESSA's *lap. She rocks him and laments.*]

Oh, oh, oh! My poor boy. It's so bewildering, isn't it? So wretched and bewildering. We're none of us what we thought we were. It's so late now. But you shouldn't panic, lovely. You shouldn't upset yourself. You upset us when you do that and we need each other now. Roland, we need each other so much. Roland? Roland?

[*She shakes him but he is in a catatonic state. Abruptly she rises.*]

Don't let his panic get you, Tessa, don't let it reach into you now.

[*She wanders around the room in a fever of distress – finally she reaches for her guitar and smashes it to pieces against the eighteenth-century chair.*]

Too late, Tess, too late.

[CRISPIN *comes to find what the noise is.*]

CRISPIN: Tessa!

TESSA: Oh, Crispin!

[*Relieved, she runs to clasp him and find comfort, but he cannot respond.*]

Aye, lad, too late.

[*She flees.* CRISPIN *collects the pieces of her guitar and places the ruins in a corner. Then he turns to* ROLAND.]

CRISPIN: Tha's frightened *now*, lad? Eh? Really frightened now. And I can't comfort thee, nor thee me, nor any of us t'other.

[ROLAND *shrinks and* CRISPIN *kneels and takes him in his arms and kisses his face as he would an unhappy child.*]

Aye, I'll tak thee in me arms and gi' thee kindness but there's nowt of comfort in me. I'm gone and messed up proper an' all. Shall I tell thee what I do, lad? Will that ease thy misery a bit? I'm so embarrassed and ashamed I can only tell thee in our dialect so's not to see the seriousness on it, so's it'll come out as a funny story. I sleep wi' owld ladies, me. I discovered one day they like me and they want me and I can gi' mesen to them. Owld passions I can drag from them, wi' me lips and me hands and a lot of gentleness. Tha canst not understand it, can tha? But it's like the glory of raising the dead to see red blood rise up in their faces and find their soft bones flutter wi' life. But they want to pay me and I takes the money and the pleasure on it turns to shame and disgust and I swear I'll not touch them again but I do. In the shop, they come and they look at me and they seem to know and their eyes plead and I go again. And there's shame and disgust and pleasure and it's all consumed me. Unnatural passions! They take out guts from a man. Aye, I knoa you can prettify it, give it justification, say the times they are a-changing. But times never made the soul, did they, lad? Eh? That's a constant that is, the soul, through all times, and what offends it today offends it tomorrow an' all. And I've destroyed mesen I have; offended and confused the soul see? Denied mesen the right of saying owt to any man. [*Pause*] It's a good dialect, ours, ent it, Roland? We've noan on us got it still but it's a good, rich dialect from your smoky north. I think I'll keep it by me. Aye, tha's taken it badly, lad. And it's not ower yet. The morning'll bring its tempers, eh? Its snapping and snarling. We'll kick each other before t'day's through, that's for sure. Nay, there's nowt of comfort in me. [*Rocking, rocking, Fade.*]

## SCENE FOUR

*Morning.*

TESSA, MANFRED, CRISPIN, SIMONE, MACEY *and* ROLAND *are ranged in different corners of the room:* SIMONE, *more isolated from the rest, is still in her dressing-gown;* ROLAND, *huddled at the side of the bed, is dressed as in the previous scene;* MACEY *is sunk in the winged-backed armchair, his*

*suit crumpled now. The rest are dressed in black.* MANFRED *sits by his desk.*
CRISPIN *fiddles with his 'toy' by the window.* TESSA, *back to the audience,*
*stands hugging herself in the centre of the room.*

TESSA [*turning*]: You look awful, Simone. Go away and dress.
SIMONE: Yes, Tessa.
    [*She leaves. Silence*]
TESSA: Oh, I feel so old this year and not very wise.
MACEY: Well, and what are you going to do now?
TESSA: What's left worth the while to do, Macey?
MACEY: What a rag-bag of shabby doubts you lot are.
MANFRED: Don't fight.
MACEY: You think you've asked a question of such importance.
MANFRED: Please.
MACEY: But it's so thin, your question, so feeble and thin; such a
    peurile catechism to measure the world with.
MANFRED [*moving to sit by the bed*]: Don't fight, please don't fight.
MACEY: And when are you going to bury her? Will it be a Jewish
    cemetery, Manfred?
    [*Silence*]
TESSA [*to* CRISPIN]: We've no children, that's what it is. We're
    barren, we're all barren; brought forth nothing, sterile. 'Barren'
    and 'sterile': beautiful words, Macey. Too frightened to make
    babies, weren't we? They would bind us, couldn't have that, not
    us. Too beautiful we were, too important to be bound down. Dead
    lovelies, us. [*Pause. Takes toy from* CRISPIN.] Toys you made. For
    other people's kids. Lovely madness. The nearest *you* ever got to
    paternal instincts. [*Returns it.*]

    [SIMONE *returns. Somehow, with the exception of* ROLAND *and*
    MACEY, *the positions of each shift into a pattern where* SIMONE *is*
    *left isolated and the others seem ranged against her.* SIMONE *senses*
    *this, the others not.*]
SIMONE: So, the mistress is dead and I'm the first to go.
    [*The others are caught off balance with this perception by* SIMONE
    *of what they are forced to realize was their subconscious feeling.*]
TESSA: What does that nonsense mean?

SIMONE: Oh, I don't know, a feeling I have.

TESSA: You have a knack of making people feel what they don't feel simply by suspecting them of feeling it.

CRISPIN: She's such a sensitive delicate soul.

SIMONE: It's not nice what you're all doing now, not just.

CRISPIN: And she goes on and on misusing words. 'Nice'! Such an indifferent word: 'nice'.

SIMONE: But *why* are you all so hostile?

CRISPIN: Another word: 'hostile'!

SIMONE: I'll go then.

TESSA: Oh stop it, Simone. Can't you understand for once?

SIMONE: And can't I be understood for once?

CRISPIN: She's complaining about being rejected now.

SIMONE: Talk to *me*, Crispin. I've got a name, I'm in the room.

CRISPIN: If I talk to her directly she'll think I'm in love with her.

SIMONE: You're very cruel, you, with your 'pace, pace'.

CRISPIN: Don't prompt me.

SIMONE: I don't understand, Macey.

MACEY: Nor me, none of it.

SIMONE: Suddenly, they're all turning on me.

TESSA: And stop whining.

SIMONE: I'm sorry about my voice, I can't help that, but it doesn't alter the meaning. You're miserable, all right, so am I. I haven't got any less feelings because I come from an upper-class family. We've got past that surely, Tessa?

TESSA: Well we haven't, so there! My father's a railwayman and yours is a company director and nothing can change that.

SIMONE [*hardly daring*]: Except the fact that *you're* a company director.

MACEY: Ah ha! She has fight. That stings you, doesn't it. Tess!

SIMONE: Oh, Macey! It's all so unworthy.

TESSA: TAKE HER AWAY! Go, Simone, for God's sake go. Go and maybe by some miracle this room'll go with you. Out – get out, out – out – OUT!

[*Long pause*]

Oh, Simone. I'm sorry. You know we don't mean it. None of us. It's shock; Esther's dead and suddenly we're old and we're none of us what we thought we were and that's not easy now, is it? Don't cry, Simone. I've never been so cruel before, have I? [*Pause*] Oh dear mother, what's happened to me? It's stuck to me, this anger, I'm prisoner to it now, me. It used to be a joke for you all, I used to get angry to make you laugh, that was my role. But it's no laugh now. There's no getting rid of it, this croaking, I'm blotted with it now, for keeps. Oh dear mother, I wish I was a girl again.

[*Silence*]

MANFRED [*as though just discovering it*]: There is about us all such a great poverty of intention. Such a great poverty of intention.


CRISPIN: Simone, I'm sorry if I –

SIMONE: I don't care for the sound of your voice just now, Crispin.

CRISPIN: I wanted to apologize, that's all; say I'm sorry. Peace – I want to make peace.

SIMONE: You only want to make peace because you've discovered a need for old women and you disgust yourself.

TESSA: SIMONE!

SIMONE: He won't give *us* his favours because he sells them.

TESSA: Shut up!

SIMONE: Can't be harsh to the world now, can you?

TESSA: Leave him alone.

SIMONE: Guilt's drained your energy away and you can't ask the world to be better than you are.

CRISPIN: I found this need.

SIMONE: Tenderness?

CRISPIN: Old women, lovely sad old women.

SIMONE: Ha! You need tenderness all right.

CRISPIN: I could make girls out of them.

TESSA: You rejected, sour bitch, you. What've you said?

CRISPIN: But it's true. How can you tell the world how to live when a passion like that takes you up?

TESSA: Have pity on yourself, Crispin. There's no shame there.

SIMONE: I didn't say it to give him shame.

TESSA: Oh you've taken up a great responsibility now, Simone. A great weight you've taken now.

SIMONE [*softer*]: I'll give you tenderness, Crispin. [*Both turn away.*] Macey, help me.

MACEY: How? Help you! Help you! How?

SIMONE: They started it, not me. I didn't want any bitterness.

MACEY: Bury the girl! What are you all standing around for?

SIMONE: They're disappointed and so they start resenting me.

MACEY: Is that all you've got the courage for? Bury the girl!

SIMONE: They think I'm silly, insignificant – a little bourgeois girl.

MACEY: At a time like this you turn on her. You need a thrashing, each one of you. Esther, bury Esther.

[*An attack is now gathering force from* SIMONE *and* MACEY.]

SIMONE: Look at them! Jumped-up downcast proles!

MACEY: They go around evolving their little panaceas and then get all depressed because their mums and dads didn't listen.

SIMONE: With their half-digested bits of self-taught education.

MACEY: The innocent charms don't work now, do they?

SIMONE: They've confused themselves.

MACEY: Why should your labouring fathers and tight-lipped mothers come to the shops anyway? What would that've solved?

SIMONE: They think I can't tell them anything.

CRISPIN: S'e's been drinking all night.

SIMONE: But I can. If they'd let me I'd tell them such things. I love them all so much, Macey; they've needed me and I've worked and loved the n and I know what matters.

TESSA: What matters, Simone? You tell us.

[SIMONE *is caught off balance but struggles for a reply. Unfortunately her terror of them makes her inaudible, she cannot even look at them and uses* MACEY *to talk through.*]

SIMONE: Manfred shouldn't despise the working class.

TESSA: What was that?

SIMONE: And Crispin shouldn't be ashamed of his passion.

TESSA: I can't hear her, can you?

SIMONE: And Roland should stop hopping from one cult to another.

TESSA: What matters, Simone? We're waiting.

SIMONE: Justice.

TESSA: *What* did she say?

SIMONE [*still barely audible*]: I said 'justice' – and the pursuit of happiness.

TESSA: But what's she mumbling for?

MACEY: She said 'justice and the pursuit of happiness', that's what she said.

TESSA [*incredulously*]: But what's that got to do with anything at this moment?

MACEY: Well give her a chance, she knows what she means. Tell them, Simone.

[SIMONE *is petrified by now and continues mumbling into* MACEY *as though he must translate it to them. She is clumsy and touching and pathetic.*]

SIMONE: You see what I want to tell them is that order matters because –

TESSA: What's she saying now?

MACEY: She's saying order matters also, now quiet.

CRISPIN: 'Order'?

TESSA: It's becoming a nightmare.

MACEY: I bet that frightened you, didn't it?

CRISPIN: Yes it did.

MACEY: Well you haven't earned the right to anarchy yet. You've created confusion and chaos and the habit of discontent and you haven't earned the right. Now, what do you want to say, Simone?

SIMONE: Tell them order is not uniformity or sameness. Tell them you can make order out of different things.

TESSA: For God's sake tell it to us, Simone. Mumbling away in that old granny's ear.

SIMONE: I'm just saying that order doesn't necessarily lead to uniformity or sameness.

TESSA: Yes –

SIMONE: And that you can make order out of different things.

TESSA: Yes – and so?

SIMONE: Well don't you see? There's a difference between the order that cripples and the order that liberates.

TESSA: Yes –

SIMONE: And that's what we're looking for, isn't it? The possibility of infinite variety? Isn't that –

CRISPIN: Noble?

SIMONE: Yes! Noble! So many blossomings. Noble! And what's more – there's room for failure when you've got order, and for weaknesses and – and –

CRISPIN: For everyman's fallibility?

SIMONE: Yes, Crispin, I don't mind being fed words, despite the manner in which they're offered. Everyman's fallibility.

CRISPIN: She's mad. She's been drinking all night and she's mad.

SIMONE: Oh, Crispin, isn't there anything in my madness touches you? Don't I deserve a little love for such loving madness?

MACEY: It's so terrible she wants to thrash your gloom from you?

SIMONE: Deny me that also?

MANFRED [*tenderly*]: Not now, Simone, not at this moment.

SIMONE: Yes, now, Manfred. Please let me go on, please.

MANFRED: It's all wrong to go on like this. I know you're distressed, you want to help, but it's all wrong.

TESSA: And irrelevant.

MACEY: Let her talk, Tessa.

TESSA: But she's talking about order and nobility and Esther's lying there dead and it's all irrelevant. Look at this room, look at the lovely order we've cluttered ourselves with. Dead and ancient riches, PERFECT!

[*She throws over the eighteenth-century chair.* SIMONE *rushes to pick it up, lovingly.*]

I can't bear this room any more. We've built too much of ourselves into it. Singing, plotting, loving – such a lot to be remembered, arrangements, smells, odd bargains – all that spent love and devotion – too rich, too too rich. And now we're trapped, hung up by it all. Bits and pieces of us all over the place.

SIMONE: You should love it.

TESSA: *Love it?*

SIMONE: Memory, the past, signs of human activity – you should cherish them – I adore this room.

CRISPIN: Millions starving and we've surrounded ourselves with thefts.

SIMONE: And would these poor bits and pieces feed starving millions? Is that the solution? More little gestures.

CRISPIN: Property is the theft, Simone, don't you know that?

SIMONE: Nonsense!

MACEY: Nonsense!

SIMONE: Nonsense! Nonsense!

MACEY: The *acquisition* of property may be theft, but er –.

SIMONE: But the proprietorship of personal things? Little personal things? That's theft? Where's the logic in that? Look at this chair. [*Points to eighteenth-century chair.*] It's got to be somewhere, it can't be everywhere. Is the man who *wants* it and *has* it near him for most of the time a thief? Does wanting necessarily imply theft? . . .

MACEY: It's not him wanting that's wrong, it's others not having.

SIMONE: After all, what does him 'wanting' that chair mean? It could mean that he's responding to beauty.

MACEY: That's bad? That's immoral?

SIMONE: Don't you see the silly confusions you've got yourselves into?

TESSA: The apple doesn't fall far from the tree, does it?

CRISPIN: She's returned to her class.

MACEY: Ah ha! Class! Class, class, class! And what a mess your lot made of that issue. I'll handle this one, Simone! The working class is deprived, you said, our society is unjust, 'stunted growth' you cried; 'promise unfulfilled'. And then – now listen to this lunacy, Simone – then, in the process of trying to redress the balance look what they did: they defended those very same stunted growths, called them working-class values and applauded them! And then they attacked bourgeois values as decadent. So tell me this, you idiots, you: if bourgeois values were only decadent and working-class values were only beautiful, then what were you complaining about in the first place? One minute you claim the need for revolution because inequality has left the people ignorant and the next minute you claim you want to do nothing but what the people want. But why should you want to do that which an ignorant people want? What kind of logic is that?

SIMONE [*swinging in on* MACEY'*s excitement with confidence now*]: That chair is beautiful because a craftsman exercised his craftsmanship on it. If an unjust society enabled one man to give another man the money to create a beautiful chair, does that make a chair a decadent work of craftsmanship?

MACEY: The trouble with them is, Simone, [*almost whispering to her*] they've taught the people to despise the wrong things and it's boomeranged right back at them. That's why their mums and dads ignored their shops.

SIMONE [*pulling him round to her, collaborators in mocking them*]: You can't come to the people and claim that the things you like are superior to the things they like, because that will then place *you* in a class that you're asking *them* to overthrow.

MACEY: And you can't pause to argue subtle distinctions like that from a political rostrum –

SIMONE: Or in the middle of mountain battles –

MACEY: Or in the middle of mountain battles –

SIMONE: There's not enough time –

MACEY: The revolution's got to be done today –

SIMONE: To gain the people's full support they must pretend the people are aware and conscious of everything –

MACEY: Worthy to be listened to on all matters –

SIMONE: And so they find themselves involved in committing acts they despise in order to prove that the people are worthy to be listened to.

MACEY: On all matters.

SIMONE: And so you despise yourselves. For in this *you've* committed the most 'counter-revolutionary' act of all: in your haste to mobilize support you've given blessings and applause to the most bigoted, the most loud-mouthed, the most reactionary instincts in the people. [*Pause. No response. Tries again and then moves to switch on light over Esther's bed.*] But *she* was a revolutionary, a real woman and a real revolutionary. She wasn't obsessed with being responsible to the twentieth century. Twenty centuries of sensibility, the accumulation of *that*, that's what she felt responsible to. The past is too rich with human suffering and achievement to be dismissed. In the end there's such sweetness, she said, in hidden places, someone is always rising up, taking wing, and I want to be there. [*Pause. No response. Turning on them*] It's not me who's confused, because I've only ever spoken about what the working man *could* be and felt anger that he's abused for what he *is*. [*Pause. No response. Then with sad defiance*] Then know this, *I* will neither wear cloth caps not walk in rags nor dress in battledress to prove I share his cause; nor will I share his tastes and claim the values of his class to prove I stand for liberty and love and the sharing between all men of the good things this good earth and man's ingenuity can give. Now shoot me for that.

[*The others now seem chastened and mellow, though more touched than convinced.*]

MACEY: They listened, Simone.

[*After a long silence:*]

MANFRED: Yes, Simone, we've listened. But that's not the half of it. Our mess is made of other things, like fears, pretensions and disappointments. It's not made of our confusion about who should own eighteenth-century chairs, it's made of – the silly things we've added to the world: easy achievements, ephemeral success. It's not because we've forgotten about injustices and the pursuit of happiness, it's because of little damages we've done to each other and a terrible sense of defeat and time passing and appetites fading and intellect softening. Our mess is not only made of Esther's dying, but the knowledge that this is a once and only life more than half over, and if you want to thrash the gloom from us then you'd have to give us back youth and the strength not to despise ourselves. Not all your haranguing us to order political priorities can clear up such a mess as that. It can't be ignored, that one, not that one.

SIMONE: THAT'S NOT GOOD ENOUGH! [*She runs to the dead Esther and throws back covers.*] She wanted to live.

ROLAND: LEAVE HER!

[ROLAND *snatches the body and hugs it to himself.*]

SIMONE [*dawning on her*]: You've been wanting to do that all the time, haven't you? But you didn't dare, did you?

[*A strange scene begins; at first it seems hysterical, then macabre, but finally must become the natural actions of people trying to find their*

*own way of both showing their love for the dead and trying to overcome
their fear of death, or at least trying to come to terms with the knowledge
of death.*

*Everyone is electrified, uncertain, but sensing* SIMONE *is about to do
something outrageous. She watches them as though gauging how far
she should go and then, cheekily rather than hysterically, raises a dead
arm, making it 'wave' at the others.*]

She wanted to *live*.

[*She waits to see what effect it has on them.* ROLAND *is mesmerized,
gripping Esther's body fearfully from behind. Now* SIMONE *makes it
appear as though he is embracing her as she forces an arm to reach back
and pull down* ROLAND's *face to kiss the neck. The body seems to
have life.*

[*Whispering tenderly and reassuringly to* ROLAND] She wanted to live.

[*How are the others affected? She watches.* ROLAND *is slowly
affected and makes the dead hand blow a kiss. At last a faint smile
appears from each one and they shift in embarrassment and shyness, as
though caught doing an improper act.*]

[*Realizing she's broken through*] She did! She wanted to live.

[SIMONE, *encouraged, pushes them further by rushing to bring
'Esther's chair' to centre of room, and facing it towards the portrait of
Lenin.* ROLAND *understands and carries the dead Esther to sit in the
chair.* MANFRED *also understands and runs for a cushion to prop up
her head. The understanding spreads as* TESSA *hurries to pick up a
stool to lay for her feet.*

MANFRED *kneels and bends Esther's hand into a clenched-fist salute.
The arm slowly falls.* CRISPIN *finds a book to place in her hands.*

*Thus seated, the others are forced to accept the presence of the dead
among them. Slowly they relax and one by one kiss her cheek, then –*
MANFRED *returns to his model;* TESSA *and* CRISPIN *go to the bed
to fold away the blankets;* ROLAND *sits by Esther as though guarding
her.* SIMONE *begins to clear away coffee cups and dirty ashtrays.*
MACEY *watches them a while, reaches for his jacket, half leaves,
turns to smile at* ROLAND, *returns to kiss Esther, leaves –*
*– and a slow, slow fading away.*]

# THE OLD ONES

This edition differs from the original, having been revised by Wesker based on his own production of the play in Munich in 1973

## AUTHOR'S NOTE

Everyone except JACK and the THREE YOUTHS happens to be Jewish; nevertheless this play is essentially about defiant old age.

The songs referred to on page 135, 'Zog Nit Kein Mol' and, the main one, 'Auf ein reigsteit a boym', are recorded by Nehama Lifshitz on CBS S.63626.

FOR OUR CHILDREN
LINDSAY JOE, TANYA JO AND DANIEL

First performed at the Royal Court Theatre, London on 8 August 1972, directed by John Dexter, designed by Douglas Heap, with the following cast:

| | |
|---|---|
| EMANUEL | Max Wall |
| GERDA | Amelia Bayntun |
| BOOMY | George Pravda |
| SARAH | Patience Collier |
| TERESSA | Wanda Rotha |
| MILLIE | Rose Hill |
| JACK | George Tovey |
| ROSA | Susan Engel |
| RUDI | Leonard Fenton |
| MARTIN | James Hazeldine |
| THREE YOUTHS | Terry Burns |
| | Stephen Grives |
| | Martin Skinner |

Revised version directed by Arnold Wesker on 27 February 1973 at the Kammerspiele, Munich, designed by Rudolph Heinrich, with the following cast:

| | |
|---|---|
| EMANUEL | Peter Paul |
| GERDA | Else Quecke |
| BOOMY | Wolfgang Büttner |
| SARAH | Maria Nicklisch |
| TERESSA | Inge Birkmann |
| MILLIE | Barbara Gallauner |
| JACK | Paul Verhoeven |
| ROSA | Heide von Strombeck |
| RUDI | Helmut Pick |
| MARTIN | Edwin Noël |

In this production nine local school children were used for the classroom scenes.

# CHARACTERS

EMANUEL, aged about 70
GERDA, his wife, about 68
BOOMY, his younger brother
SARAH, his sister, about 71
TERESSA, Sarah's friend, about 68
MILLIE, Sarah's friend, about 71
JACK, Sarah's neighbour, about 72
ROSA, Sarah's daughter, about 32
RUDI, Sarah's nephew (son of a dead sister), about 40
MARTIN, Boomy's son, about 28
THREE YOUTHS, aged about 16

# THE SETTINGS

There are seven different settings:

The garden and verandah of Emanuel's house
Boomy's room in Emanuel's house
Sarah's council flat – the front room/kitchen
Millie's council flat – the kitchen
Teressa's attic/living-room in an old Victorian
   house
A street
The classroom

I visualize two revolves, one containing three, the other two, interior sets, with the space between left for a street and the classroom.

# ACT ONE

## SCENE ONE

*Darkness. A garden, a verandah, a hammock between two trees. Then, the thin light of a hazy, summer dawn, just enough to catch the figure of a distressed old man walking round and round. He cannot sleep. He moans. Which way must he turn, what must he say? He can decide neither. He screams, a harrowing confused sound, the pain incomprehensible to him. Exhausted, he crumbles to his knees; the light is growing, the night over. An old woman limps into sight.*

EMANUEL: Warnings! All I can do is cry out warnings. What's that for a life?

GERDA: Torturing yourself again?

EMANUEL: But there's no light.

GERDA: You torturing yourself again?

EMANUEL: Crying out in the darkness. Typical!

GERDA: And you're torturing me also.

EMANUEL: No light, and no one there. Nothing!

[GERDA *stands by him to cradle his head.*]

GERDA: You think I'm not tired?

EMANUEL: There should be an echo, a coming back or something.

GERDA: It's not enough already?

[EMANUEL *screams.*]

MANNY!

[*He disentangles himself and lumbers about. Frantically he searches the garden. Two stones; he knocks them together, waits between each sad, stinging sound; three times. Searches again. An old kettle, a piece of wood; he rattles the one in the other, rapidly. Silence. Stillness. He is full of helpless pity for what seems lost, wasted, irretrievable.*]

EMANUEL: Ah! Gerda. I'm reduced to such simple sounds. Noises, that's all.

GERDA: Come, Manny. Sleep.

[*He allows himself to be drawn back to the hammock.*]

It's not a way to grow old. Like this? A madman? You're not a madman and you know you're not a madman. Sleep.

[*She enters the house. He returns to sleep. Slowly, the bright sunlight and sounds of morning.* GERDA *comes from the house, across the porch, with a tray of tea, toast and boiled eggs. She wears an ortho-paedic shoe. A few hours have passed.*]

[*Pouring.*] China tea! A new madness. Every morning a thin cup of smelly tea.

EMANUEL: Mornings my mouth is like I've been through a sand-storm. I need a delicate taste.

GERDA: Delicate taste! My delicate man!

[*She slices his eggs.*]

EMANUEL: You know, I must stop sleeping out at nights.

GERDA: Now he's decided.

EMANUEL: It's too cold and I'm too old to camp out.

GERDA: Who says you're too old?

EMANUEL: You're cantankerous, you know that?

GERDA: Cantankerous! Cantankerous! Here, I heard a new quotation on the radio. [*Gives him a torn-off piece of paper.*]

EMANUEL: Show me. [*Reading from it.*] 'All things fall and are built again. And those that build them again are gay.' Ha, ha! He won't have one to match this, not so early in the morning. [*He crosses porch to the room and bangs on a wall.*] Boomy! You listening? [*Pause.*] You there? You awake yet?

BOOMY'S VOICE: I'm awake.

EMANUEL: 'All things fall and are built again. And those that build them again are gay.'

BOOMY'S VOICE: Who wrote it?

EMANUEL [*to* GERDA]: Who wrote it?

GERDA: Bates.

EMANUEL [*to* BOOMY]: Bates!

BOOMY'S VOICE: Bates?

EMANUEL [*to* GERDA]: Bates?

134

GERDA [*uncertain now*]: Gates?

EMANUEL: Gates? [*Pause.*] Yeats, perhaps?

GERDA: Yeats!

EMANUEL [*calling to* BOOMY]: Yeats!

[*Silence.* EMANUEL *interprets silence as victory and is about to return to his breakfast.*]

BOOMY'S VOICE [*mumbling*]: '. . . and those that build them again are gay'. [*Pause.*] 'For, alas, what is Contract? If all men were such that a mere spoken or sworn Contract would bind them, all men were then true men, and Government a superfluity. Not what thou and I have promised to each other, but what the balance of our forces can make us perform to each other; that, in so sinful a world as ours, is the thing to be counted on.'

EMANUEL: Who wrote it?

BOOMY'S VOICE: Carlyle.

EMANUEL: Carlyle! Still Carlyle. You've been reading him for two months now. I'll give you three more quotations from him and then you've got to find your proofs of doom from somewhere else. You hear me?

[*He returns to his breakfast but on the way picks up a tailor's dummy with an uncut suit on it. He pins and unpins this while eating his breakfast.*]

GERDA [*calling*]: Boomy! You want breakfast?

BOOMY'S VOICE: In my room.

GERDA: Come out and eat, it's sunshine outside.

BOOMY'S VOICE: Too hot!

EMANUEL: Get some sun on you.

BOOMY'S VOICE: In my room, please.

EMANUEL: He keeps me alive, my brother. With his philosophy of doom he keeps me alive.

[GERDA *enters the house. Alone, shyly,* EMANUEL *takes a portable tape-recorder, rewinds it a little and plays back the last snatches of himself singing a Socialist song. Delighted, he turns to a new part and records another, this time Hasidic song, in Yiddish. He sings into the microphone with gestures as though before an audience – it's obvious this is what he's wanted to do all his life. When finished he winds everything back and replays. He returns to the work on his dummy and talks while listening to himself sing.*]

[*To unseen* GERDA] Your son wants a suit? He shall have a suit. Your grandchildren want coats? They shall have coats. [*Stands back from dummy.*] You know, I once worked with a machiner, Joe! Joe – er – Joe – er – names! I can't remember names. What's the matter with me? Was a time I remembered everything, everything! Anyway. Joe. A rotten machiner. Didn't like the work. You can't do well what you don't like and he was proof. But a talker? An intellect? Mustard! From him I got the habit of reading and through him shaped what I'd read. Between us we should have done great things. Only we didn't. [*Pause.*] Anyway, one day, he looked at my dummy and he said, 'Manny,' he said, 'the other day the dummy spoke to me.' 'Get on with your work,' I tell him, 'we're behind.' 'It spoke,' he said again, 'and it asked me "What of your life?" Imagine! the dummy asked me to justify myself.' 'And did you?' I asked Joe. 'It's very disturbing.' he says, 'not a nice question to be asked.' And that was all. For the rest of the day he said nothing more, absolutely nothing more. [*Pause.*] A man of sweetness and a big forehead. [*Shouting to his brother.*] Boomy! You should work in your old age. Stop thinking so much.

## SCENE TWO

SARAH'S *council flat. It is full of healthy pot plants. We see the front room, partitioned into kitchen, and a balcony on which her nephew,* MARTIN, *is erecting the ' Succah'. The ' Succah' is a symbolic ' tent' with a partly covered roof of branches. We will learn more about it as the play progresses.* MARTIN *has nailed together a rather shaky wooden frame around which he is now pinning a white sheet.* SARAH *is watering her plants.* ROSA, *her daughter, is reading aloud from a little book about the Jewish festival of ' Succoth'.*

ROSA: 'The festival of Succoth, known as "The Festival of Tabernacles", begins on the 15th day of Tishri, lasts for eight days and is called "The Season of our Joy".'

SARAH: That's how I remember it. Joyful! Your grandfather was a very joyful man. Your uncle Manny takes after him.

ROSA: 'Judaism recognizes the natural instinct of joy and makes no attempt to repress it, but rather to encourage natural self-expression.'

MARTIN: Good! I like that.

ROSA: And I like this. Listen: 'To draw away from a natural instinct of gladness with the fear that gladness might lead to vice is an admission of inability to exercise that restraint which requires strength of character.'

MARTIN: Very Jesuitical.

SARAH [shaking frame]: It's got a bit of a wobble.

MARTIN: I'm not trained as a 'Succah' maker, Aunt Sarah.

SARAH: But it'll do.

ROSA: 'The Bible, through the law of the Succah, brings man face to face with the realization of the frailty of human life and the transience of human existence.'

MARTIN: I thought it was a harvest festival.

ROSA: It is. But, says the book, 'In the season of plenty the Jew rejoices in his prosperity and the rewards of his labours and is inclined to delude himself into thinking that life is secure and durable. So the Psalmist feels it's necessary to warn people who are misled into trusting their wealth.

MARTIN: Very wise.

ROSA [To MARTIN]: ' – And for this reason it is essential that the "Succah" is built in a manner which enables it to provide more shade than light because man – ' Ah! Mother, you wanted to build the 'Succah'? Then listen to this: 'because man should not have confidence in his own strength nor in his own fortunes but should place his faith in Divine providence, therefore the covering of the "Succah" with plants and leaves should not be laid on too thickly so that the heaven and the stars should be visible, for, as Psalm XIX says, the heavens declare the "glory of God".'

MARTIN: 'The glory of God'! What do you say to that, Aunty?

SARAH: Let the heavens declare the glory of God, we'll build the 'Succah' to declare the glory of man.

MARTIN: Bravo!

SARAH: And to remember my father.

MARTIN: That's my Sarah.

SARAH: And for your Aunty Gerda who likes these things.

ROSA: But, Mother, that's hypocrisy.

SARAH: She's insulting me again. What's hypocrisy about it?

ROSA: You don't believe.

SARAH: I don't believe.

ROSA: But suddenly! Out of the blue! The rituals of belief.

SARAH: Suddenly! The blue! The rituals of belief.

ROSA: It's not logical.

SARAH: It's not logical.

[*Stubborn pause.*]

ROSA: Actually, maybe it is logical. After all, I suppose it's very human to want to remember your father.

MARTIN: And Aunty Gerda.

SARAH: She's a good girl, my daughter. If you let her argue long enough on her own, she gets to agree with you. [*Picking up an old refrain.*] She's got a job as a careers-advisory officer, you know, with the Ministry of Education. Such a profession.

[ROSA *tries to out-talk her by picking out something else to read from the little book.*]

ROSA: 'We cannot measure life quantitatively. It is not the number of years but rather the quality that determines whether life is transient or permanent. The Rabbis had this thought in mind when they said: "In one brief hour a man can achieve eternity." '

SARAH: She went to university, got degrees, honours, I-don't-know-what, but she couldn't decide on a profession for herself so she took up advising others. I'M GOING SHOPPING!

SARAH *has the last word as she leaves.* ROSA *joins* MARTIN *to help with the 'Succah'.*]

ROSA: Mothers! And how's Uncle Boomy?

MARTIN: My father and I also quarrel. He wants me to stick to my research.

ROSA: And stay out of student politics.

MARTIN: And stay out of student politics. 'You'll make me into a

138

neurotic,' I tell him. 'So what?' he says, 'there's plenty analysts, aren't there?'

ROSA: And you've left Moira and the baby for good?

MARTIN: Who knows what's for good?

ROSA: We've both made a mess of our marriages.

MARTIN: You should have married me.

ROSA: Cousins?

MARTIN: We'd have kept our qualities in the family.

ROSA: And weakened the strain.

MARTIN: Everything has a price. [*Kisses her.*]
    *Pause.*

ROSA [*leafing through the little book*]: Do you think *we'll* turn to rituals after fifty?

MARTIN: Ecclesiastes! He keeps quoting Ecclesiastes at me. [*Imitating Boomy.*] 'It is better to hear the rebuke of the wise than for a man to hear the song of fools.'

ROSA [*reading from the little book*]: 'Men learned in the law came to the Besht – the founder of Hasidism – on an errand of dispute. "In times gone by," they protested, "there were pious men in great numbers fasting from Sabbath to Sabbath, and inflicting their own bodies with self-devised torments. And now your disciples proclaim it, to all who care to listen, that much fasting is unlawful and self-torment a crime." The Besht answered, "It is the aim and essence of my pilgrimage on earth to show my brethren by living demonstration how one may serve God with merriment and rejoicing. For he who is full of joy is full of love for men and all fellow-creatures." '

## SCENE THREE

*A section of* TERESSA'S *dishevelled attic living-room: an armchair in which she lives surrounded by books, papers and a typewriter, most of which are on an adjustable table.* TERESSA, *a heavily built, once beautiful, elderly woman, enters in her petticoat. A dress is over her arm, a roll of toilet paper in her hand. She lays the dress over a chair; hoists her petticoat and proceeds to wrap the toilet roll round her middle.*

TERESSA: You never know when you may need what.
[*She puts on a record of Beethoven's 'Streichquartett' Op. 131, slips on her dress, moves to a mirror to adjust her hair and heavily cosmeticize her face. Surveys herself before mirror at which she constantly talks. Her accent is deeply Slavonic.*]
All dressed up and nowhere to go. [*Pause.*] It's not funny, darling. If I wasn't an educated woman I'd understand, but I'm educated! A reader of books! A translator! [*She idly reaches for a piece of paper and reads from it.*] 'Wanda Wilczynski was born in 1857 in the market town of Lashkowitz in Poland. To this town my father went in terror of his life to sell his goods' [*corrects a mistake and becomes involved*] 'and he brought back news of this strange poetess whom everyone thought was mad. My father's passion became mine and for this reason I have felt it a duty to undertake the translation of her poetry into this the most harmonious of languages.' 'Harmonious'? That's a way to describe the English language? 'Lyrical'! A better word. [*She scribbles the alteration but it's a casual stab at work.*] Ach! Books! Thoughts! [*Stops record.*] If they live in your head and you can't use them – useless! Mocking! Fifteen years I've been translating you, Wanda my darling. [*Moves again to mirror.*] Look at my face. When did you last see a face that said *so* much. It's all there, Teressa, full of lines, And I can tell you which line is which. [*Pointing.*] Disappointment, bitterness, self-hatred, heart-ache, fear. Sour – all sour, my darling. [*She turns away unhappily; then, defiantly.*] I want to look beautiful! [*Shrugs. Moves to cut a slice of bread; eats it with a lump of cheese, indifferently. Full mouth.*] Silly woman! Silly, silly

woman, Teressa. [*Pause.*]What's silly about wanting to be beautiful again? Vanity? I've had my children, I've had my heartache, now I want to look in a mirror and get pleasure. I tell you, with that kind of pleasure I'd be so generous, so generous and calm and dignified. Sweetness, darling, there's such a sweetness in beauty. Oh dear. Oh dear, dear me. [*Pushes away food.*] Who can eat? [*She picks up papers again.*] 'Her life was a tragedy. At the age of thirteen she was sent to a sanatorium where it was thought to cure her of tuberculosis. One day her parents received a telegram; the postmaster had been ill and a boy had been taken on for the day to deliver the mail. Telegrams being unusual in small Polish towns the mother tore it open without checking the envelope'; [*but she knows it all by heart and has no need to refer to her notes*] 'the boy had taken it to the wrong address. It had been meant for the apartment next door and by strange ill-fortune the telegram read, "Come at once your child is very ill." The child next door had been staying with relatives and died without seeing its parents. Wanda's parents packed at once but their speeding carriage was involved in an accident that proved fatal. These events hung like an accusative hand of God over her life.' What a life! And no one cared then and no one cares now. Not about your poetry nor my translations.

[*The* LIGHTS DIM *down.*

*A banging on a wall is heard. It is* BOOMY *calling for* EMANUEL'S *attention.*]

BOOMY'S VOICE: Manny! You listening? 'I Kahelth, I the preacher was king over Israel and Jerusalem. And I gave my heart to seek and search out by wisdom concerning all things that are done under heaven; this sore travail hath God given to the sons of man to be exercised therewith. I have seen all the works that are done under the sun; and behold, all is vanity and vexation of spirit . . .' Ecclesiastes.

[*A return of banging.*]

EMANUEL'S VOICE: Boomy! You listening? 'If the zaddick serves God,' says Rabbi Nahman of Bratzlav, 'but does not take the trouble to teach the multitude, he will descend from his rung.' From Martin Buber.

141

## SCENE FOUR

*The classroom.* ROSA *enters with a chair and briefcase. She is a Ministry of Education careers-advisory officer, and is addressing a rowdy group of school-leavers from a tough neighbourhood. She's tentative, apologetic and finally ineffectual amid their assorted sighs and rasping sounds. It is her first confrontation. Note: It is essential that* ROSA *does not appear to be addressing the audience.*

ROSA: Now my task isn't easy, now is it? So some quiet, please. There are a lot of you boys and I don't know you each individually and so I can't really know what's the best job you're suited for and we need to talk about it. Nor is it only a matter of what *you're* suited for, is it? But what suits you. After all, I think insufficient attention is paid to what is likely to make us feel fulfilled. Society isn't very good at that yet, is it? It's a bit of a monster actually. Eats up everything, indiscriminately. [*Mocking laughter.*] And so, my task is all the more important and what I propose to do is outline the kinds of jobs that are open to you, roughly, very roughly you understand, and then for the next week I'll be available to speak to you individually. Those who want that is. Does that sound all right to you? [*Growing offensive noise.*] Does that sound like a good approach? Have you any suggestions for another method? I'd gladly listen. [*Pause, into which the sound swells.*] That's all right then. Good.

   [*The noise is overwhelming.*]

## SCENE FIVE

SARAH's *council flat. At this moment she is cutting up fruit and raw vege-tables for another nephew,* RUDI, *tall wild-eyed and bearded. He's a com-pulsive talker of half-finished, disjointed thoughts, constantly accompanied by gestures. He is setting up an automatic slide-projector from which will be projected, throughout his talking and eating, slides of his gaudily coloured, tortured, primitive-type paintings.*

SARAH: You see the 'Succah'?

RUDI: I see it. She's become religious. A religious socialist!

SARAH: I'm doing it for your Aunt Gerda.

RUDI: *Two* mad aunts.

SARAH: I need some branches with leaves to cover it.

RUDI: So?

SARAH: So can you get some for me?

RUDI: Leaves? It's early autumn.

SARAH: We've got an Indian summer. There's still leaves.

RUDI: Leaves! Get leaves, she says. Where can I get leaves from? My garden? Who's got gardens these days? A room, a kitchen and a bathroom with three other people that's what I've got. Can you grow trees in a bathroom? Pot plants maybe, but not trees.

SARAH: Don't make jokes, Rudi.

RUDI: Jokes! Who's making jokes? What's funny about anything?

SARAH: Rudi!

RUDI: All right! I'll find you some leaves. [*Referring to projector.*] I'll show you.

SARAH: Eat!

RUDI: Forty-two pounds it cost, but this way a man can show who he is, what he is and no doubts, you know what I mean?

SARAH: Stop talking and eat.

RUDI [*taking her to a chair*]: In the garment factory they laugh. So! They laugh! What's laughter?

SARAH: What you doing?

RUDI: A projector! Watch! Automatic and – no touching.

[*Switches off room light, switches on machine; we receive the first shock of his 'work'. Satisfied, he sits to eat.*]

There! Photographs! You don't have photographs? No one believes you. Saves a lot of talking, explaining. Like this you show them, they can see, it's your work, your name. I get tired talking; lose breath, waste time, you know what I mean? You want to see some of the paintings? There's one in Hackney library and half a dozen in a new Israeli restaurant, Stoke Newington end of Northwold Road. Open ten in the morning till one, two, maybe three in the morning, for three weeks. But I'm not forcing you to go to not go you please yourself. Who can force people? Force people you make enemies, they get annoyed, they start lying – who can be bothered? People always have excuses why they can't go – they're busy, they've got appointments, they're ill – I never knew people could be ill so many times. You got commitments? I understand. What can I tell you? That you're my aunt? That you *must* go because you're family? So what? That's no reason. You please yourself. You go because you *want* to go, you're interested. You know what I mean? It won't stop me. Nothing stops me. I go on because I know if you don't go on for yourself you've had it; with jealousy from this one from that one, you wouldn't believe people can be so jealous, in every place, over everything, one person watching you, another one frightened in case you get more marks than them, you know what I mean? Like this I paint and I keep track where the paintings go. No one lets their work go somewhere without them knowing, you can be swindled, but me? I got photographs, with my name, on both sides, and it's proof and one day they'll sell and I'll earn money enough to take no notice of the lot of them. And they want me, you know that? To give my paintings. They chase me, write to me, the librarian, to bring, to hang. Because people, you know, they don't like reality, they hate reality, they're frightened. That's why there's all these goings on with revolutions and riots and violence.

[*Now* SCENE *6 begins to merge into this scene. It is* MILLIE'S *council flat. She's an old woman, tiny, withering, with a cracked voice. She is humming to herself and pinning up old sepia photographs of her family, her mind wandering.*]

But it costs money – for paints, for hardboard, for framing. Me. I don't give them to frame anymore, I do my own the way I want them because one painting I gave and I said I wanted it in ten days' time and the girl wrote it down 'ten days' for Saturday but I went and nothing was done. 'The boys didn't know,' she said. They didn't know! They didn't *care*! They don't want to do any work, just to get paid while they flirt around, so it wasn't done and I took it away because who can wait while they mess things up for you? Everyone's busy messing things up for you. I could tell you stories. In every business. Twisting and dishonesty. One bloke says to me 'Take one of your paintings down and pretend you sold it, fool the people.' But who can remember such things? This story, that story – how long can you go on doing that before you get found out – you know what I mean? Me, I can't work that way.

MILLIE: And where are my brothers? I had brothers, where are they? A funny thing. They stay away. Who tells them to stay away? [*Puts on a kettle of water for tea.*]

RUDI: The other day I walked in the street and I found a wallet so I picked it up and I could see people watching me, waiting to see if I was gonna put it in my pocket. But I counted the notes, the pound notes and the pennies and all the receipts – packed with receipts, you could see she did the football pools – and I took it to the police-station and there there was forms, forms, you should see the forms, and every penny was counted and noted down and they told me if there was no claim in fourteen days they'd write to me. But she claimed and I got the letter with inside a postal order for ten shillings and it was worth everything to me, more than all the values.

MILLIE: No answer. No one makes an answer.

RUDI: Who understands art?

MILLIE: Terrible, terrible, terrible.

RUDI: People listen to other people, no one comes to see the work and then they want you to explain: 'what does it mean?'

MILLIE: Who am I talking to?

RUDI: What does it mean!

MILLIE: *I* don't know anymore.

RUDI: They don't *know* what it means?

145

MILLIE: I don't *know* anymore.

RUDI: They can't *see* what it means?

MILLIE: Ach! leave me alone.

RUDI: It means what I understand!

MILLIE: I should worry! Brothers! [*She finds herself by the phone. Dials.*]

RUDI: You know what I don't like doing? Portraits! A man can only show one kind of face when he's made to sit and think: sadness.

   [SARAH *picks up phone.*]

MILLIE: Sarah?

SARAH: Who is it?

RUDI: One day the Kosher butcher asks me to paint Dayan.

MILLIE: It's Millie, Millie, Who else?

SARAH: You all right?

RUDI: Why Dayan?

MILLIE: I'm all right, but where are my brothers?

SARAH: What brothers?

RUDI: 'Paint Dayan please, it's a Jewish neighbourhood!'

MILLIE: My brothers. I had three brothers.

SARAH: Millie, your brothers are dead.

RUDI: So I said, 'How can I paint Dayan? I don't know him!'

SARAH: Millie?

RUDI: 'From a newspaper,' they said.

SARAH: Millie!

RUDI: A newspaper!

MILLIE: Dead?

RUDI: 'Give me a real live photograph,' I said, 'maybe I can do something.'

MILLIE: I know they're dead.

SARAH: Millie!

MILLIE: So, they're dead. And your husband?

SARAH: What are you talking about! My husband is also dead.

MILLIE: Also dead! Shoin!

SARAH: You know that, Millie.

MILLIE: Of course I know. I know everything. Terrible. Terrible.

   [MILLIE *replaces receiver and sits looking about her.*]

SARAH: Millie!

MILLIE: So good-bye then.

[SARAH *dials back.*]

RUDI: The man in the restaurant asks me to paint his sign – I don't
mind that I'm an artist and he asks me to paint his sign, but when
it's only half done he says he can't get a ladder to finish the job. He
*says.*

[MILLIE *picks up the receiver.*]

SARAH: Millie?

RUDI: But maybe it's not true.

MILLIE: Who is it?

SARAH: She doesn't know me.

RUDI: Maybe he doesn't want to *pay* me.

SARAH: It's Sarah.

MILLIE: Sarah? How are you? I never hear from you.

RUDI: And maybe I won't ask to *be* paid.

SARAH: She's wandering.

RUDI: But all of a sudden he can't get a ladder.

SARAH: You just phoned me, you forgotten already?

MILLIE: Of course I'm all right.

SARAH: Millie, stop it. You mustn't forget things.

MILLIE: Yes, yes, yes.

[MILLIE *replaces her receiver.*]

SARAH: Millie!

RUDI: So, the sign's only half done.

MILLIE Funny woman, she is. So many years my brothers are dead
and she doesn't remember. [*Goes to make tea.*]

[SARAH *has replaced her phone, and sits, unhappy, uncertain.*]

RUDI: I tell you, two things I don't do: I don't jump into other
people's business and I don't jump into other people's fights. Who
knows what it's all about, you get caught up, *you're* the good one,
and *you* get murdered! By mistake.

## SCENE SIX

*Now this scene comes fully into its own.* MILLIE *is about to pour out tea. Thinks. Climbs on a chair to reach for a pot on top of a cupboard. Inside are five-pound notes. She counts and throws them on the floor.*

MILLIE: Five pounds, ten, fifteen, twenty, twenty-five, thirty, thirty-five ... [*Counts on in mumbles, scattering the notes like seeds.*] seventy-five, eighty, eighty-five, ninety. [*Stops. Looks. Long pause. Descends. Moves to pour tea. Adds milk. Looks back to money on floor.*] It's good to have money. [*Takes her tea and stands looking vacantly out by the window. Long silence.*] My brothers. My poor brothers. Where are my poor brothers?

## SCENE SEVEN

*Darkness.* EMANUEL's *garden again. Again the light of dawn and again he comes from the hammock on the porch, howling.* GERDA *follows to comfort him once more.*

GERDA: You'll kill me, Manny. I promise you, you'll bring me to an early grave.

EMANUEL: Night again! Always when no one can hear.

GERDA: For weeks now, night after night, for weeks.

EMANUEL: There must be something.

GERDA: Pills. Take pills. That's something.

EMANUEL: Perhaps in the morning – in all the newspapers, on the headlines, they'll say something.

GERDA: Stop it! You're trembling.

EMANUEL: On every headline in every newspaper, all over the world – something to reassure us.

GERDA: Not the world. Not the whole world. Can't I make you understand? No man can think about the whole world in his little brain. It's a little brain you've got, I've got, everyone's got. It'll crack, Manny, listen.

[*She leads him back to the hammock.*]

EMANUEL: Freedom! It's so important – it's got to be dictated.

GERDA: All my life.

EMANUEL: Justice? Force it!

GERDA: All the time we've been married you've never given yourself a moment's real happiness.

EMANUEL: Contradictions!

GERDA: You know that? All my time with you, not a moment's peace.

EMANUEL: Chaos and contradictions!

GERDA: And what are you?

EMANUEL: What's that for a life!

GERDA: A tailor!

EMANUEL: What's that for life!

GERDA: A little Jewish tailor!

EMANUEL: Chaos and contradictions!

[*She goes wearily into the house. He returns to sleep.*
*Morning, its sounds and a slow, slow sunlight.*
GERDA *brings him his usual breakfast of eggs, toast and china tea.*
*A few hours have passed.*]

GERDA [*pouring*]: Pea water it looks like.

EMANUEL [*in rising from hammock, has small tussle with entangled blankets*]: It's started! I've woken up! Problems!

GERDA: You heard? They've landed on the moon.

EMANUEL: I'm very happy. The farther out they reach the more left behind I feel.

GERDA: You're trembling.

EMANUEL: I'm trembling! I'm trembling! I marvel, so I tremble. The earth they leave is the ground that falls away from *me*. I didn't have an identity *before*? *Now* I've got nothing. [*Shudders.*] I should stop camping out at nights.

GERDA: Stop saying. Do!

EMANUEL: I'm too old to camp out.

GERDA: Who says you're too old?

EMANUEL: Look at that sky. I'm just getting used to the earth they

149

give me the moon. I haven't enough problems? So, I marvel and I tremble. [*Reaches for book in hammock.*] Boomy! I need to have a go at my fraternal Doomsday Book.

GERDA: Manny!

EMANUEL: And have I got a quote!

GERDA: You know what I'd like to see? I'd like to see *you* two quarrel. Say two words of your own to each other.

EMANUEL: It starts my day.

GERDA: You've been having quarrels through other people's books for years now. Yell at him in your own voice for a change.

EMANUEL [*banging on wall*]: Boomy? You listening? [*Struts and declaims in playful harangue.*] '. . . religious difference causes no trouble today . . . The Jew, the Catholic, the Greek, the Lutheran, the Calvinist, the Anabaptist, the Socinian, the Memnonist . . .' The Socinian, the Memnonist? [*Shrugs.*] ' . . . The Socinian, the Memnonist, the Moravian, and so many others, live like brothers in these countries, and contribute alike to the good of the social body. They fear no longer in Holland that disputes about pre-destination will end in heads being cut off. They fear no longer at London that the quarrels of Presbyterians and Episcopalians about liturgies and surplices will lead to the death of a king on the scaffold IT – WILL – NEVER – BE – REPEATED. Philosophy, the sister of religion, has disarmed the hands that superstition had so long stained with blood, and the human mind' [*approaching triumph now*] 'awakening from its intoxication is *amazed* at the excesses into which fanaticism had led it.' The undisputed crown-king of reason. VOLTAIRE.

   [*Silence.*]

What's he doing? [*Calling.*] Did you hear it? You still think all can't be well with the world? [*To* GERDA.] Is he awake?

GERDA: I took him his breakfast and he looked at the eggs and he said, 'Children who weep at the death of the first chicken they see killed laugh at the death of the second.' And he ate.

BOOMY'S VOICE: 'They who protested that all is well are Charlatans . . . glance over the human race . . . behold these battlefields, strewn by imbeciles with the corpses of other imbeciles. See these arms, these legs, these bloody brains, and all these scattered limbs;

it is the fruit of a quarrel between two ignorant ministers' [BOOMY *enters, book in hand, declaiming in a mock histrionic voice*] '. . . Enter the neighbouring hospital, where are gathered those who are not yet dead . . . and then tell me all is well. Say the word if you dare . . . over the ruins of a hundred towns that have been swallowed up by earthquakes . . . fancy yourself amid the floods and volcanoes that have so often devasted so many parts of the world; amid the leprosy and the plague that have swept it. And do you, who read this, recall all *you* have suffered, admit that evil exists, and do not add to so many miseries and horrors the wild absurdity of denying them.' [*Pause.*] Voltaire.

[*He has walked slowly round them and has gone with his last words.* EMANUEL *is upset. He brings his tailor's dummy from the room to the porch.*]

EMANUEL: Work! Look! My hand doesn't shake. It can still cut cloth. My fingers are strong. I can still sew. Your son wants a suit? He shall have a suit. Your grandchildren want coats? They shall have coats. [*Pause.*] He should still have been reading Carlyle.

## SCENE EIGHT

*The street.* MARTIN, *Boomy's son, paces up and down.* BOOMY *appears.*

BOOMY: You couldn't come into the house? What's this! A clandestine meeting outside where I live!

MARTIN: I was arrested yesterday.

BOOMY: Come into the house, your aunt will make you some food.

MARTIN: I'm only out on bail.

BOOMY: You should leave politics alone.

MARTIN: I might get a prison sentence.

BOOMY: I've told you – it's the age of computers, the problems are different. Come inside.

MARTIN: I need some money.

BOOMY: A thick ear you need.

MARTIN [*exploding*]: Take me seriously.

BOOMY: Secret meetings with my children I should take seriously?

MARTIN: A hundred pounds and you'll never see me again.

BOOMY: A hundred pounds for the pleasure of not seeing my son again? That's sense? That's an intelligent, responsible person talking?

MARTIN: *You're* a responsible person I suppose.

BOOMY: I've read too much! I've seen too much!

MARTIN: Well that's you, not me. Stop drowning me with your experience of men.

BOOMY: My quarrel is with God not men.

MARTIN: Good! You quarrel with God about important jobs – earthquakes, cyclones, droughts – I'll quarrel with men about trivialities – poverty, injustice, social orders – only lend me a hundred pounds, please.

BOOMY: I can't be expected to get excited about students' liberties.

MARTIN: There's a crisis.

BOOMY: There's always a crisis.

MARTIN: Yes! Always! That's how it must be in order for things to get better.

BOOMY: You mean like Stalin telling the German communists not to worry about Hitler, I suppose. 'Comrades! Hitler will create the right crisis for the German proletariat to take over?' Madness! The worse things are, the worse they get! What did women do when they got the vote? Two world wars we've had.

MARTIN: One. Women got the vote in 1928.

[*They smile at one another. Tension relaxed. Relieved father hugs son.*]

BOOMY: You want freedom? Show me you can use it.

[*Sweetly said, but ill-chosen words. The quarrel slowly mounts again.*]

MARTIN: There's nothing I've ever done that you've made me feel proud of.

BOOMY: You want revolution? Show me your plans for the new world.

MARTIN: You made everything seem like an act of delinquency, and every time I listened, thinking you were maybe right.

BOOMY: You want to make people happy? Where's your wife, where's your child? Are *they* happy?

MARTIN: At no point have I behaved impetuously, no matter how much you've tried to make me think I have.

BOOMY: Have you learnt how to be a husband yet? A father? Show me these things.

MARTIN: But I'm not a delinquent and I'm not a fool, and I will, I will follow my conscience.

BOOMY: Show me these things, maybe I'll trust you.

MARTIN: I've STUDIED! I've studied and I've studied responsibly. I've thought and I've thought carefully. When I worked in the holidays didn't I share my earnings with the house? I do not like what I see. That's not unnatural and if doing what you disagree with is called irresponsible then irresponsible I am! [*Moves to go, turns back. Softly.*] The truth is, and you know it, *you're* the failure. A self-pitying, malicious failure and I won't believe in the image you've given me of myself. [*Leaves.*]

BOOMY [*calling after him*]: 'That which is crooked cannot be made straight, and that which is wanting cannot be numbered . . . For in much wisdom is much grief; and he that increaseth knowledge increaseth sorrow.' [*Pause.*] Ecclesiastes!

[BOOMY, *heartbroken, goes back into the house. The* LIGHTS DIM. *We hear a banging on the wall.*]

EMANUEL'S VOICE: Boomy! You listening? I'm reading from Martin Buber again. 'Rabbi Leib, son of Sarah, used to say about those rabbis who only *expound* the Torah that: "A man should see to it that all his actions are a Torah and that he himself becomes so entirely a Torah that one can learn from his life." '

## SCENE NINE

SARAH's *flat. She is preparing to bake a cake and is whipping the eggs. A bell, like that of an old town-crier, is heard ringing to the accompaniment of a sing-song voice.*

JACK'S VOICE: It's Jack-o-bell ringing, Jack-o-bell ringing. His warning his ringing.

SARAH: Ah! Jack, Jack!

JACK'S VOICE: Don't come you near me, don't come you near me,
the plague is upon me, the devil is in me.

[*Ringing continues, dying away at times as though he's walking backwards and forwards outside her door.*]

SARAH: I tell him. Does he listen? They'll take him away one day
and he's not mad.

JACK'S VOICE: Jack is a-dying, the young folk is living, Jack is a-
going, the young folk is coming. Don't come you near me, the
plague is upon me, the devil is in me, the young folk is living.

[*Abrupt silence.* SARAH *goes to the door, leaves it open and returns to
her preparations: unwraps packet of butter to put in separate bowl.
Adds sugar and salt.*]

[*After a long pause* JACK *stands by the door, struggles with himself
but then comes in. He sits by her, an old cockney neighbour. Silence
then –*]

SARAH: They'll take you away.

JACK: Do I care, Missus?

SARAH: Everyone on the new estate is old. You're not the only one.

JACK: I've lived a terrible life, Missus, wicked. Nothing you'd ever
dream about.

SARAH: We've all been angels, I suppose.

JACK: Born a bastard, I was. Parents who didn't want me. Now wot
abaht that? Ain't that a plague? A real, right, plague that little
fact is. Mustn't contaminate people with that, Missus.

SARAH: Who do you think takes notice these days, silly man?

JACK: This silly man. All me life. Plagued me. And I beat me wife
for it and drove me children from their own doorstep. Wot sort of
a bloke's that?

[SARAH *takes glass and half-bottle of whisky from a cupboard. Pours
him a tot.*]

SARAH: Don't tell anyone.

[SARAH *begins tapping flour through a sieve over the butter in the
bowl.*]

JACK [*drinks in one gulp*]: Do you know, Missus, when I was in the
war, in the jungle, I let a man die? A mate. Let 'im die. We was
sent to round up snipers, a group of us, each with our little bit of

ration, for three days. And this bloke, 'ee got it on the first day, in the side. The 'ole of 'is side out. And as I pass 'im 'ee calls, 'Got a drop o' water, mate? Just a drop.' And I looks at 'im and I thinks: 'ee's only got another hour or two in 'im, and me, I got another forty-eight hours to go. I need that water. And I leaves 'im. Now, Missus, wot sort of a bloke am I to leave a dying mate go thirsty, eh? A wicked life. Twenty-three years a rotten sergeant, bullying, foul-mouthed; nothing lovely abaht me at all. Contaminated!

[*Silence.* SARAH *rubs fat and flour together.*]

SARAH: I'm baking a cake for my daughter.

JACK: You're always doing something, Missus. Cooking, cleaning, watering plants, making us sign petitions. *I* never seen you still.

SARAH: You think *you're* wicked? I'll tell you a secret. To keep you company in wickedness, I'll confess. You know one of my greatest pleasures? I'm ashamed to tell you, but listen. [*Pours another drink.*] You've never met my son-in-law, have you? My daughter you've seen, she's got a job as a careers-advisory officer with the Ministry of Education, such a profession! She went to university, got degrees, honours and I-don't-know-what, but she couldn't decide on a profession for herself so she took up advising others. [*Pause.*] Still – her husband, you know what he does? I didn't think such a job existed but it does – he's a soil expert. True! A soil expert! He looks at earth through a microscope to find out how to make things grow. A clever man. I'm not saying he's not a clever man. He works hard but – he's a climber. Imagine! won't even leave his wife in peace – thinks she ought to go into television or newspapers or make more degrees. I also think she ought to do something better, but I don't nag her and I don't care so much so long she's happy.

JACK: And is she happy, Missus?

SARAH: She's not happy, Missus. 'Missus!' – What's that for a name?

JACK: Can't call you Sarah, Missus. 'Missus' is polite, ain't it – Sarah?

[*Her smile is shy, his – cheeky.*]

Don't that deserve another drink?

SARAH: *You're* not mad.

JACK: Didn't say I was, just said I was wicked.

SARAH: I'm telling you a confession. This son-in-law of mine, in his house, is full with boxes with different soils. And all the time he's planting, planting, and cutting and mixing and adding things to the earth and – you know what? There's not a flower in the house [*Laughter.*] Can't make a thing grow. Boxes, that's all, with soil. Nothing grows. [*More laughter.*] And it gives me such pleasure. Every time he comes here I make sure I've got a new plant or a new bud and I show him. 'What do you think?' I say. 'Big surprise! I did nothing to it and look – a new shoot!' [*Both in full laughter.*]

## SCENE TEN

*A different class.* ROSA *addresses them, with more firmness but still the wrong approach; still too reasonable, open to derision.*

ROSA: All right, all right! So you make noises and send me up. But what's the point? Look, you've all got another sixty years to get through. I mean that's a long time, that needs thinking about. What you decide now can affect your whole life. I can't understand why you don't care about that. [*Noises of mock surprise.*] Listen, look at it this way. You're sixteen now. How many of you have friends of fourteen? You're different from them, aren't you? They're almost like kids to you. And at fourteen were you the same as you were at ten? And so, can't you imagine yourselves being different in the future? When you're twenty, twenty-five, thirty-five, fifty? Can't you imagine that you'll feel differently, think differently, have different needs? That's got to be prepared for, hasn't it? Can't you project yourselves forward, with your imagination. Can't you use your imagination to put yourselves into another situation? [*Noise.*] No, I don't suppose you can. I must be bloody mad.

[*Crescendo of noise, mock applause.*]

## SCENE ELEVEN

TERESSA'*s room. She sits amid the chaos of her table, working on her translations. A record of Beethoven is playing.*
TERESSA [*reading from a sheet*]:

> For Oh the wind like hammers hound
> And mock my life with warning sound;
> Those winds who for all others sing
> Prepare for me an inevitable ending.

'Prepare for me' or 'prepare me for'? There's a difference. Or is there? Problems! [*Takes off the record.*] Always the same question. Should I translate the exact words or the exact meaning? The exact words would be: 'The winds sing for everyone else but I am to be prepared for they whisper "dying, dying".' The sense is poetic but the word's aren't. Or are they? What about:

> Those winds who for all others sing
> Whisper to me of dying, dying.

But then you lose her intention to show how the winds of life are preparing her for what she believes is the inevitable retribution of death. She feels guilty for her parents' death and she sees all life as her trial. Suppose we say:

> Those winds who for all others sing
> Prepare my death with whispering.

But then you see, Teressa darling, she repeats the words 'dying, dying' so that it also *sounds* like the wind. You'll lose all that. Well, something is always lost I suppose. I wonder, would it matter if I made it a verse of five lines instead of four?

> Prepare me for my death
> With their whispering, whispering.

So:

> For Oh the winds like hammers hound
> And mock my life with warning sound;

Those winds who for all others sing
Prepare me for my death
With their whispering, whispering.

God knows! Enough now. You've been working on that verse for two months now. Leave it alone. Come back to it next week. [*Pushes papers aside and puts on the record again.*] Now what should I do?


## SCENE TWELVE

*The street. Afternoon.* MILLIE, *wandering, humming, sometimes backing away from what she peers at, surprised, finally walking round in circles.*

MILLIE: Sarah? Is that you? Have you moved? You used to live near here, somewhere. [*Nods and hums to imaginary passers-by.*] Good afternoon, good afternoon.

> THREE YOUTHS *approach and begin to mimic her distress. She peers at them as though she doesn't see or understand their presence.* TERESSA *appears on her way to Sarah's. The* YOUTHS *depart.*]

TERESSA: Is that you Millie?

MILLIE [*peering at her*]: Sarah?

TERESSA: It's me, darling, Teressa. You going to Sarah's?

MILLIE: I'm not going to Sarah's. Why should I be going to Sarah's? She got a tea or something? Sarah always has a tea, with people, always full with people.

TERESSA: Were you out for a walk?

MILLIE: Where does she find them, so many people?

TERESSA: Were you lost?

MILLIE: Lost? Me? I was going to the shops, to buy bread, a little chicken and – things. I got to shop, can't stop shopping.

TERESSA: Come, Millie. I'm going to Sarah's, come with me.

MILLIE: Funny thing. I was also going to the same place.

> [*Moves in the wrong direction.* TERESSA *guides her back.*]

TERESSA: This way, Millie.

MILLIE: This way? She moved? I didn't know Sarah moved. She tells me nothing, all these years, she's supposed to be my friend, nothing.


## SCENE THIRTEEN

SARAH's *flat.* JACK *is hanging things on the 'Succah'.* SARAH *reads a letter.*

JACK: It wobbles.
SARAH: I know it wobbles.
　　[TERESSA *and* MILLIE *knock at door.* JACK *stands up, alarmed, backs to the wall.*]
JACK: Tell them to stay away. Wait till I've gone out. Not contaminating no one, I'm not.
SARAH [*at door*]: It's only Millie and Teressa. [*Returns to push fried liver through mincer.*]
TERESSA [*has entered with* MILLIE]: She was wandering, you know that? Lost. Good afternoon, Jack.
JACK: Afternoon, Missus.
SARAH [*to* MILLIE]: It's Jack. You remember Jack, my neighbour?
MILLIE: Jack? Jack? I don't know no Jack.
SARAH: You must remember, Millie. Think!
MILLIE: [*one isn't certain if she's pretending*]: Jack? Jack?
SARAH: On about half a dozen occasions. [*Pause.*] You *must* remember. It's *not* too much for you to forget. You've seen him here, in this very room – and always by the wall. Teressa, make tea please. Come away from the wall, Jack, and stop being a silly man. I'm surrounded by silly people. Millie, you mustn't forget things. You mustn't forget! Make your mind think, think! Forget things and you'll go to pieces. Look at her, as if she doesn't hear me. Sit, both of you.
　　[MILLIE *wanders over to the window to gaze out.* JACK *remains glued to the wall.*]

Ach! I should care. [*Returns to mincing.*]

TERESSA [*preparing tea*]: Three young thugs were teasing her. God knows what would have happened if I hadn't come. [*Pause.*] The sons of your working class.

SARAH: Leave me alone with 'your' working class. *My* working class! She's always on to me. Look! [*Picks up a letter.*] A letter from my brother in Lithuania! Someone had to bring it to my door, how do you think it got here? Carrier pigeon? You're making tea, you've got milk, every morning there's a pint of milk at my door. Who brings it? Prince Philip? And who do you think got it from the cow? His wife? Look! [*Switches light on and off.*] Light! How did it get here? [*Moves to telephone.*] You want to speak to your sister in America? Speak! Turn this, wait a little, a voice answers. Who's putting you through? Who does it? Everywhere you look – new buildings, new roads, new cities – who puts them there? So leave me alone about my working class. [*Continues mincing.*] That's shut her up.

TERESSA: Nothing shuts me up, I must warn you. You know what they say: those near the grave have nothing to lose but their life. A very funny saying, I've always thought, but it means something. Me, I've never had much to lose anyway, so I've always talked. Why shut up? People close their ears anyway so it's necessary to keep talking or you'd forget language. Very important, language. Without language men think with their fists.

SARAH: You see, she's contradictions. Half her pension she sends to left-wing charities. Can't make up her mind which side she's on.

TERESSA: I know which side I'm on, but who says everyone that's on my side I should like? Jack, you owe me ten shillings.

[JACK *is staring uncertainly at* MILLIE, *she fascinates him. Then, to her* –]

JACK: You know wot they do with the foreskin of Jewish babies, Missus?

SARAH: Jokes like that aren't nice, Jack.

JACK: Send them to Israel to plant under trees.

SARAH: She won't understand.

JACK: Forest upon forest. Honest! And that's wot makes the trees grow straight.

SARAH: You're a crude man.

JACK: I'm making her laugh.

[MILLIE *is ignoring him.*]

SARAH: She's laughing, look!

JACK: I'm wicked, always was and always will be.

[TERESSA *sets down a tray of tea and biscuits.*]

It's here.

TERESSA: What's where?

JACK: The ten shillings. Up me leg.

TERESSA: Did he say 'leg'?

JACK: Pull up me trouser-leg.

TERESSA: *I* should pull up your trouser-leg?

JACK: You ain't never met a man wot's mean like me. Can't bear to part with nothing. Me 'ands won't bring themselves to part with a thing. You wants it, you 'as to take it.

[*Amazed.* TERESSA *moves to raise his trouser-leg.*]

A handkerchief. See it? Tied round me calf. In there.

[*She unties a handkerchief that's attached to his leg.*]

Should be two pound notes and some silver. Take it, 'cos I can't give it.

[*She extracts some coins and puts the handkerchief back in his hands. He ties it back.*]

Can't believe it, can yers? I told you, Missus. I'm wicked. A man born a bastard remains one, and all your fighting 'gainst it won't help. [*Picks up his bell and leaves ringing it.*] Jack's a-dying, the young folk is living, Jack's a-going, the young folk is coming.

SARAH: Your tea!

[*Door slams. We hear* JACK *from outside ringing and chanting.*]

JACK'S VOICE: Don't come you near me, the plague is upon me, the devil is in me, the young folk is living.

EMANUEL'S VOICE: 'All things are literally better, lovelier, and more beloved for the imperfections which have been divinely appointed, that the law of human life may be Effort, and the law of human judgement, Mercy.' John Ruskin.

## SCENE FOURTEEN

BOOMY'S *room. It is filled with books and the bits and pieces of a large children's computer set and a semi-dismantled T.V. set.* BOOMY *is helping* GERDA *to make his bed.*

GERDA: I'm waiting for an answer. [*Pause.*] I've got to live between two brothers always quarrelling?

BOOMY: I was eight when our father brought us over.

GERDA: You were nine, you've forgotten. You were nine, Manny was ten, Sarah was twelve. So?

BOOMY: Did you know our father was rich?

GERDA: Comfortable, yes. Rich, no. But that he wasn't careful, *that* I know.

BOOMY: He was rich *and* he was careful. [*Turns to fiddle with T.V. set.*] Before leaving Lithuania he converted his money into diamonds and gave them to a Gentile friend to take to Amsterdam; and from there, every year, his friend brought a few in for him. And slowly he built up a business in Black Lion Yard off the Whitechapel Road. One day – a robbery! An ordinary common-or-garden robbery and our father, bless him, for all that he was wise and careful, was not insured. Still, it was not the end of the world. There was one last bag expected from Amsterdam and those, our father said, were for us to pay for our education. He was a frugal man, needed very little – his sons would provide. And to Manny, because he came first, he gave the little bag of diamonds.

GERDA: Of this I knew nothing.

BOOMY: Wait, there's more you don't know. Did you know Manny was one of the first members of the Communist Party?

GERDA: Communist! Communist! He keeps saying he's a Communist, he refuses to join any of the groups and he quarrels with everybody.

BOOMY: But in those days he joined. [*Gives up fiddling with T.V. set.*] A founder member. And you know what happened?

GERDA: O-my-God-no-he-gave-them-to-the-party-funds.

BOOMY: Ah! Gerda. I knew you'd think that. And so would every sane-minded person have thought it; and if he'd done that I think I'd have understood better – I might even have been proud. But no, that's not what happened. One day he says to me – I was sixteen at the time, the father dead, school finished, we were planning university – and Manny says to me: 'Boomy, come for a walk, let's see London, how much of London do we know?' So we walked, through Spitalfields to Liverpool Street, down through the city to Mansion House and out along the embankment to Westminister. What a walk that was, exhilarating! And we stood on the bridge and talked and talked about the future. How I was going to study medicine and he was going to study economics, perhaps go into Parliament – young men's talk, brave, happy. You ever stood on that bridge and looked at London? Wordsworth wrote a poem from it, the river bends, a wide sweep, you can look up and look down – beautiful! [*Pause.*] And we talked. [*Pause.*] And suddenly Manny says: 'But Boomy,' he says, 'everything we do must come from our own hands. You agree?' And of course I agree, 'cos I thought he was only talking about the efforts we would have to make in our studies. 'Good,' he says, and he embraces and we cry and before I know it he's thrown the bag of diamonds into the river. [*Pause.*] You're paralysed, aren't you, Gerda? Can you imagine what *I* felt? I nearly choked him on the spot. 'Little, lunatic,' I yelled at him, 'lunatic!' And he kept saying 'but you agreed, you agreed' until I had to run away and he kept shouting after me, 'You agreed!' Agreed!

[*Long silence.*]

GERDA: And haven't you done enough to each other?

BOOMY: It's so bad, eh?

GERDA: Make peace.

BOOMY: I thought the worst was over. We don't scream like we used to. It's only a ritual that's left. Funny, even.

GERDA: But no friendship. Forgive him. You're both old now.

BOOMY: I'm not very good at being old. Some people are like that; only a certain period in their life suits them. Some are lovely children and rotten adults. Me, I was good at being young, not because I enjoyed it so much – I couldn't stop being bitter – but because I had strength, I could fight. That's my weakness, I can't bear being defenceless. You know things? Defence! You got a profession? Defence! You can talk? Defence! Instead? Tailors. Little schneiders. And now look at me, playing with T.V. sets in order to start understanding things. Now! Sixty-eight years old. Like a senile Doctor Faustus. You noticed that about our family? Look at our nieces and nephews: Rosa, trying to knock awareness into young people; Rudi, all his savings on night classes, psychiatry, engineering, singing and now – a painter. Dabbling! My brother has made of me, of our children, of himself – a dabbler. Even Martin, my son. A revolutionary! From love? No! From hate. Hatred of me. One thing leads to another! [*Returns to fiddling with T.V. set.*]

GERDA: Forgive him.

[GERDA *leaves. Sound of banging on the wall.*]

EMANUEL'S VOICE: 'Be more humane when you speak against fanaticism, anger not the fanatics; they are delirious invalids, who would assault their physicians. Let us make their ways more gentle, not aggravate them.' Voltaire.


## SCENE FIFTEEN

*The street.* GERDA *is on her way to shop.*
*The* THREE YOUTHS *approach and begin to mimic her limp. She is not afraid but retraces her steps. They continue to follow till she turns to face them.*

GERDA: Silly boys. What do you want? To mimic me? Mimic then, it'll help you be thankful you've got strong legs.

[*One* YOUTH *does a specially cruel and grotesque imitation for the amusement of his companions.*]

Good! You feel better? Then let me pass.

[*They menace her.*]

You want to frighten me? I'm too old to be frightened, go home.

[*They limp round her in a circle.*]

It's really *me* you want to bash? Little bash-boys? *I'm* the biggest 'enemy' you can find? Look at me. Look at yourselves. Three of you. That's brave? I'm the biggest conquest you can make? Go home. Brave boys, go home!

[*Her reason intimidates them. Both sides watch each other. She seems to have won and leaves them.*]

[*Alone there is nothing to feed their valour. One tries to revive the rest by another imitation. It fails. He does it again, more violently. It begins to work. A third time he does it, stamping around as though beating a signal for attack. The other two pick it up and go off with their loud limping mockery.*

*Silence. A scream.*

JACK *walks by clanging his bell.*]

JACK: Jack-o-bell ringing, his warning he's ringing, the plague is upon me, the young folk is living, Jack is a-dying, the young folk is coming, the devil is in me, the young folk is living.

# ACT TWO

---

## SCENE ONE

*SARAH's flat. Chairs on table.* SARAH *is binding sheaves of dried wheat.* BOOMY *is tying them to the 'Succah'.*

BOOMY: And he didn't even go to the police. 'Youth makes mistakes' he says. Mistakes! His wife gets beaten up and he calls it high spirits. You know your brother's trouble?

SARAH: *My* brother and *your* brother.

BOOMY: You know our brother's trouble? He doesn't understand evil. He can't come to terms with the existence of evil. He's always looking for explanations. Some people are colour blind – he's evil blind.

SARAH: It could have been worse.

BOOMY: Can you imagine it? A mind so simple that it has to find reasons for everything, and because of that he doesn't act.

SARAH: A few bruises, that's all.

BOOMY: If *he* was confronted with a man about to strike him he wouldn't react like an ordinary man. He wouldn't raise his hand, reach out to grab something, hit back. No! He'd be paralysed by principles and by trying to work out why it was happening and in the meantime he'd be killed.

SARAH: She's strong, she'll survive.

BOOMY: Principles he's got!

SARAH: In a few days she'll be up and about but in the meanwhile they'll both stay with me. It'll be a pleasant change. Company. You want to stay also?

BOOMY: Principles! The trouble with principles is they make you take a stand about the *one* situation you know you're defeated in.

SARAH: I tell you something? I'm glad it happened. She'll be more careful next time.

BOOMY: And you can't use reason to talk your way out of it.

SARAH: Like this she's learnt and it won't happen again and with luck she'll live to be a year older.

BOOMY: *Why* can't you use reason to talk your way out of it?

SARAH [*handing him a sheaf*]: Instead of talking, help!

BOOMY [*taking the sheaf*]: Because that same reason also tells you you're not in a reasonable situation involving men of principle. Oh no!

SARAH: Did I tell you the fright I had the other day?

BOOMY: You're in a maze. Created by bigots!

SARAH: I phoned Rosa and there was one of those recorded voices at the other end.

BOOMY: And you're trapped.

SARAH: She'd made a tape.

BOOMY: Between your reason and your principles – trapped!

SARAH: A little speech!

BOOMY: Principles! Everyone has principles!

SARAH: You know what it said? 'This is a recording. Mrs Rosa Luxemburg is dead. If you have any messages speak now and we'll do our best.'

BOOMY: The trouble is everyone imagines he's going to have to defend his principles in a romantic situation, where right will prevail.

SARAH: My daughter!

BOOMY: Beautiful!

SARAH: A joker!

BOOMY: But most situations are sordid, confused, Created by idiots or dogmatists or fanatics or psychopaths who *have* no principles – and there you are!

SARAH: We'll have a nice supper.

BOOMY: Caught!

SARAH: They're all coming.

BOOMY: You know what I think about principles?

SARAH: The first 'Succah' the children have ever had.

BOOMY: Principles are like loves and friendships – precious, special.

You should only apply them where they're deserved, sparingly.

SARAH: I'd almost forgotten how to decorate it.

BOOMY: And don't tell me a principle's a principle and that the nature of a principle is that it should be applied in all situations or else it's not a principle. That's the argument dishonest men give you in order to undermine you.

SARAH: I'm making chopped liver –

BOOMY: That's why men of principle are vulnerable –

SARAH: – strudel –

BOOMY: – they can always be defeated.

SARAH: – you'll see!

BOOMY: You want to be principled? Then make a principle of using your scruples only in an emergency, when they're *most* needed, when everyone else can understand them.

SARAH: You think there'll be enough room?

BOOMY: She should have screamed.

SARAH: That's the trouble with this flat, it's too small.

BOOMY: Straight away – she should have screamed. 'Help!'

SARAH: I keep telling Rosa 'Thank you for getting it but it's too small.'

BOOMY: 'Help! Help!' So everyone could have heard. 'Help!'


## SCENE TWO

TERESSA's *flat*.

TERESSA: Perhaps if I do physical things I won't feel so lonely.

[*Her flat is a shambles. She begins pulling clothes off here and there stuffing them away.*]

Work! they say. Keep your body working! As if growing old can do all the things you could when you were young [*But on bending she strains herself.*] Aaah! Work! they say. Give me a new body – I'll work! [*She moves to a cupboard lined with medicine bottles. From one she takes a pill.*] So! And that's for my lumbago. And what shall I take for the pain behind my ears, and my weak bladder, and my coughing fits and the pain in my chest and my fear? Fear? Who's got pills against fear? [*On the table are a box of dominoes. She builds with them.*] You know, darling, when a person *really* feels lonely? Not when they're alone and no one comes to see them – in such a case you can go out to people, even if they don't ask. No, it's when they don't have in their heart one little bit of a wish themselves to see other people. It's *not* having appetites for contact, that! That, my darling, makes for real loneliness. You, you're lucky, you're *not* lonely – you *want* contact. But who? That's your problem. And where? And when? [*Pause.*] And why? I always forget why. Such a memory! My memory is so bad that when I went to a psychiatrist to get it seen to I'd forgot why I came. [*Pause.*] No! That's not true. It's funny but it's not true. Who can afford a psychiatrist? Jokes! Even jokes I have to tell myself, and *that's* not funny, darling. My poor darling.

[LIGHTS DIM. *There is a banging on a wall.*]

BOOMY'S VOICE: 'Man is not what one calls a happy animal.' Carlyle.

## SCENE THREE

SARAH's *council flat.* MARTIN *is knocking more nails into the 'Succah', ineffectively trying to strengthen it.*

MARTIN: I'm afraid it'll always wobble.

SARAH: Let it. So will I always wobble.

[RUDI *enters carrying a bundle of branches tied with string.*]

RUDI: Trees! Get trees, she says. Where can I get trees from? My garden? Who's got a garden? One room and a kitchen I've got, with a bathroom for three other tenants to use – and their friends. I'm lucky if I get a bath once a week. [*Sees* MARTIN.] It's Martin?

MARTIN: Hello, Rudi.

RUDI: After all these years it's Martin.

MARTIN [*helping to untie bundle*]: And where *did* you get them from?

RUDI: Can you grow trees in a bathroom?

SARAH: They're just right.

RUDI: Little pot plants, maybe. But trees?

[*They begin to lay them over the 'Succah'.*]

And how's my student? So many years you've been a student. When does a student stop being a student?

MARTIN: It's too long, isn't it?

RUDI: Who says it's too long?

MARTIN: You're right.

RUDI: I'm just asking.

MARTIN: It *is* too long.

SARAH: It's never too long to study. Study. You won't be sorry.

RUDI: You want to know where I got them? In the place where I go to evening classes they've got a big oak tree. Two in fact. I asked the caretaker. A few coppers, you know, on the side. Everything costs a few coppers. And he cut some for me. It needs pruning, he says. Pruning! And if it didn't need pruning? He'd still cut them! For coppers! Everything's possible for coppers.

MARTIN: Be careful how you lay them. It wobbles.

RUDI: Everything wobbles. You seen a piece of furniture these days that doesn't wobble?

SARAH: Study. Great learning. It's an honour.

RUDI: You know I go to evening classes?

MARTIN: I know. To study singing.

RUDI: That was last year. You see how long I don't see people in this family? A cousin! And he still thinks I'm singing.

MARTIN: What is it then?

RUDI: Painting. I paint. Oils, watercolours, gouache. You know what I mean?

SARAH: Study! It's a blessing to know things. My father was always telling me. Knowledge is light, ignorance is darkness.

## SCENE FOUR

MILLIE's *flat.* JACK *is with her. She gazes, as always, out of the window.*

JACK: No, Missus, I ses to meself, that lady can't be mad. Wot, that
little frail thing? I seen women frail like that before but they out-
lived their men they did. Little things they were, pellets of steel.
Pellets like them don't go mad, I ses to meself, and there's one of
'em. [*Waits for response. None comes.*] So I comes, leaves me bell
behind and looks her up. She'll give me a cup of charley, I ses, and
talk a little, an' the day'll pass and be the better for it. [*Still no re-
action.*] Wot should I do? Stay at home? Ring me bell? You think
a man don't tire of his own bell-ringing? So 'ere 'ee is, your Jack-o-
bell. Tea I got, your good company and homemade bread pudding
into the bargain.

MILLIE: My daughters were evacuated to Wales, you know. In the
war. Five daughters I had. My poor husband! No son! And three
were big. Big girls – worked in armaments. But the youngest? A
place called Tredegar, in a little stone cottage, no electricity, no
water, no nothing, miles from anywhere. My poor children. And
this woman – you talk about madness? – this woman made them
do strange things every night. One night combing her hair,
another night rubbing her back, then washing her feet – funny
woman. Who knows where your children go in wartime, eh?
And *she* ended up in a home, my daughter told me, she went back
one day and found her, in a room, padded, her hair sticking out
like a tree, and my daughter said, 'You remember me?' and she
did. For a second, she called her name, Becky, and then she forgot.
Strange, yes? The whole place was strange. In the school the teacher
used to tell them 'Because you're Jewish your nose will get longer
and horns will come out of your head!' My poor girls. They be-
lieved him. Did you ever see? Horns! And each night they used to
look in the mirror and it was true. They were growing girls and
their noses got bigger! And all the time they were waiting for the
horns. And all the time this woman, this mad woman, kept saying,

'Maybe your horns won't grow, maybe because you're in Wales they won't grow!' But the teacher kept saying, 'They must! They must!' Is that a teacher I ask you? And one day they came home for a holiday and my husband, God rest him, could see they were unhappy so he asks them, 'What's the matter?' And they told him and he says, 'Silly girls, look at me, your father, have *I* got horns?' And they looked and he was right, they could see, no horns!

[*Pause.*]

JACK: Yes Missus, I ses to meself, you'll get a cup o' tea, a bit o' company and the day'll be the better for it.


## SCENE FIVE

SARAH's *flat. A depressed* ROSA *is replacing chairs from table to floor.*

SARAH: You shouldn't let it upset you.

ROSA: I just can't break through to them.

SARAH: You'll try again.

ROSA: The problem's so immense.

SARAH: With another lot – you'll learn.

ROSA: And they can see, those little monsters, even before I begin, that I'm defeated. And wham! They step in.

SARAH: Who knows about things in the beginning?

[ROSA *kisses her mother, sits, takes off shoes from aching feet.*]

ROSA: One day, Sarah, we will die.

SARAH: *You*, silly girl? *You're* at the age when you'll never die.

ROSA: It's the most terrible fact I know. Every lovely, lovely thing I cherish will, for me, one day, be ended. And I don't know when it will be, or how, or where. I try to think of it, imagine the circumstances, but I can't, there are too many possibilities. And it's such a pain, that loss, of you – and me. You can't imagine how much I dread it. Says Boswell: 'But is not the fear of death natural to man?' Says Johnson: 'So much so, Sir, that the whole of life is but keeping away the thoughts of it.' [*Pause.*] I won't ever die happily; no matter what splendid life I lead I can't see myself smiling sweetly with my last breath; I'll rage – that's for sure. But could I rage less? What could I do to make me rage less? I don't know. I ask myself but I don't know. I can't even recognize which is the real problem. Capital versus labour? Computer versus individual? Rich world versus third world? Affluence versus spiritual poverty? Which is it? One or all or something else? And if I find out, what can I do? And those cruel little cripples – who'll be the real victims, you know – they block me.

[SARAH *breaks away from her and throws a big white tablecloth over the extended table.*]

SARAH: A white cloth!

[ROSA, *her mood spent, takes the other end.*]

Nothing like a white cloth, fresh, clean, happy.

ROSA: Happy! Happeeee!

[ROSA *now begins unpacking a box of drinks.*]

SARAH: What you doing?

ROSA: Drinks! I've bought you a little arsenal of socializing equipment. All those thirsty tipplers you entertain.

SARAH: Take it back.

ROSA: It's a present. I got an income-tax rebate.

SARAH: You've got money? Keep it! You may need it one day.

ROSA: Cointreau! Your favourite! Cointreau, gin, Tia Maria, cherry brandy, brandy – only half-bottles. Indulge yourself.

SARAH: It makes me ashamed. Me, an old-age pensioner in a block of flats for old-age pensioners.

ROSA: A *few* bottles.

SARAH: It's immoral. A couple of pounds they've got to live on and I've got a brewery inside here.

ROSA: And why do I love to see full cupboards? You! Got it from you.

SARAH: Me! Me! Always me.

ROSA: You! You! Always you. I used to love unpacking *your* shopping-bags, and now when I go shopping it's terrible, I can't stop. Biscuits from one shelf, tins from another, and cheeses – all those different cheeses. You never know who's coming. And I feel so ashamed. The children see me, taking, taking, taking – in a fever. What will they grow into, I think? [*Pause.*] Psst! I'll hide them under the bed.

SARAH [*dusting chairs*]: You're a good daughter, not everyone's got good daughters, take them back.

ROSA: Mother, there's not a law against having good daughters.

SARAH: You mean well, I'm very grateful, don't argue with me and take them back.

ROSA: There's no logic in you.

SARAH: She's starting on me again. Something else wrong with me.

ROSA: I'm not starting on you, I'm criticizing you.

SARAH: You're always criticizing me.

ROSA: No, *you're* always criticizing *me*.

SARAH: There! Another thing wrong I've done. I made a new year's resolution – no more quarrelling with the children.

ROSA: Will you stop being paranoic.

SARAH: Don't be crude.

ROSA: I'm not really criticizing you. How could I? Everything *you* are, *I* am.

SARAH: Calling me names.

[ROSA *stops her in her work and embraces her from behind.*]

ROSA: Everything! The little I respect in myself I've inherited from you.

SARAH: A terrible life I gave you.

ROSA: You! Generosity, tolerance, intolerance, sanity, insanity. You!

SARAH: Leaving you alone to go out to work.

ROSA: The weather gets overcast – I'm depressed! You!

SARAH: Not caring enough for your education.

ROSA: When I lose my temper confronted with bloody-mindedness? You!

SARAH: You think it pleases me that you've inherited my faults?

ROSA [*casually stepping up on to a chair*]: I read about the terrible things men do to each other – wars for gain or prestige, massacres for religious principles, cruelty to children, indifference to poverty – and then, one morning, one person, one, does something beautiful and I say, 'See! people *are* good!' You! [*Jumps up on to the table.*]

SARAH [*slapping her off*] I was a fool? I brought *you* up to be a fool.

ROSA [*stepping from chair to chair like stepping-stones*]: The pompous action that makes me giggle? You! My laughter, my ups, my downs, my patience, my impatience, my love of music, mountains,

174

flowers, knowledge – a reverence for all things living? You! You, you, you! [*Leaps into her mother's arms.*]


## SCENE SIX

*The street.* JACK *and* MILLIE.

JACK: Come, Missus, tonight's the night. With a hop, skip and a jump. Look! [*There's a children's chalked game on the ground.* JACK *hops through it.*] You do it, Missus.

MILLIE: You're a very funny man.

JACK: Too late for lying, Missus, too old to pretend. I rings me bell, they can go to hell.

MILLIE: A poet he is.

JACK: Quite right, little missus, little pellet of steel. A poet! With a hop and a skip and a jump. [*Hops through the game once more and turns to face her.*] Hated the army, hated the war, hated employers and all their sweet smiles; and I learned that a man's got ter give 'is warning and cry stinking fish sometimes. But – I loves London and I loves England and I loves the little foreigners like you wot they let in to mix the blood a bit. Come, Missus, me arm. I'll escort you safe and sound to the other little Jewish lady wots my neighbour.

[*She takes his arm, shyly.*]
And wot a neighbour she is, she is. A fighter, a real little pellet of steel she is. Pellets of steel all you lot are. Come.

[*They walk on.*]

## SCENE SEVEN

SARAH's *flat. A restless* MARTIN. *Both are involved in preparing for the dinner.*

SARAH: If I had a hundred pounds, I'd give you. Stay for a Friday-night supper and see your father.

MARTIN: I can't face him any more, Sarah.

SARAH: A lonely, old man. What harm can he do you?

MARTIN: He thinks he's tough, but he's gloomy.

SARAH: You've got a court case hanging over you. Speak to him.

MARTIN: I try. I always try. 'Leave politics alone!' He screams at me.

SARAH: Prison. It might mean prison.

MARTIN: All that tough gloominess? It's soft really. And the softer he becomes, the harder I must be.

SARAH: Idiot's logic.

MARTIN: I look at him and I see myself. That softness? I'll catch it from him and it'll destroy me.

SARAH: You think you're not already? Your studies, your wife, your family – abandoned! That's not destruction?

MARTIN: It only looks like it.

SARAH: I'm losing patience.

MARTIN: They're leaving us no alternatives.

SARAH: They! They! Always someone else. And you think you're not doing just what *they* want? Window smashing, burning, insulting – everyone and anyone – little gestures?

MARTIN: They arrested a friend, Sarah; a sweet, frail young man. For months I'd been talking to him; arguing, explaining, making him read different books, giving him courage. He took nothing I said without checking, without counter-argument, without asking others. I worked so hard to persuade him that I grew to love him. He had the reddest hair I'd ever seen, was brilliant – much more than me – and diabetic. And when they arrested him they took one look at his long red hair and refused to *believe* he was a diabetic. He died.

SARAH: An exception!

MARTIN: I wish it were.

SARAH: You can't make policies from exceptions.

MARTIN: I could tell you more.

SARAH: You can't tell me anything will excuse these actions.

MARTIN: Now *I'm* losing patience.

SARAH: If your family rots, your beliefs will rot.

MARTIN: I don't know what you want from us. You *taught* us to respect human beings, didn't you? To revere knowledge and despise gain? You and Uncle Manny? Well, didn't you? 'If a man is hungry while you eat you won't have peace,' you said. 'When you see injustice, protest?' Manny used to pack me off to school saying, 'Don't fight and don't let misery stop you laughing, but if you see a bully – stand up! Always stand up and be counted!' And he'd tell me, 'Take no notice of your father, he's a good man but he doesn't like himself.'

SARAH: So! Your father's *made* mistakes.

MARTIN: Mistakes?

SARAH: All right! He was wrong. Not right-minded with a few natural mistakes – but wrong! From start to finish, wrong! What must you do? Scream insults at his old age? Spit on him? That's lovely? You shriek untenderly at him that he had no tenderness? You handle him violently for his violence upon you? That's inspiration? Leadership? You must have strength to ignore Boomy's weaknesses and leave him a little bit of useless old peace. What do you imagine *your* children will say at the sight of such ugliness in protest against ugliness? What must they learn from such a spectacle of your revenge? That's what you build new worlds with? What's this for revolution? Lovely! Oh, very lovely! Lovely, lovely, yes!

MARTIN: Do you think I enjoy the conscience you all gave me?

SARAH: Stay and speak with your father.

[*He leaves.*]

## SCENE EIGHT

*Another class.* ROSA *enters. She is determined to control them and does.*

ROSA: I'm here once and once only. And when I'm gone I'll not care
one bit about any of you but you're going to care about and remember me. You, each one of you, are nothing in this society.
Nothing! You are poor, used, nothings who will mostly end up
unhappy, frustrated and thoroughly defeated. You *think* you're in
control, that no one can shove you around, that you're God al-
mighty free Englishmen but you're not. You can bash each other
and pinch sweets and knock old women on the head but the great
world goes on and ignores you or knows and cares little for you
just as you boast that you know and care little for it. What, what is
there you can do? Can you take a yacht round the world? Can
you fly to wherever you want? Can you speak another language,
split an atom, transplant a heart, live where you like, climb a
mountain? You won't even find the job you want, most of you.
So get that straight, firm, in your heads. It's a big world in which
control rests with other people, not *you. Not* you. [*Pause.*] Good.
You're listening. It makes a change. I don't say any of these things
happily. Do you think I like how we're forced to live with each
other? But someone must warn you. Who knows, one of you
might even listen. One of you might rise to the challenge and have
done with his tiny ambitions of petty kingships and turn in on himself and find his real strengths. And it will *only* be one of you – the
rest will end up on the scrapheap of dead-end jobs with dead-eyed
wives. [*Pause.*] You hate me, don't you? I can see from your eyes
and clenched mouths that you hate every part of me; the sound of
my voice, what I say, the way I dress, the life you imagine I lead.
I'm sorry about that. Hate's a sterile emotion. Useless! It'll take
you round in circles while others go straight for what they want.
Still, I suppose that's the diet most of you will live with from now
on. Hate. Sad. BUT HERE! Here is a book. Books! Take them. Use
them. Other men may build an alien world out there you never

dreamed of. [*Softly, without hope*] Defend yourself! Books! Centuries of other people's knowledge, experience. Add it to yours, measure it with yours. They're your only key to freedom and happiness. Books! [*Forlorn, weary*] There is no other. I promise you. There – is – no – other!


# SCENE NINE

SARAH's *flat. Everyone except* MARTIN *is there surrounding and listening to* ROSA. *Only* GERDA *is apart and bandaged on a couch.* ROSA *finishes relating the story. From here, this scene and all its characters must be full of energy, for these are people who eat and bustle while they talk.*


ROSA: And then I went on to talk quickly about jobs and when I left them I was so nervous and shaking that I had to rush to the lavatory to be sick. So feeble. So bloody feeble.

BOOMY: And you'll lose the job?

ROSA: With luck, yes. You're not supposed to talk like that to the pupils.

[*Silence.*]

SARAH: Good! *You* were sick? Gerda here got a good bashing? Let's eat!

[*Everyone attempts to settle.* SARAH *attempts to serve.*]

RUDI: And the 'Succah'? We made a 'Succah'. I don't know why we made it – I mean who's orthodox? I'm not orthodox, I'm just Jewish. But we made it! So now what do we do with it?

[RUDI's *question brings everything to a halt.*]

TERESSA: We've got no cuples, we've got no prayer books.

ROSA: It was only meant to be a gesture.

SARAH: To please Gerda.

TERESSA: And *is* Gerda pleased?

GERDA [*too late for anything to please her*]: And is Gerda pleased!

TERESSA: It's sacrilegious. I mean, we don't even remember.

RUDI: Doesn't anyone remember?

SARAH: Who can remember? We were children.

EMANUEL [*reading from the little book*]: 'The "Succah" gave ample opportunity for hospitality, and in the words of the Zohar [*directing this at* BOOMY]: "It is necessary for man to rejoice within the 'Succah' and show a cheerful countenance to guests." '

BOOMY: So? What you waiting for? Go inside. We'll pass you in some food, you start eating and then you show a cheerful countenance to the guests!

EMANUEL [*continuing reading*]: 'It is forbidden to harbour thoughts of gloom and, how much more so, feelings of anger within the portals of the "Succah" – the symbol of joy.'

BOOMY: Joy! Joy! You know what book belongs to 'Succous'? Ecclesiastes! So! Go read Ecclesiastes and be joyful!

JACK: Perhaps I should go.

SARAH: Not you. You're the guest.

BOOMY: To whom must be shown the cheerful countenance.

EMANUEL: And a fat lot of cheer he or anyone'll get from you! Sarah, is the water hot for a bath later?

SARAH: What kind of a question's that? The water's always hot.

ROSA [*who's taken the little book from* EMANUEL]: A procession. It says you must make a procession.

SARAH: Still not eat?

ROSA: You wanted to celebrate 'Succoth'? Then follow the instructions.

BOOMY [*sitting*]: I'm not going to be party to such mockery, to such irreverence, to such childishness.

EMANUEL [*sitting*]: Nor me!

BOOMY [*standing*]: Maybe I'll change my mind.

EMANUEL [*standing*]: See how easy it is to get him to do things?

ROSA [*reading*]. 'Josephus in his work *The Antiquities of the Jews* stated that during the offering of the sacrifices in the Temple "every one of the worshippers carried in his hands a branch of myrtle and willows joined to a bough of the palm tree, with the addition of the citron".' Here, Mother, you can hold the lemon.

SARAH: I'm beginning to feel embarrassed.

TERESSA: I must tell you, I think we should only do this in a synagogue, not in a home.

ROSA: 'The Talmudic regulations which give detailed instructions as to how the plants should be held indicate that the custom of "waving" the plants and of bearing them whilst in procession during the service was widely in use before Mishnaic times.'

[ROSA *meanwhile has been giving everyone a branch of some sort to hold in their hand.*]

MILLIE: We going somewhere?

RUDI: So! We walk and wave the branches.

[*He begins to move and waves his branch. Everyone excepting* JACK *slowly, awkwardly, self-consciously, follows him. They move in a circle.*]

Then what?

TERESSA: But where's the service? We don't know the right prayers or the right songs.

RUDI: Who knows the right prayers and the right songs?

TERESSA: In a *synagogue* they'd know the right prayers and the right songs!

MILLIE: Where we going?

BOOMY: You don't even know what it all stands for do you?

EMANUEL: Tell us, O wise one.

BOOMY: It's man. Every different plant stands for a different part of the body. The palm is the spine, the myrtle is the eyes, the willow is the lips.

JACK: Beautiful.

ROSA: And the lemon?

BOOMY: I don't know.

GERDA: The lemon is the heart. Bitter.

EMANUEL: Nonsense! It represents the unity of differences.

BOOMY: The unity of differences!

EMANUEL: The unity of different abilities and different races – that's what it means. Judaism was a universal religion.

BOOMY: That's what those German Jews said. Trying to make themselves acceptable to everyone.

[*Everyone is brought to an abrupt halt.*]

ROSA [*reading*]: 'Rabbenu Bahya ben Asher, the medieval moralist, says that traditions which have their roots in the past must not be dismissed as obsolete but must be revived by the language and minds of new generations.' That's me! *I'm* supposed to tell you what to do?

[*Pause.*]

GERDA: Sing. Perhaps you should sing?

EMANUEL: Now that's a good idea.

BOOMY [*throwing down his branch*]: Madness!

ROSA [*to* GERDA]: We tried.

GERDA: I'm grateful.

SARAH: Let's eat.

[*Everyone, except* RUDI, SARAH, ROSA *and* MILLIE, *takes a place at the table.* RUDI *serves the wine,* SARAH *and* ROSA *fetch plates of chopped liver and* MILLIE *collects branches to replace under the* '*Succah*', *keeping one for herself.*]

BOOMY: 'Then I beheld all the work of God, that a man cannot find out the work that is done under the sun; because though a man labour to seek it out, yet he shall not find it; yea farther, though a *wise* man think to know it, yet shall *he* not be able to find it.' Ecclesiastes.

EMANUEL [*preparing to light the candles*]: 'For wisdom is a defence, even as money is a defence; but the excellency of knowledge is, that wisdom giveth life of them that have it.' [*Pause.*] Ecclesiastes!

[EMANUEL *lights the candles.*]

BOOMY: There's no cover on his head, no prayer on his lips and he's lighting candles.

EMANUEL: My head is covered with grey hairs and there are more prayers on earth than was ever dreamt of in Heaven.

ROSA: Enough. Uncle Manny. Let's eat.

EMANUEL: I was mad! All my life I've been depressed. Depressed! What was I depressed for? Sarah, is the water hot for a bath later?

SARAH: I've told you! It's hot, it's hot. What's the matter with him?

EMANUEL: And so one morning I woke up and I said, 'Manny,' I said, 'you're not young any more!' And I went out and bought myself a tape-recorder and started singing. And you know what? I got a good voice. [*Standing.*] Pass the salt someone, please.

BOOMY: Brother mine, answer me a question. Do I exist?

EMANUEL: Do you what?

BOOMY: Exist.

EMANUEL: I sometimes wonder.

BOOMY: Prove it.

EMANUEL: Prove what?

BOOMY: That I exist.

EMANUEL: You doubt it?

BOOMY: I doubt it.

EMANUEL: So! You exist.

BOOMY: That's not evidence, that's faith.

EMANUEL: You idiot, you. The fact that you doubt is proof that you exist because you exist to doubt it. The salt, please.

BOOMY [*arrested*]: Mmm. I'll come back on it.

EMANUEL [*reaching for a tape-recorder*]: Who would like to hear me sing?

SARAH: Not now.

GERDA: Look at him, it's not fair, such energy.

EMANUEL: 'What've you been depressed about?' I said.

GERDA: I grow old and he grows young.

EMANUEL: 'What! You've committed crimes? You've done harm? Betrayed people? All right!' I said, 'so the world's got troubles, but someone's got to remember how to be happy. You mustn't lose the habit of joy,' I said. 'Someone's got to carry it around.'

GERDA: So they chose my Manny.

EMANUEL: People need it!

GERDA: People! People! Don't talk to me about people.

EMANUEL: Seventy years a madman.

GERDA: There's a silliness, a – a – nastiness to people which – Ach! Explain to them, tell them things – for what? What do they understand? A little bit of niceness? Kindness? Nothing! Nothing they feel and nothing they know. Hot angers they've got, about grubby little things. So leave me alone about people, all my life I've had people.

[EMANUEL *goes to her, partly to pacify her, partly to bring some food.* ROSA *and* SARAH *now move to ladle and serve the soup.*]

EMANUEL: Eat! Eat and be happy!

GERDA: Look at him. I grow old and he grows young.

EMANUEL: Shuh! Shuh!

TERESSA [*collecting dishes*]: That's what makes you grow old, darling.

Eating! We eat too much *and* the wrong things. The body works overtime. Eat the wrong things – your body works the wrong way. Look at Shaw, a vegetarian, lived to nearly a hundred.

EMANUEL: And did you read about those farmers in Georgia? Honey and yoghurt – lived till a hundred and forty.

JACK [*standing*]: I think it's sex.

TERESSA: Did he say 'sex'?

JACK: Sex makes you grow old. It's been proved. Look at nuns and monks. Beautiful. [*Sits.*]

BOOMY: And *I* think it's just living. The longer you live, the older you get!

MILLIE [*moving to fix her branch into the 'Succah'*]: Me, I've got three grandchildren, a boy, a girl, a boy; and listen what happened. It was after a bath and the girl put her hand between her legs and said – this is children for you – she said, 'I'm only nine and I've already got hairs.' And so the youngest, of course, had to say something, and so he looked and found four or five; but the eldest, the eldest says, 'Well, what about me, I'm only ten and I've got a forest?'

[*General laughter.*]

TERESSA: My granddaughter calls them 'public hairs'.

ROSA [*to SARAH*]: *Your* granddaughter asks me to lend her the nail varnish because she wants to paint her 'testicles'!

[*Great laughter.*]

TERESSA: Ah! Laughter, laughter, laughter! You know, on the Continent they think the Englishman has the greatest of all senses of humour. But I'm not so sure.

JACK: You can't beat an English joke!

TERESSA: I'm not talking about jokes. Jokes are jokes, little stories, nothing important; but humour, real humour, to look at a situation and find humour *in* it – *that* the Englishman can't do.

BOOMY: Nonsense! You've never heard of English satire?

TERESSA: Oh, he can mock. Very good at mocking. And being rude.

BOOMY: Look at more television. That's where you'll see what makes the Englishman laugh.

TERESSA: Precisely! Rudeness! Someone insults someone else – they laugh! Someone punches someone else – they laugh! A husband calls his wife a nit – big, big laughter! Very subtle! And now it's sexual jokes. The Englishman has to prove he's sexy, so there's innuendoes about things that stand up and fall down. Stand up, fall down, put in, take out. All very subtle. What lovely soup.

RUDI: I'm missing somebody. Rosa. Your husband the soil expert.

[Pause.]

BOOMY: Rosa, Rosa, where's your husband the soil expert?

RUDI: Have I said something wrong?

ROSA: You've said nothing wrong, but my husband the soil expert is trying to cross an oak with a rose to strengthen the one and colour the other and he's not having much luck. All he can produce is mud.

RUDI: And where is Martin?

[Pause.]

ROSA: Boomy, Boomy, where's your Martin?

RUDI: Have I said something else wrong?

BOOMY: Your cousin! Huh! Have you got a cousin.

RUDI: I've said something wrong.

ROSA: Our cousin is on his way to prison.

RUDI: Nobody tells me anything.

ROSA: He'll spend six months in prison because our uncle there thinks it'll make him a *mensch*.

RUDI: Who says prison makes a *mensch*?

BOOMY: He'll learn: you can't apply to Britain what you can in other countries.

RUDI: That's a funny idea that is to think prison makes a *mensch*.

BOOMY: A thousand years this country hasn't been occupied. A thousand years to grow, unmolested – it means something. You can't change it overnight.

RUDI [*standing in order to begin collecting dishes*]: You let your son go to prison to be made a man?

BOOMY: He wants to change Britain? Good! Find other ways. He'll spend six months in jail and come out a *mensch*.

RUDI: Funny ideas people have.

BOOMY: Rudi, you're a fool.

RUDI: Don't call me a fool. Nobody calls me a fool.

SARAH: Stop it, enough now.

[SARAH *and* ROSA *now begin to ladle out the chicken dish which they hand to* RUDI *who serves during his story.*]

BOOMY: I've got a family of fools.

RUDI: Anybody calls me a fool and they know what's coming, you know what I mean?

BOOMY [*mocking*]: 'You know what I mean?'

RUDI: You had a clever son, educated, I wish I was educated like him, what did you send him to prison for?

BOOMY: What did *I* send him to prison for!

RUDI: One day he comes to me and he says, 'Rudi,' he says, 'there's a fortune to be made out of simple ideas.' 'What's simple about anything?' I tell him. 'Listen,' he says. 'Look around you. What doesn't function properly?' Funny question. 'The lights work,' I say. 'The trains run on time, or nearly always,' I say. 'The planes stay up in the air, the clock goes,' you know what I mean?

BOOMY [*mocking echo*]: 'You know what I mean?'

RUDI: 'No, no!' he says. 'Simple things! Simple things!' 'All right!' I say, '*you* tell me.' 'A nutcracker,' he says. 'You ever seen a nut-cracker that cracks nuts properly?' You ever hear? 'In this day of rockets to the moon,' he says, 'they haven't got a tool to crack nuts!' Of course, I knew what he was talking about because I've studied electronics, studied it, you see. So then he says, 'I'm going to go to a nut-cracking factory and find out how they do it. But', he says, 'they won't part with their secrets so I've got to pretend I'm a school-teacher and take a party of kids on a trip.' So what does he do? He rounds up half a dozen kids, gives them five shillings each to play truant and takes them to a nut-cracking factory.

[*Silence. Everyone waits.*]

BOOMY: So?

RUDI: So what?

BOOMY: So what happened?

RUDI: How should I know what happened? *You* sent him to prison. [*Uproar. All are now eating.*] I haven't seen him again. I never see this family except once in a blue moon when I go to *them*. I'd die and no one would visit me.

[EMANUEL *and* GERDA *have been whispering together in subdued tones. Suddenly their conversation erupts.*]

EMANUEL: And I'm telling you I *will* be cremated.

GERDA: Never! You can stand on your head but you'll lie by *me* when you're dead.

EMANUEL: And if *you* die first I'll make my own arrangements.

GERDA: And if *you* die first?

EMANUEL: The arrangements are made.

GERDA: I'll change them. We slept together alive? We'll sleep together dead.

EMANUEL: Countermand my orders and you'll be dishonouring the dead.

GERDA: Why didn't you tell me?

EMANUEL: A dozen times I've told you.

GERDA: Never! You've never said a word till now.

EMANUEL: You don't listen.

GERDA: We've paid for the plots.

EMANUEL: *You've* paid for the plots.

GERDA: I won't let it happen. I want you by me. You'll see.

EMANUEL: *You'll* see.

GERDA: All these years paying for nothing. Cremated! Dust!

EMANUEL: Ashes.

GERDA: Ashes! In the wind. Nothing left.

EMANUEL: You think I'll stay whole in the earth?

GERDA: I don't care!

EMANUEL: I'm going to have a bath. A lovely supper, Sarah, but you'll excuse me, please. [*Storms off.*]

SARAH [*calling after him*]: *Now* you're quarrelling with her?

GERDA: Leave him. He needs a bath. May it be too hot for him, then he'll know about cremation.

TERESSA: As if there isn't enough violence in the world!

BOOMY: Violence! Violence! Who wants more wine?

GERDA: Here, here. I've got a thirst.

BOOMY [*rising to uncork and serve the wine*]: Everyone's talking about violence – a big mystery! What causes it! Whisper, whisper, whisper, pssssssss! Why don't they ask me? Ask me, I'll tell them.

[*Silence.*]

ROSA [*finally*]: We're asking you, Uncle Boomy.

BOOMY: What! They've never heard of cultural intimidation?

ROSA: Whew!

BOOMY: I'm not of course referring to your so-called 'magnificent primitive working man' – we all know nothing can intimidate him. I'm referring to the men of *real* inferiority, men who suspect their own stupidity. That's where violence comes from. The anger of self-knowledge. Self-knowledge that he's a pig and then – everything intimidates him: a tone of voice, a way of dressing, a passion for literature, a passion for music, for anything! He hates it! One little speck of colour on a man's personality unleashes such venom, *such* venom.

RUDI: Give a man more money.

BOOMY: Money! Money! Money he has, security, a good job, a house, a car – everything. Not riches, I'm not talking about riches, but like us – enough. And still, and yet, his whole body, every corpuscle in his thick blood is on fire and alive to the slightest deviation *from what he is*. Can't bear it! Grrrr! Hit it! Smash it! He'll show who's superior and who's not. Wham! And there it is, all round him, the intimidation – bookshops, television, flamboyant actresses, Cabinet ministers who went to university, protesting students with long hair, trade-union leaders with big cars, black leaders with clenched fists, pop singers, Hippies, Yippies, Queers, Yids! 'Know thyself!' everyone says. 'Unto thine own self be true!' What's that for advice? We *know* ourselves. Only too bloody true we know ourselves. That's the trouble. We know ourselves too well. Grrrr? Can't bear it! And there they are, the intimidated, squirming in their factories and shops, missing it all. The adverts tell them! Missing it and hating it and hating themselves for missing it. Trapped! All over the place, in little black holes, trapped! Grrrr! Who can I smash? Who's fault is it? Someone's got to suffer as well as me. Wham! Nigger, Jew, Artist, Student. Lynch 'em! Send 'em back! Bring back the gallows, the whip, anything I – hate – them! I – hate – me! Hate! Grrrr! [*Pause.*] Violence? They want to know about violence? Me! Ask me.

[*Silence.*]

SARAH: Boomy, you're a very depressing man.

[*Silence.*]

JACK [*rising to get a drink of water*]: Dogs! Have yous ever thought about dogs?

TERESSA: Dogs? Did he say dogs?

JACK: Do you know a dog has a smell wot's a hundred times more sensitive than ours? Fact! So, wot's old Jack been thinking to hisself? Can you not, he thinks, can you not give a dog music through smells?

TERESSA: Music? Did he say music?

JACK: Take an organ. Wot does an organ do? A piano you knocks, but an organ you puffs. I knows, yer see, 'cos I used to work where they made 'em. You puffs out air and yer puts a tube in the way. And if yer puts a big tube in the way it makes one kind of sound and if yer puts a small tube in the way it makes another kind of sound. Now, suppose yer puffs through your tube and yer puts a special *smell* in the way?

TERESSA: Is he serious?

JACK: A different smell, like a different note. And if the tube is big yer puff a big smell and if the tube is small yer puff a small smell. And music makes yer *feel* things, same as smells, so – smells can be puffed out to make a dog feel things.

TERESSA: He *is* serious.

JACK: Would not that, I ask you, breed a special kind of dog?
  [*Silence.*]

MILLIE: He's a very funny man.

  [JACK *shyly retreats to the wall.* SARAH *goes to lay out strudel on the plates.*]

TERESSA: Yes, well, everybody's got a funny something with them. You need it! To survive! [*Rises to begin collecting the dishes.*] I tell you – I escaped from the Germans in the war, with my family. We went to live for a little while in Denmark. Did I say 'live'? Hide! Who could live in Europe during the war? Anyway, with me was a mad woman and she was also Jewish; but beautiful? Like you've never seen. And – *she* was lucky. A famous Danish poet – he's dead now but I won't mention names – an old man, about sixty-five, agreed to marry her to save her from the Gestapo. Only once they married she began to claim her conjugal rights! What do you think! An old man of sixty-five and she began to make demands like that on him. It's not a joke. 'I insist,' she used to say, 'I insist that he honours me with the traditional performance in bed.' And she used to whip him with her breasts, beat him, a poet! This little woman! On the run from the gas chambers! Making love! I ask you!

ROSA [*rising*]: A toast! Ladies and gentlemen, a toast! In the eighteenth century in France there was a famous woman called Madame d'Epinay. And she was the centre of great learning and great men. Among the many ways she helped them was to keep up a corre-spondence with some of them. But one by one they died, those keen minds of Europe, and she became sadder and sadder. But with one, a lively Abbé in Italy called Abbé Galiani, she maintained the longest and probably the last of her letter-writings. And as those great men about her died, she reported it to the Abbé and she wrote: 'I'm made of iron. Everything hurts me, nothing kills me.' To my mother.

[*Everyone rises, and turns to a surprised* SARAH *as she is about to serve the strudel.*]

ALL: To Sarah!

SARAH: Me? Me?

[JACK *has been fiddling with the tape-recorder and suddenly we hear* 'MANNY' *singing.*]

JACK: It works!

ROSA: Leave it playing.

[ROSA *takes the tray of strudel from* SARAH *and places it on the table from which she picks up a table napkin and offers an end to her mother. The others join in humming and clapping while she and* SARAH, *shyly, begin a delicate Hasidic dance.*

*Suddenly,* EMANUEL *bursts in covered by a towel. He rushes to switch off the tape-recorder.*]

EMANUEL: I got it! I got it! The answer! Listen everybody, I've been thinking and I've been thinking and at last it's come to me. In the bath.

GERDA: He'll catch cold the lunatic.

EMANUEL: Evil! It doesn't exist. It can't.

BOOMY: He's a tryer. I'll say that for him.

EMANUEL: Listen! Evil is when you want to be cruel – right? And

cruelty – now listen carefully – [*slowly*] cruelty is when one man is trying to create a situation in which *he* is not suffering pain.
    [*Silence.*]

GERDA: I didn't hear.

EMANUEL: Cruelty is when one man is trying to create a situation in which *he* is not suffering pain.

BOOMY: What new nonsense is this?
    [*General commotion, everyone asking each other what he means.* JACK *decides at this moment to leave as though it's all too much for him.*]

JACK [*on his way out, ringing*]: Jack's a-dying, the young folk is living, Jack's a-going, the young folk is coming.

ROSA: Uncle Manny, it's brilliant.

BOOMY: It's nonsense!

GERDA: Go back to your bath, you'll catch cold.

EMANUEL: You don't understand, you're not listening. Don't you realize the significance of what I'm saying?

SARAH: Jack! Jack! Supper isn't over yet. [*But he's gone.*] It's like a madhouse here.

EMANUEL: Think about it, for Christ's sake, think about it.

BOOMY: What? What? Think about what? 'Vanity of vanities, all is vanity.'

ROSA: What's vanity got to do with Uncle Manny's definition of cruelty?

BOOMY: 'A fool's voice is known by a multitude of words.'

ROSA: But his definition was brief, very succinct, don't be so ungenerous.

BOOMY: 'Better is a handful with quietness than both the hands full with travail and vexation of spirit.'

EMANUEL: I produce an original thought and he quotes me Ecclesiastes.

BOOMY: 'The thing that hath been it is that which shall be,
And that which is done is that which shall be done,
And there is no new thing under the sun.'

TERESSA: It's very beautiful.

EMANUEL: I know it's beautiful but I can't bear people who quote it all the time. You have to earn the right to find the world a vain place. [*Takes* ROSA *on his side*.] But he *enjoys* quoting it, he *loves* it, relishes it. Listen to him roll all that juicy gloom on his lips. 'All things toil in weariness' – aaaah! All things, that is, except *him*. You don't catch him reciting wearily – no! There's an energetic ecstasy in *his* voice. He *loves* it. Pronouncements of doom. Revelations of futility. Declarations of life's purposelessness. Except for *him*. *He's* got a purpose. A lovely purpose. The easiest of all purposes – to inform that no purpose exists! Catastrophe-monger!

GERDA: He'll have a heart attack, I promise you.

EMANUEL: *He's* made no impression on the world? So! It's a flat and dreary world. *He's* failed to live a life he can respect? So! It's a vain life. *He's* approaching death? Therefore it must all have been for nothing.

GERDA: Go back to your bath, you'll catch cold.

EMANUEL: No one wants to die, *I* know that; it's a rotten time, old age; just when you're at peace you've got to go. But *that's* a reason to plague youth with our disappointments? We must warn them before they begin that it'll all be for nothing?

BOOMY [*taking* RUDI *on his side*]:

> Rejoice, O young man, in thy youth;
> And let thy heart cheer thee in the days of thy youth,
> And walk in the ways of thine heart,
> And in the sight of thine eyes . . .

EMANUEL: It's as though he doesn't listen.

BOOMY: But know thou that for all these things
God will bring thee into judgment . . .

EMANUEL: Let them read it later, when it's got meaning for them.

BOOMY: Therefore remove sorrow from thy heart,
And put away evil from thy flesh;
For childhood and youth are vanity.

EMANUEL: CATASTROPHE-MONGER! [*He begins to press* BOOMY *round the room*.] 'The chef who day-dreams his dishes, must he love those who eat them?'

BOOMY: He *never* gives up.

EMANUEL: 'And if some are indifferent to his tastes, must he cease to concoct them?'

BOOMY: More nonsenses.

EMANUEL: Quiet. It's my turn to quote. 'The architect who designs houses, and plans cities, must he love those who dwell in them?'

BOOMY: What now?

EMANUEL: 'And if the inhabitants are blind to the city's beauties, must the architect offend his own sight and create monstrosities?'

BOOMY: What's this got to do with anything?

EMANUEL [*pressing him on*]: 'If a man reasons and struggles to legislate for the well-being of his neighbours, must he needs love all his neighbours?'

BOOMY: Come to the point.

EMANUEL: 'And if they are insensitive to the change he has helped bring to their lives, must he cease to reason for that change? If all action seems vain, must we cease all action?'

BOOMY: The point! The point!

EMANUEL: 'I tell you verily – verily I tell you – he has no choice. The chef, the architect, the man of reason, do what they must because men must apply what is in them to apply. And so –'

BOOMY: And so, and so?

EMANUEL: 'And so, to cry "vanity of vanities" at foolish or evil men and then to abandon your true work is to abandon not them but yourself; it is to be guilty of an even greater vanity: for you knew what they did not.'

BOOMY: Who said all that?

EMANUEL: Guess.

BOOMY: Joke me no jokes, who said it?

EMANUEL: Me!

BOOMY: You?

[MANNY *acknowledges the applause of his family.*]

EMANUEL: Me! Me! Meeeeee! [*On his way out he turns on recorder of himself singing.*] And listen to that!

[ROSA *jumps up again. Again she flicks the napkin to* SARAH *who rises and again – they dance. Slowly, slowly and sweetly – to the low humming and clapping of the others, while* BOOMY *takes a seat to eat his strudel alone and calls after* EMANUEL *– who continues to laugh* *and mumble, 'Me, me, mee', creating a contrapuntal background to:*]

BOOMY: 'Because to every purpose there is a time and judgment, [*Laughter.*] therefore the misery of man is great upon him. [*Laughter*] For he knoweth not that which shall be; [*Laughter.*] for who can tell him when it shall be? There is no man that hath power over the spirit to retain the spirit, neither hath he power in the day of death ... [*Laughter.*] ... neither hath he power in the day of death ... [*Laughter.*] ... neither hath he power in the day of death ...'

[*The* LIGHTS *have been slowly* DIMMING *on the dancing and the shouting and the singing.*

*Now –*]

THE CURTAIN

# LOVE LETTERS ON BLUE PAPER

Based on the author's story and T.V. play
of the same title

FOR MIKE AND ORNA KUSTON
WITH LOVE FOR THEIR FRIENDSHIP

World première presented by Syracuse Stage, Syracuse, U.S.A. on 14 October 1977, directed by Arthur Storch, designed by Eldon Elder, with the following cast:

| | |
|---|---|
| VICTOR | John Carpenter · |
| SONIA | Myra Carter |
| MAURICE | Richard Clarke |
| T.U. OFFICIAL | Jay Devlin |

U.K. première presented by The National Theatre on its Cottesloe stage on 15 February 1978, directed by Arnold Wesker, designed by Bernard Culshaw, with the following cast:

| | |
|---|---|
| VICTOR | Michael Gough |
| SONIA | Elizabeth Spriggs |
| MAURICE | Kenneth Cranham |
| T.U. OFFICIAL | Timothy Block |

# CHARACTERS

VICTOR
SONIA
MAURICE
T.U. OFFICIAL

## AUTHOR'S NOTE

All SONIA's letters must be recorded and put through speakers, as many of which should be placed around the auditorium, to give the effect of SONIA's voice speaking gently to each member of the audience. (See note at end.)

*A composite set in an open space.*

*Most important is the bedroom, then the kitchen, the lounge, a hospital singles ward, [which should be out of sight until needed] a clothes line for a spacious outside garden. It is summer.*

*While waiting for the play to begin an almost luminous white light is spotted on the four, full pillows puffed up and cosy on the bed in the bedroom. As the audience lights fade this spot is the last to go.*

*When the stage lights come on focused on the bedroom,* VICTOR MARS-DEN *is sitting up in bed, patiently leaning forward while his wife* SONIA *is sternly changing the last semi-starched pillow-slip.*

*The room is cluttered with paintings leaning here and there, and pieces of sculpture and busts propping up unframed canvases.*

*Standing by is their slightly bewildered friend* PROFESSOR MAURICE STAPLETON, *who's obviously just come in because he stands with his briefcase still in his hand.*

VICTOR *is a retired Yorkshire trade union official, about 65, mischievous, fiercely intelligent.* SONIA *is matronly, a large self-assured presence.* MAURICE *is 45, a professor of the history of art,* VICTOR's *one-time protégé, warm, sympathetic.*

SONIA *finishes pushing the pillow into its slip, adjusts it behind* VICTOR, *slams her way out, and goes to the lounge area where she sits, in the shadows, by a desk, as if writing.*

*As soon as she is gone both men come to life and begin talking at once,* MAURICE *while taking off his coat.*

MAURICE: She didn't seem to know you'd called me.
VICTOR: Maurice lad! Take that chair –
MAURICE: Didn't you tell her you'd called me?
VICTOR: Throw those books on the floor –
MAURICE: She seemed so surprised to see me.
VICTOR: You've chosen a good day to come.
MAURICE: Why didn't you tell her you'd called me?
VICTOR: Been rotten lately, not well at all.

MAURICE: In fact she seemed furious to see me!

VICTOR: But today! Ha! Look at that sun, wild, eh? It's gotten right into me. Full of youth. Luverly!

[*He breathes deeply, exaggeratedly, which forces him to cough.*] Shouldn't be misled by sunlight. Makes you want to take breaths you haven't got.

MAURICE: And why didn't you tell me you'd been ill?

VICTOR [*reading from a notebook*]: You've come just at the right time –

MAURICE: *I've* come?

VICTOR: Listen to this.

MAURICE: *You* called!

VICTOR: Listen. 'The genuine creative instinct is and always has been a celebratory one. The earliest known forms of painting and ritual *may* have had to do with magic born of ignorance but – beginnings should not be mistaken for truths. Art *may* have begun in the belief that the act of mimesis contained magical properties but, *once* discovered, man looked at himself in wonderment, delighted in it, and thenceforth excelled in it *only* when his motivation was celebratory. *This* modest history of art will attempt to prove such.'

MAURICE: I'm impressed. It's a very good beginning. A very generous theory to want to prove. Congratulations, but first tell me why you're in bed?

VICTOR [*irritated, he throws book on floor ignoring the question*]: It's rotten! Clumsy and illiterate. Like me. Written in the language of the negotiating table. Once a trade union bureaucrat always a trade union bureaucrat. [*Mercurially changing to a mischievous grin, enthusiastic again as* MAURICE *returns the book*] But it *is* a beginning, I suppose.

MAURICE: Please, Victor, I want to talk about . . .

VICTOR: It won't ever be an erudite work, such as *you* could write, but art *is* celebratory and no one, not even you, Professor Maurice Stapleton, has attempted to prove why. So, old Victor, with his W.E.A. background, his self-taught smatterings and crazy passion [*Waves an arm at his bedroom exhibition. But his enthusiasm dies away.*] Trouble is, no one's interested in art. Even artists have been made to feel guilty, diminishing their roles like old-fashioned sinners.

'Me, an artist? Oh no, mate, not me. I'm just ordinary, like you and him. Nothing special. I'm sure you could write War and Peace if you tried, or the Sonnets, or paint like Leonardo. Nothing to it, mate. All men are artists . . .' Cant! And if you've not got even the artists on your side, well . . .

[VICTOR *angrily pummels his cushions as if they were to blame. But his anger doesn't fit the crime. Something else must be wrong.*

MAURICE *gently moves to help put the cushions in place. As he leans close and intimately to* VICTOR – *suddenly, wearily*]

I'm dying, lad.

[MAURICE *is paralysed*]

Six months, nine months, a year. They're not certain, but soon.

[VICTOR *hardly notices how stunned* MAURICE *is. Having reminded himself, actually said it, he now turns inward and away.*

*There's a long silence, after which they talk almost on top of one another.*]

MAURICE: I'm shattered, I can't say anything, I –

VICTOR: Aye, don't worry –

MAURICE: It's unforgivable but –

VICTOR: Nay, 'twere me, the way I told thee –

MAURICE: I mean, Victor. it's terrible –

VICTOR: Thoughtless of me.

MAURICE: Don't apologize, for Christ's sake –

VICTOR: What did I expect thee to do –

MAURICE: I just don't believe it, it's ridiculous, they've made a mistake, they always do, I mean I know of a case, cases, doctors calculate a year and patients go on and on and –

VICTOR: Maurice don't bumble! I'm dying! It's myeloid leukaemia! I waited three years for these last months and they've come and that's that. Now, let me talk. [*Pauses to gather strength*] Oh, I'm frightened. No doubt about that. And bitter. Look at that sun, listen to those sounds, look at those books. Who'd want to leave all that? [*Picks up newspaper*] Despite all this. [*Reads*] 'Allegations of torture to prisoners of war in North Vietnam.' Never stops does it? 'Man batters child to death. Youths batter old man to death. Quarter of London's homes without baths, and heating. Sectarian killings in Belfast. Famine in India . . .'

[*He's said it all in one breath which makes him cough and his irritation increase.*]

[*coughing*] Still! Still, still, still! After what we did. All we did!
[*Long pause*] And yet – I don't want to leave any of it. I'd live with it all – just so long as I lived. [*Pause*] Retired me from the union just in time didn't they, eh?

[VICTOR *gets out of bed.* MAURICE *attempts to help. He refuses it. Puts on dressing-gown. Begins talking. While talking he takes a medicine, and potters, reshuffling stacked canvases, replacing a bust. Rearranging the order of things.*]

I'll tell you a story. Told me by the head of one of the largest unions in West Germany. Fantastic fellow he was, still is, I suppose. God knows! Lose touch with them. You share a special conference or something together, bosom pals, console each other through dreary affairs – and you know we used to get some boring old sods at those conferences, self-righteous little functionaries they were – but not Heuder. Wolfgang Heuder. Very vivid *he* was. Dragged into the Wehrmacht when he was fifteen, last months of the war. I was probably chasing him in one of my tanks! It was him told me this story. Seems their regiment picked up a deserter, some poor scrawny old man who'd been out of the thing but now they were taking in anyone who could hold a rifle. *He'd* no appetite for the glorious Third Reich right from the start so he'd precious little urgency to die for it in its last gasps. Who would? And off he scarpered. *He* could smell defeat. But – he'd no energy. Food supplies low, foot-sore, wheezing – he was caught, court-martialled, and sentenced to a firing squad. That depressed everyone it seemed. No one had stomach for it, not even the regiment commander. But he was an old soak, duty was duty, regulations was regulations. There had to be a trial, it had to be a fair trial, there had to be a sentence, it had to be carried out. Victims of law and order when all law and bloody order were crumbling round them. Madness, eh? [*As he switches over two paintings*] Do you like it? One of the students at The Royal College. Still, the commander was an honourable man and he asked the prisoner if he had any last wishes. You know what the poor bugger asked for? A plate of barley soup! Wanted to eat before dying. To go off on a full stomach as it were.

It were staple fare and there were some left to be heated up in the kitchens so they give it him. What he'd asked for. A plate of barley soup!

[VICTOR *bends to exchange position of one bust for another,* MAURICE *rushes to do it for him.*]

Change them over, please. And when it were finished, now listen to this, when it were finished he asked for another plate! That were unprecedented but, nothing in the rules to say a condemned man couldn't have as much of his last request as he wanted, and rules were rules! So, another plate was called for and the man ate it slowly. And when he'd finished, yes, he asked for another plate and this time they had to wait while it was being made because they'd run out of the previous night's left-overs. And he ate! And he ate, and he ate, and he ate! Barley soup! More'n he wanted, more'n he could take. Anything so long as it delayed the moment of his death. And you know what happened? The Russians came. The sentence couldn't be carried out. Everyone fled. He lived! He couldn't have known he'd live but some instinct kept him eating. Eating to stay alive! Ha! Simple!

[MAURICE's *eyes are welling*]

I've given you a real shock haven't I, lad? Terrible. [*Cheerfully*] Look at those pillows. Fresh every day. She changes them. Every day. Believe it or not I get into fresh sheets every night. [*Wearily climbs back into bed*] I tell her there's no need but she takes no notice. 'You spent good money on a washing machine' she says, 'I'll use it then!' Love it, of course. [*Pause*]. I'm sorry, lad, you look quite pale. Daft bugger, me.

MAURICE: Don't start being sorry for me, for Christ's sake! That's absurd, that's ... Oh, Victor, Oh Jesus, Victor! I wish at this moment I was a religious man. I wish I could tell you about an after-life, heaven, reincarnation, something!

VICTOR: Right! That's it! What I really meant to talk about. That's why I've called you. To talk about that, after-life, just that. But how about a cup of tea first, eh? Go to the kitchen and ask Sonia to make us some tea. Oh –

[*He mechanically puts his hands in his dressing-gown where he finds a blue envelope with a letter inside, written on blue paper.*]

– and while she's doing it go into the lounge and read this. I'll have a rest meanwhile. Tire quickly these days. Only for Christ's sake don't let Sonia see you reading that letter, and don't tell her anything. She doesn't know.

[MAURICE *stands up, moves shakily to the door, but has to sit on a chair nearby.* VICTOR *laughs heartily.*]

Unsteady legs? Ha, ha! I've given him unsteady legs. Ha, ha! Oh dear! [*Long chuckle*] I haven't yet learnt how to be sombre all the time. Sacrilegious isn't it? Confusing!

[LIGHTS DOWN *on bedroom,* UP *in kitchen and lounge.*

MAURICE *leaves and goes to the kitchen to which, during the laughter,* SONIA *has also made her way and begun preparing tea-things as if she'd heard.*]

SONIA [*sourly*]: What was all the laughing for?

MAURICE: War-time stories, Sonia. He's full of them. I never tire. Victor asked me to –

SONIA: I know what Victor asked you.

[*He's still bewildered by her hostility*]

MAURICE: I'll wait in the lounge.

[SONIA *doesn't bother to reply.* MAURICE *leaves her to go to the lounge where he sits on a swivel chair by the desk and takes out the letter to read.*]

SONIA'S VOICE [*tentatively*]: I was thinking the other day. I used never to be able to call you 'darling'. Do you remember?

[LIGHTS DOWN *on lounge. As the letter is being read* SONIA *makes morning tea. A ritual. While waiting for water to boil she cuts four slices of 'cut-and-come-again' cake, heats pot, counts out three tea-spoonfuls of tea, pours in boiling water, covers with tea-cosy, sets out on a tray. Finally her hand rests on tea-cosy, pausing to feel the heat, then she picks up tray and moves into hall.*

*Over all this has been* SONIA'S *voice continuing with the reading of the letter.*]

SONIA'S VOICE: When we first met I was really plain. Plain-minded I mean, not looking. I was pretty looking but I felt daft saying darling and sweetheart and those things. Took about two years before I could bring myself to call you any but your name. And I only ever gave in because you bullied me. Got proper annoyed in fact. You *made* me say the word, forced me. Remember? I do. It was after we'd been to have tea with my grandmother. A Sunday afternoon. One of those big spreads. Everything thrown on the table, you know, from home-made pickled onions to thick old crusty rhubarb pies. And she was making her usual fuss of me. Adored me she did and I did her too, and she was teasing me and saying 'She's a little darling, *isn't* she a little darling? She's *my* little darling.' And when we walked home you turned on me and said 'She can say the word why can't you?' 'What word?' I asked. 'Darling!' you yelled. 'Go on, say it!' You *did* look funny, your face all angry while your mouth was saying words of loving. Didn't go together somehow. '*Say darling*' you shouted at me and made me giggle. And the more I giggled the more angry you got. But you won, you made me say it. Darling! Sweetheart Victor, dearest Victor, darling Victor, darling, darling and my heart. I was re-membering. Just today. For no reason. While I was outside cleaning the windows.

[MAURICE, *the letter finished, hears the rattle of tea-things, puts letter away and goes into the kitchen. He looks at* SONIA *with even greater bewilderment, seeing a different woman. So do we. He's not absolutely certain the letter was from her, yet he must regard her differently. She however remains indifferent to him, moving to the lounge.* LIGHTS DOWN *in kitchen,* UP *in bedroom.*

*He moves from her to* VICTOR's *bedroom.* VICTOR *dozes. The noise of* MAURICE *entering wakes him.*]

VICTOR: Tea! Tastes and senses. I'm really sensing everything now. When I gave up smoking all tastes came back. *Now* ... the lot's coming back. Tastes, colours, shapes. Everything's vivid, stands out. And everything has to be special, too. Little things, like tea. Has to be the real thing, not your old tea bags. And coffee, has to be real beans, ground, none of your mean instant. And food, must have food with its own flavours. I get neurotic if cabbage tastes weedy, watery, or the lamb gets shredded like old shoelaces.

[*They've been pouring out their tea and arranging plates. Now before they sip and munch,* MAURICE *returns letter.*]

MAURICE: Sonia?

VICTOR: Aye, Sonia.

MAURICE: Strange. All those years, almost like a second mother, and not know her . . .

VICTOR: Came a few days ago with the rest of the post, fully stamped.

MAURICE: A wife sending such a letter to her husband?

VICTOR: Posted from our own post office at the bottom of the road and written, presumably, in the lounge while I was here in the bedroom.

MAURICE: Just like that? For no reason?

VICTOR: Oh don't ask me about her. The children always used to tease her. 'Frustrated messenger from God!' Graeme once described her. 'Yes' Hilda would say, 'overweight from underwork!' She loved their teasing.

[*Long pause. They drink tea in silence.* MAURICE *knows his friend wants to talk about his illness, and waits.*

   VICTOR *dips his cake in the tea, sucks the juice from it, bites, then begins.*]

VICTOR: It began about three years ago. In the middle of a strike. I began to suffer from headaches and dizziness.

MAURICE: The hospital workers' strike?

VICTOR: Aye. Remember? Daft government policies. What a time that was. All-night discussions about compromise, open-air gatherings up and down the country – the lot! So, blood pressure, I thought, and went for a check-up. Nothing! Blood pressure was high but not pathological. My general condition was good. Next day, a phone-call. Specialist's assistant. Would I go in and see them. Something's cropped up. When I saw the specialist next day he told me: high white corpuscle count. Just like that! Almost angrily, as though I were to blame. Like being told I'd an overdraft. And then, well, I was – curious. I was curious about what I was going through. Curious, you know, like a bystander. It were strange. I'd no sense of shock or fear, no sweating or increased pulse. Just a great slowing-down of time. Everything . . . in slow motion. No, don't ask me to be logical about it. I only know what happened. In this order, as I'm telling you. And then, into this slow-motion, came this great increase of . . . don't laugh, it's difficult for me to say it . . . but, this . . . great increase of love. I didn't feel it. It wasn't that. But I had, suddenly, a better *sense* of it. And then, relief. I was aware of how tired life had made me, how tired I was of myself and how, now, now I could be held responsible for nothing more. Ever again. Sonia asked what it were and I told her it were the strike. But she'd seen me in strike times before, so I had to tell her half the truth, that I'd seen a doctor and he'd told me to go easy because of high blood pressure. Anyway, 'We're not certain', the specialist said, 'but all the evidence points to myeloid leukaemia.' I knew the implication of that of course, but I wanted to hear it spelt out. 'Fifty per cent of the people in your condition live for three years,' he said, 'of the other fifty per cent many live for five, some for ten. A few have been known to live for twenty but that's rare. Some have died within the year but that's just as rare. You have my answer.' Ha! I had his answer all right. But, as you said, they can be wrong. It's been known. So I saw someone else. And what a bastard he turned out to be. A diehard old Tory who'd obviously always hated my guts. When I asked him for a prognosis he said: 'If you've got some papers that need signing you can leave them, but if you've got a fortune to make I'd start making it right now.' I ignored all that and just asked about the possibility of cure or spontaneous recovery. And you know what he said? 'Cure is a dirty word!' A right bastard he were. It was from my own doctor, my own old GP that I managed to find a little comfort. I remember he embraced me first and then said: 'Vic, you aren't *worried* about it are you? *You're* not going to die of leukaemia. A heart attack, maybe, a plane crash, anything! But not leukaemia. Myeloid leukaemia', he said, 'for a person in your condition and at your age is a benign ailment. Eat very well. Go to bed early. Get up a bit later. Avoid infections. Keep outdoors as much as possible, and don't tell anybody, it only creates the wrong atmosphere.' Great man, that. Restored my sanity. So, there it is. I belonged to the fifty per cent who last three years. My time's up. The Myleran and Purinethol are having less and less effect. I'm up and I'm down. I recover but I recover more slowly. It still just looks like high blood pressure to Sonia but *I* know. I *know* what's happening.

[VICTOR *is obviously exhausted.* MAURICE *rises, anxious*]
It's all right, just a turn.

MAURICE: You look so – so grey.

VICTOR: Grey is it? Ha! I'll be all right after a sleep. But you'd better go. Come again soon. Tomorrow, the day after. Leave the bloody students. Attend to me. I really need you, Maurice lad. But don't I beg you, don't tell Sonia.

[LIGHTS DOWN]

SONIA'S VOICE: You used to tease me about God.

[LIGHTS UP *in garden area. Sound of brisk wind and crack of linen on a clothes line.* SONIA *comes to hang up dazzling white sheets and pillow-slips*]

Soft brain I had in them days. Could I help it though? My soft brain, yes, but not my religiousness. That were my upbringing. No one can be blamed for that, though they do say the sins of the fathers shall fall upon the sons, but that's cruel and unreasonable. Not that you were like that, you weren't cruel and unreasonable no never I'm not saying that. But you teased and you shouldn't have done because I was very badly hurt by it. You didn't know that I was, but I was. Very hurt. To begin with. Then my brain got hard.

[SONIA *turns to go back for more linen but in turning finds she's facing the sun. She closes her eyes, basking in it, as the voice continues*]

'God is one man's invention to frighten other men into being good' you said. 'But no one's good if they're frightened.' That's what you said and it sounded very reasonable to me. Besides, there was the war and all of them soldiers being gassed and slaughtered and then it happened to my brother Stan so I couldn't much believe in God. But I missed him. I don't mind telling you I missed God. Used to give me lovely pictures to think about. It was a long time before I knew what it was you gave me. Better. You know that don't you?

[LIGHTS DOWN *in garden area.* UP *in* VICTOR's *room. He looks unbearably sad and is cuddling one of the huge pillows to him, using it for memory.*]

After the teasing and tormenting my brain got harder and I grew proud of what I got to understand and how I could listen to you and your mates arguing and saving the world and make up my own mind. Did you *know* I grew? Couldn't talk or argue much or write but I grew from God to you. Became a woman. For a while at least.

[MAURICE *enters as* VICTOR *rises and moves to 'window'. Turns*]

VICTOR: Can't bear heavy skies. Sooner imagine it was night time than face morbid bloody clouds. Look at those stunned starched over-fed cushions. They reproduce themselves when I'm not looking. [*Pause*] Well?

MAURICE: Yes. [*Thinking he means* SONIA's *second letter*] Extraordinary. Worth publishing.

VICTOR: No! Not that daft thing. My notes I mean. The notes for my book.

MAURICE: Ah, yes, well, those are very well worth publishing. [*Hands him folder*]

VICTOR: Aren't they a mess!

MAURICE: All first drafts are a mess, Victor, not even erudite me gets it right first time.

VICTOR: A mess! Confused. Gibberish. [*While complaining nevertheless he takes a hole-cutter and hard-back file for filing away his notes*] When I wrote all that down I thought it was the beginning of a profound inquiry that would unravel why everyone concludes it's a rotten life. [*He gives up trying to punch holes – his fingers can't bear pressure, passes file to* MAURICE *who does the job for him*] Have you noticed that? Everyone says it's a rotten life, 'People are rotten!' Life, literature – all filled with characters whose experience of the world is depressing. So – who upsets them? Speak to the man who they say has upset them and you find *he* also thinks the world is a rotten place and that people are rotten. And who's upset *him*? Where does it begin? Everyone knows it's a terrible life only it never seems possible to lay your finger on the culprit, the cause. I know people have got answers – religious, political, philosophic. But at the end of everyone's life, whether he's a revolutionary leader, a dictator, a pope, a millionaire – a worker, a prime minister, a socialist citizen, a citizen of the West – a great artist, a great scientist, a great philosopher – for all of them! Terrible life! By the end of it they're all weary and disillusioned and dispirited. I mean listen to Ruskin. [*Reaches for a book*] Who could want to have achieved more? But was *he* happy? [*Reads*] 'I forget, now, what I meant by "liberty" in this passage; but I often used the word in my first writings in a good sense, thinking of Scott's moorland rambles and the like. It is very wonderful to me, now, to see what hopes I had once: but Turner was alive then, and the sun used to shine, and the rivers to sparkle.' [*Pause*] Too late, Maurice lad. Were a trade union leader too long. Should've given up at forty and started to study for me book then. But not now.

MAURICE: Now, come on.

VICTOR: Not even with your help.

[*Long pause. Suddenly* –]

Tell me about someone dying.

MAURICE: About *what*?

VICTOR: Someone dying. Someone you knew.

MAURICE: Victor that's morbid.

VICTOR: No it's not. It's sensible.

MAURICE: Look, we should be talking about your carefully filed-away gibberish.

VICTOR: My carefully filed-away gibberish can take care of itself. Tell me.

MAURICE: I can't. I'd be embarrassed.

VICTOR: It's no use me ducking it. And besides, I *want* to talk about it.

MAURICE: Don't make it more difficult to me than it is, for Christ's sake.

VICTOR: I want to know. Familiarize myself with it. Tell me. Was there anyone? A friend? A relative? Someone close who you watched? [*Pause*] A parent? [*Pause*] There was your mother wasn't there? [*Pause*] I remember that time. [*Pause*] Tell me.

[*Long pause*]

MAURICE: She didn't know she was dying. Her kidneys . . . She was constipated and vomiting all the time. No appetite. Victor, I can't.

VICTOR: Please.

MAURICE [*haltingly*]: It was her bewilderment distressed me most She was living with us by this time, and as the days went by she'd eat a little, complain of pain in her gums, vomit while I held her head and then say 'When? When, when will it be over, done, finished with?' She couldn't understand. 'I've *never* been so ill. Never!' She'd be angry but she'd make jokes. On her good days, when she could eat and not feel nauseous, she'd sit up, hold out her hand and cross her fingers. 'Don't say anything', she'd caution, 'just hope!' And when I'd give her her umpteen pills she'd say 'Well, I'm a good pill-taker at least.' Once when the doctor came and she was particularly flat out, she collapsed utterly into her pillows, and he asked in that special breezy voice doctors reserve for the dying 'And how are you today?' she replied with her special brand of gentle self-mockery, and holding her aching gums: [*Imitating her exhaustion*] 'Oh, very well, thank you!' I remember once when I was sitting by her she held a little hand-mirror in front of her and after looking for a while she said: 'How could I become such a face, how?' and she clutched at the side of her head and rocked it as though trying to shake her mind and memory back into place. Then she stopped, and said simply, 'I want no fuss, you know what I mean? No fuss. It's got to come sometime or other, sooner or later.' I pretended she was talking nonsense. Got angry with her, even. But she persisted. 'I might go any time. Suddenly. Plonk! Finished! What can you do?' I didn't think I'd ever weep, but I did. It was an absurd time. Weeping. Everything about her and everything associated with her became very vivid and unbearably dear to me. As though my unhappiness gave each detail of memory an extra meaning. I had to keep driving to her flat to look for mail, reassure the neighbours, collect her pension, and even driving up to the council estate, even just the act of swerving the car into the curb, an action I'd done a hundred times before, caused me to swallow hard because I associated it with driving to see her and finding her writing her diary, watching television, cooking or just standing in front of the gas stove hoping the warmth from the upper grill would ease the pain in her gums. Memory of her flooded back at every corner. I was covering ground I knew she'd never cover again. It was all poignant, full of loneliness, that quadrangle of other old people, looking out of windows, waiting. Full of loneliness and a sense of time past. Sad. I can remember an overwhelming ache to be young again with her, cooking for my friends, telling me off for late hours, joining in. And she'd make it worse by trying to make it seem the most natural thing in the world. Which it is. Only it never seems so. 'I don't mind', she'd say. 'Only peace, let there be peace in the world, and friendship in the family. Stay together. Don't be sad. I don't really mind.'

[MAURICE *climbs on to the bed beside* VICTOR.]

As she became worse the pain in her gums increased and she needed to be kept on Palfium drugs. Morphine based. She'd get high, lose her memory, construct strange or unfinished sentences. 'I'll soon tell you, I'll soon tell you all about it.' About what? God knows! She never finished. Once I went into her room and found her sitting up and clutching at something in the air, as though reaching out for a person, and she said, 'Suddenly, just then, I felt that really I was alone.' In the end not all the pills I gave her helped, so I sat close to her and cradled her in my arms instead, holding her hands. 'Ah, warmth, warmth!' she said, 'there's nothing like warmth.' [*He cradles* VICTOR.] 'Get into bed' I said, 'that'll make you warm.' 'Not warm like this' she said. [*Pause*] A few days before she died I went into her room – I'd go there first thing as soon as I got up – she was sitting with her hands behind her head, her eyes bright. 'I feel so excited about something', she said. 'I want something to happen, some event, some special event.' I took her downstairs, walking in front of her, holding her hand, high up, to steady her. She descended, slowly, sedately. 'The bride!' she said. [*Pause*] And all the time the vomiting, the pain in the gums, the jokes and the bewilderment. [*Pause*] Jokes and the bewilderment. [*Pause*] Jokes. [*Pause*] She was a tiny thing. So sweet. [*Pause*] I adored her.

[*They exchange smiles. It is a moment of gentle rapport.* SLOW FADE OF LIGHTS. *Sound of telephone. It's picked up. Sound of* MAURICE'S *voice.* LIGHTS UP *on lounge.* VICTOR *on phone.*]

MAURICE'S VOICE: Victor?

VICTOR: Aye, it's me.

MAURICE'S VOICE: I'm sorry, Vic, but I won't be able to come when I promised. I have to go to the States.

VICTOR [*sourly*]: Are you trying to pretend that'll be an unpleasant labour for you?

MAURICE'S VOICE: Don't be angry with me, friend. It's only two weeks. A colleague's gone down with a sudden appendix and I've got to take over this lecture tour.

VICTOR: I'm sure you'll have a terrible time.

MAURICE'S VOICE: Of course I won't have a terrible time. Don't begrudge it to me. I've not been abroad these last five years. But I'll come and see you as soon as I return. Even jet-lagged.

VICTOR [*whispering*]: Listen, I've had another of those letters.

MAURICE'S VOICE: From Sonia?

VICTOR: Aye. A third one. I'll send it you. Read it on the plane. Ssh. No more, she's coming. Safe journey.

[*Puts down phone.* SLOW FADE OF LIGHTS.]

SONIA'S VOICE: The only time I ever swore was a night you got more than normal drunk and wept because things weren't going right in the union and you began complaining at me. You told me 'You don't care about me or my state or the fact that I'm losing me nerve and failing me mates, do you? And you haven't a care for rights nor conditions nor wages nor nothing.' Remember that?

[LIGHTS UP *in the kitchen where* SONIA *is laying out two cups and saucers on a tray where there is already a pot of tea and jug of milk. Then from out of the oven she pulls a platter of scones, prises off two, slices them in half, opens the fridge, takes out a bowl of double-whipped cream, some of which she scoops up and spreads over the four halves of scone, returns the bowl, bends, folds down, without bending her legs, to a cupboard for some strawberry jam, which she drips over the cream, during which –*]

SONIA'S VOICE: How you raged and wept and screamed. 'I'm going to pieces, I'm going to pieces and you don't care and you don't understand.' Very loud you were that night my love, and I railed back 'Of course I care of course I understand but I won't give consolations to a man when he's filled with pity and shit. That's what you are,' I said, 'you're filled with pity and shit.' Ha! The only time you wept and I swore that was.

[SONIA *is smiling to herself. The change from her normal sternness is stunning.*

*Now bright sunlight floods the garden area and spreads into the bedroom.* VICTOR *is putting on his dressing-gown. He wraps a scarf around his neck and moves into the garden.* SONIA *takes linen off clothes line and, though she may still be silent yet there's a happy defiant look about her. During which –*]

And that was a *tense* time. Very tense that was, my love. I'm laughing as I write it down. You looked so funny, so startled. I felt very bucked with myself to have startled you so. It was serious then but

I confess how I giggled afterwards. Went away and giggled to myself. I'm laughing even as I write about it. Oh dear. Ha ha! 'Full of pity and shit!' I said. You forgot all about your going to pieces then. Aye. You were so shocked. Pity and shit! Ha! Ha!

[SONIA *brings out tray to a garden table, facing the sun. A scarf is round her neck. She removes it and places it round* VICTOR's *neck. Feigns strangling him, a tender, playful moment.* MAURICE *arrives, helps to bring chairs to the table. When* SONIA *leaves the two friends embrace. When she's gone* –]

VICTOR: And how was the land of the bitch goddess?

MAURICE: I can't make up my mind about the American success bitch. Like many bitches, in the process of chewing you up she brings every nerve-end alive. [*Pause*] How are you?

VICTOR: Would you believe it, she wants me to get out of bed, pack a case and go with her for a week to Mytholmroyd on the moors, where we used to court. Isn't that daft? Now *that's* a daft thing for you. Doesn't she know I'm bloody dy – No! she doesn't, poor bitch! It's no good, Maurice, I can't take it. I thought I had it in me but I haven't. I'm so frightened and unhappy. You think – something will happen, someone – a discovery in time. Something always did, didn't it? Whenever we made fools of ourselves or got ill there was help, a cure, forgiveness. I can't *really* be dying! That's just plain silly. What? All this – gone, stopped, done? It's such a burden this knowledge, rotten, heavy. I feel so humiliated watching myself become frightened. No one should have to know it. It's not fair. A man's not made to live with such a knowledge. Look at it! [*Waves arm at sky and garden*] Love it! I love it, love it! I just plain and simply love it! [*He weeps*] Bloody hell! Don't let her see me like this. There'll be murder to pay. Kill me, she would.

[*This amuses him. He smiles. It grows. Into huge laughter. Which soon becomes exhaustion.* MAURICE *reaches into a brief-case and brings out a mounted drawing*]

MAURICE: Here. Found it in a little junk shop in New Bedford. Look at it carefully. What's the signature?

[VICTOR *reaches for some glasses*]

VICTOR [*peering*]: John Rushton? Who's John Rushton?

MAURICE: Are you sure it says Rushton? That's what I thought, but look again.

VICTOR [*testily*]: Rushton. It says Rushton. That's all I can see. [*Returns drawing*]

MAURICE [*whispering*]: What about – Ruskin?

[VICTOR *is suddenly alert and snatches back the drawing*]

VICTOR: *Ruskin?*

[*He takes a huge magnifying glass from his dressing-gown pocket and waves it up and down in front of the drawing, squinting*]

[*excitedly*] My God, it could be. It just could be. Now isn't that a thrill! Well, that's revived me no end that has. You're a lovely friend. Was worth pushing you through college. Forgive me jadedness, I mean – a Ruskin! Well! [*Pause*] There's no doubt about it, the soul does depend upon the body.

[VICTOR *gets up from his garden chair, takes a refill of tea and, clasping both hands round the cup, walks to the bottom of the garden. There's a huge field, a cricket-practice ground at the bottom of it. He watches the slow mechanics of the game. Though in the city, yet there's a countryside feeling to the scene. We hear the sound of birds and the knocking of the ball on wood*]

VICTOR: I've started to imagine this other place.

MAURICE: 'Avoid infections. Keep outdoors as much as possible, and – '

VICTOR: Supposing it did exist.

MAURICE: ' – and don't tell anybody' your doctor said.

VICTOR: But just supposing.

MAURICE: 'It only creates the wrong atmosphere,' he said.

VICTOR: What *could* it be like? I mean I can't even begin to imagine what it would be like visually. Where do you place it, this ... after-life? And then I think: it's not a physical place, Victor, that's where you go wrong. It's a spiritual state, a state of awareness unconfined by a physical framework. Ha! And so I lie in there trying to project myself into 'a spiritual state of awareness unconfined by a physical framework'! Ever tried to do that?

MAURICE: Often!

VICTOR: Try it some day. And then I get angry and I say to myself: 'Darkness! Nothing! When you're dead that's it. Over! Done! If you want satisfaction, Victor lad, then look to your life, your political battles, the fights you fought for other men.' But who can do that for long? Dwell on his past and go scratching for bits of victory? Eh? A smug man perhaps. But I'm not a smug man, Maurice, never was. So what's left? No after-life I can conceive of and no past to feel at peace with. And I go round and round in circles driving myself mad because even the very act of contemplating it, me! thinking about whether there's a heaven, another life, the very worrying about such things makes me feel guilty and shabby. 'You, Victor? Worrying about where you're going? frightened are you?' I taunt myself. 'Frightened? Poor, feeble-minded man, you. You who used to be so confident about it all beginning with birth and ending with death. You! Want a comfortable little heaven to go to now? Do you?' And I'm a merciless bugger you know. Really get to the heart of myself, where it hurts. Always been like that. Have you ever thought about the tone of voice your conscience has? Everyone's got a conscience which talks to them in a different tone of voice. Mine jeers. Very acidy. [*Picks up drawing*] A Ruskin. What d'you know?

SONIA [*calling*]: Victor! You haven't forgotten?

VICTOR: Noa, noa, lass! You wouldn't believe it but when there's no one in the house she's a changed woman. Becomes visibly younger, playful and tender. You know how it is when some people are angry, they turn, well, ugly. Their face collapses. Get defeated by their own irritation, become heavy, vicious. She even treats *me* like a stranger then. But when they leave she's full of outrage and she's magnificent. I love her! Even that massive bulk of hers moves elegantly. Now she's heavy as a landslide because a gaggle of old colleagues are due in half an hour – God knows what for.

MAURICE: Is that my cue to go?

VICTOR: Good God, no! Just wait out here while I change. I'm not letting *that* lot see me in bedclothes.

> [VICTOR *leaves and returns to bedroom.* MAURICE *sits back with eyes closed and takes in the sun.*
>
> SONIA *comes, collects cups and saucers in stern silence. As she is about to leave –*]

MAURICE [*exploding*]: Sonia, stop this. For Christ's sake. It's not an easy world and I'm far from being the most perfect of men but *you've* been given no cause to be so unfriendly. [*Pause*] Even if only because your husband needs our friendship you ought to show more grace.

[SONIA *is untouched. As she turns to go to the kitchen* MAURICE *grabs a scone from the tray getting his fingers sticky. With comic irritability he re-enters the lounge.*

*Meanwhile* VICTOR *calls* SONIA *to look at his drawing. She peers at the signature through the magnifying glass.*]

SONIA: Rushton?

VICTOR: What about Ruskin?

SONIA: Ruskin? *John Ruskin?* [*She peers again. She is pleased for him.*] Aren't you the lucky one!

[*He goes to his dressing.*

MAURICE *looks around the room. Sighs. Nonchalantly picks up a beautiful cut-glass wineglass, holds it up to the sunlight, twirls it round, reflects it on the palm of his hand, and is so pleased with it that his irritability fades.*

*He sits by the desk and swivels round and round until he catches sight of some familiar sheets of blue paper stuck in between the pages of a huge Oxford English Dictionary. Hesitantly, guiltily, he opens the book, lifts out the sheets, and begins to read aloud*]

MAURICE: 'The lilac is dead. Don't ask me how but its had a blight. Remember the lilac? We planted it forty-one years ago and uprooted it four times for four changes of house.

[SONIA's *voice merges into* MAURICE's]

It survived all those uprootings and now . . .

SONIA'S VOICE: I'd be lost without my garden.

[*Sunlight out in lounge.* SONIA *enters the garden. She wears garden gloves and is armed with secateurs which she uses to cut roses. Having carefully chosen about eight she returns to the kitchen, 'fills' a glass with water, snips the roses of excess foliage and arranges them. During which mime and sound of clicking the letter continues and, of course, sunlight comes to the kitchen*]

It's not just a place I potter around in you know. I think you think it is. 'Thank God she's occupied' you say to yourself. I bet. No, it's a place where I think my best thoughts, my *only* thoughts in fact even though they don't amount to many. And where I touch all manner of things like earth and leaves, squashed worms and stones and colours and fresh air and smells and winds and clouds and rain and sunlight and – the cycle of things. *You* used to be like that, loving the cycle of things. It's you I got it from. Remember how the lilac came? You brought it home one day and said we must start a garden. You'd got it from the old railway porter. It was a sucker and you told me, lilac cuttings were always suckers, from the roots not the branch. A thin thing it was with only a few whispery strands between living and dying. I didn't think it would take but you did and it started our garden off.

[*By now the 'flowers' are 'arranged'. She looks at her watch. The trade unionists will soon be here. She takes a highly polished copper tray. On it places five cut-glass sherry glasses, finds a bottle of sherry which she pours out into an exquisite cut-glass decanter. From this she meticulously measures out five just-adequate drinks. In fact in one she has put too much and sips the excess herself, which she likes, so she finishes it and has to measure another. Then, with the same care, she arranges in a neat spray ten sponge fingers around a willow pattern plate. Than, taking another glass of sherry for herself, she sits and waits. During which –*]

SONIA'S VOICE: What about those arguments we had? We had our first rows over our first garden. What shape it should be, what should grow in it, which way it should face. You would insist the sun came up in one place while I knew darn well it came up in another. So what did we do? Daft buggers we set the alarm to get up before sunrise. You were wrong of course. You've no idea how important it was to me to have been right about that. It was my first landmark. Gave me great confidence that did.

[LIGHTS UP *now on bedroom.* VICTOR *is looking through his wardrobe trying to decide which outfit to wear. To begin with he's enthusiastic about the quest, then with resignation, realizes he doesn't really care and settles for a light brown check suit with waistcoat. He takes off his dressing-gown, his pyjama top, puts on a shirt, his trousers, a tie, slowly, slowly . . . through all of which we've heard –*]

And as for the quarrels about what we should grow, well – I thought it would end our marriage. I wanted more vegies and you wanted more flowers. You said it wasn't a real saving to grow our own vegies, only an illusion. But you said, all right, we'll have more vegies only I had to keep accounts. You made me work out what it cost in seed and labour and I had to weigh all what grew and then check it with the price in markets and make a sum of it all. And I did it too. Worked all hours figuring it out. Mad people. But I loved it. Columns of figures all very neat, and grand headings. Looked very important. I got top marks at school for neatness. Loved it. And was I proud. I *was* proud. Gave me great pleasure and I was right. Again. It *did* pay to grow our own vegies. That was my second landmark. A huge garden. Planted everything in it bar the sun. When you insisted I learn to drive a car, that was a landmark. When you asked me to show the Italian delegation round London without you, that was a landmark. When you first went abroad for a fortnight and I carried my affairs and your affairs alone without you, that was a landmark. When you first put your head between my legs, that was a landmark . . . when . . .

[LIGHTS UP *sharply upon an embarrassed* MAURICE *who hurriedly pushes the sheets back into, and closes, the book.*

*At that same moment the house moves into action. A door-bell rings.* SONIA *rises and moves to lounge with sherry and flowers.* VICTOR, *dressed, braces himself and also moves towards lounge. Both* SONIA *and* MAURICE *register with shock how thin* VICTOR *looks in the clothes he's not worn for so long.* SONIA *moves to go to the door, but is stopped by* VICTOR *who sees nothing, is quite pleased with himself, in fact.*]

VICTOR: Don't rush. They can wait. One before they come?

[*Lifts a glass from the tray, raises it to them, and moves away.* MAURICE *and* SONIA *look at each other. The moment has brought them closer together. The front door-bell rings again.* SONIA *moves to answer door.*

BLACK OUT. *Sound of 'babelled conversation' on tape to carry over to –*

LIGHTS UP *on lounge, bedroom and kitchen.* VICTOR *sits exhausted in a lounge armchair.* MAURICE *tray in hand is in the kitchen with* SONIA.]

SONIA [*taking tray*]: He looked so thin.

MAURICE: It went well.

SONIA: Those clothes, they hang so – so pointlessly on him.

MAURICE: They came to ask if they could name a new trade union building in his name.

SONIA: So – alien on him.

MAURICE [*imitating*]: 'I'm fundamentally opposed to a building being named after anyone' [*Pause*] 'but I'd love to see myself made an exception of.' His performance was a joy.

SONIA: Oh aye! He could always perform for them.

MAURICE: 'On one condition' he said, 'that you assure and promise me a sum of money will be set aside for purchasing the paintings and prints of young artists to go on the walls. You've known it's been my passion to help young painters and civilize you barbarians.'

SONIA: Aye! Used to squeeze between their prejudices and bloody-mindedness like a political geigercounter. The rank and file loved him for it. Not the hierarchy, though. All they did was tire him out. Couldn't trust him. What! trust a man without political ambitions?

[*She goes to the lounge.* VICTOR *is raising himself with difficulty, she moves swiftly to help him*]

That's what they did, always. Drained you!

[*He kisses her hand as she helps him up. She withdraws it, speaking with kindly sternness as she guides him towards the bedroom. He mumbles affectionately, teasingly, under her chastisements.*]

Selfish men! You only ever surrounded yourself with selfish men who used you, built their careers on you and then left you. A once-and-only lifetime, wasted on them. Selfish men! [*Calling after them*] SELFISH MEN!

[VICTOR *turns to* MAURICE *who stands with briefcase in hand.*]

VICTOR: You're not going, are you?

MAURICE: I think you need to rest, dear friend.

VICTOR: Wait. Help me undress and then you can go. Ten minutes. What's ten minutes to you?

[MAURICE *appeals to* SONIA *with another look. She nods. Leaves, but kisses and, for the first time, smiles at him.*]

MAURICE: My first kiss from Sonia in months!

[*He helps* VICTOR *undress*]

VICTOR: She's always been like that. Anxious about abuse. Me, I never worry. Hell! It were a lonely life. In order to find one friend you had to let dozens abuse you, I reckoned. I always took it easy. Not her, though, she scowled. Let the lads come I always said, they ate a little, drank, lingered. *My* family's atmosphere was like that – open house. Not her's though. Give everything to the friends she loved, but *everything*. Mean as old socks to the rest.

[LIGHTS FADE.

LIGHTS UP *on kitchen and bedroom.* SONIA *is spreading out a newspaper on the table ready to polish brass. Puts on rubber gloves. Takes brass pieces and begins furiously and angrily polishing.*

MAURICE *patiently waits, watching* SONIA *and reading newspaper. A visitor is already with* VICTOR, *a young trade union official. Business talks are more or less over and he's looking at paintings.*]

VICTOR: And one last thing – before you go – while you're on strike losing your week's wages, which you can ill-afford, while you're being loyal and comradely and losing your wages do you know where your General Secretary is?

OFFICIAL: No, where?

VICTOR: In the bloody Canary Islands having a bloody holiday.

OFFICIAL: Bloody Canary Islands?

VICTOR: Yes, R.S. bloody D, your General bloody Secretary, having a bloody holiday and looking for a house to buy for himself out of union bloody funds for when he retires.

OFFICIAL: Bloody Canary Islands! Now isn't that just like R.S. bloody D. [*Referring to painting.*] It's nice.

VICTOR [*taking the painting from him*]: You're not appalled?

OFFICIAL: It's not a perfect world is it.

VICTOR: He's not appalled.

OFFICIAL: Aren't we being a little naive, Victor?

VICTOR: I think you'd better be off. I get tired.

OFFICIAL: Look Vic. We all know how it goes on and some of us aren't happy about it. But let's stick to the agenda, first things first. This wildcat strike. Trust me! The lads'll be interested in what I tell them you've said, you'll see, your advice is going to make great sense.

VICTOR: And I'd be obliged if you didn't misinterpret me.

OFFICIAL: Not me. They'll appreciate every word.

VICTOR: But not take any notice.

OFFICIAL: Ah well. The offer of advice and the taking of notice are two different things, as we all know.

VICTOR: As we do indeed all know.

OFFICIAL: But the lads will listen.

VICTOR: You promise me that?

OFFICIAL: Why shouldn't they? They're good lads. Bit opinionated, without thought sometimes, but you're something of a legend for them.

VICTOR: Unbelievable you mean!

OFFICIAL: They'll respect every word you said. I didn't tell them I was coming to see you, but it came to me, suddenly – ask Victor, he'll know the arguments to use for pointless strikes. I'm like that – impulsive. An idea strikes me? I'm away. Vroom! First from the pit. Vroom! Can't sleep at nights for the ideas that dance in me. Ask Victor – Vroom! Vic always knows.

VICTOR: Not always. Wish I did. Wish ideas danced in me. Vroom. Might've done more with me life, but –

OFFICIAL: More? Few people in the movement achieved more than you, Vic.

VICTOR: Yes, yes.

OFFICIAL: No, no! Don't sell yourself short. You're a yardstick for us young stars.

VICTOR: Please, I really do get tired.

OFFICIAL: Yes, of course, I do go on. But I want you to know, Vic, I'm your man in the office. Anything I can do –

VICTOR: Vroom.

OFFICIAL: Anything you want –

VICTOR: Thank you, thank you.

OFFICIAL: Ask me.

VICTOR: Yes.

OFFICIAL: I'm your man.

VICTOR: Good-bye then.

OFFICIAL: And I won't misinterpret you.

VICTOR: Of course not. Good-bye.

OFFICIAL: Someone else might've come. Taken your advice – twisted it to his own ends and given it the authority of your blessing.

VICTOR: Oh?

OFFICIAL: Not me, though.

VICTOR: Good.

OFFICIAL: I am the best person. The doctor did say blood pressure?

VICTOR: Aye, blood pressure.

OFFICIAL: I mean, we've got our own hospital, Vic. A great team of specialists to . . .

VICTOR: I know. I did help found it!

OFFICIAL: Of course. Good-bye then. Are you sure . . .? Keep well now. If you . . . Don't do anything rash.

[VICTOR *thankfully grabs the hand offered him. The* OFFICIAL *has to leave. On his way out* . . .]

The paintings read well. [*Pauses at the door and turns.*] Vroom! [*Then in the hallway calls to* SONIA] Good-bye then, Mrs Em.

SONIA: Oh, he knew he had to go, then!

[*The* OFFICIAL *pauses, waiting for her to come and see him out. She doesn't move*]

OFFICIAL: No, don't bother. I'll see myself out. [*Pause*] He's looking very well, so don't you worry. [*Pause*] Anything we can do don't you forget to contact us and we'll –

SONIA: Don't forget to close the door firmly when you go out.

[*He gives up. Leaves.* MAURICE *prepares a lemon barley water for* VICTOR.]

Patronizing little upstarts! Nothing can touch them. Watch him go back and say to his bumptious little colleagues 'Well I had a word with old Vic and he agreed with me this and he agreed with me that!' Bloody little opportunist! Unioncrats I call them. Rattie-catties. That's it, Maurice, take him his drink, he'll be needing it after that demoralizing encounter. Here. [*Reaches for brandy to lace drink.*]

[LIGHTS DOWN *on kitchen.* SONIA *slides to her place behind the desk in the lounge.* MAURICE *takes tray up into bedroom.* VICTOR *is scrutinizing his drawing through a huge magnifying glass.*]

VICTOR: My bloody eyesight's going. They told me that would go. Jesus Christ! I just have to sit here and watch myself disintegrate. But you know, Maurice, I think it *is* a Ruskin. Look, compare it with this facsimile of his signature. It's shakier than the other, that's all. Mine's an early sketch, but . . . Now how in hell did it get to New Bedford I wonder? *There's* a story for someone. What lives were wrapped around the voyage of that, eh?

MAURICE: Who was the badly-dressed, smart young man?

VICTOR: A young 'father' from one of the printing chapels. They want to come out on a token sympathy strike with the footplate men. [*Smells drink*] Whose birthday, luv? You know what the *real* problem is of industrial relations? To sort out the true militants from the holiday-makers. There's a lot of them. And they're bullies with it. Cheap Chicago-style mobsters. When I told that fellow his union boss was buying himself a house in the Canary Islands out of union funds you know what he did? You won't believe it – he grinned and he nudged me and he said 'Now isn't that just like R.S.D.!' Admired it! He admired his union boss being like all the employers so's to show they could screw their way into power and affluence same as them! Doesn't that depress you? Depresses the hell out of me. Can't win now, Maurice. Capitalism has created an enemy in its own image, monstrous as itself. [*Pause*] Hurts. What a mess, eh? What a waste. What a life! [*Pause*] Would you get the Ruskin framed for me, please?

MAURICE: Surely.

VICTOR: For Sonia.

[*Both men realize they're looking at the made-up bed with its dazzling white sheets and high-stacked white pillows.*]

I mean, sometimes I feel guilty for dozing on it of an afternoon. I fear she might come up and change it *twice* a day.

[VICTOR *picks up top blanket and wraps it round his shoulders, as if for comfort. It's obvious* VICTOR *wants to say something special.* MAURICE *waits*]

They want me in hospital. A few days, week maybe, for preliminary tests, you know the sort of thing. Think they may have found a new drug.

MAURICE: Found a new drug! What good news! Why look so down? Don't you know what scientists can do these days?

VICTOR: You think so? Well, I could more easily bring myself to believe in the possibility of a cure than an after-life.

MAURICE: You still dwelling on such morbid prospects?

VICTOR: Even if I'm cured, Maurice lad, it won't ever stop me thinking about the after-life. Been too near to leave off contemplating it now. Here.

[*He gives* MAURICE *one letter on blue paper and holds on to another*]

VICTOR: Two arrived in one day. How about that?

[MAURICE *reads.* LIGHTS UP *in lounge from where* SONIA *reads aloud.*]

SONIA: On the day we got married I thought you hated me. I must tell you that, because it's the only time I've ever seen hate in your eyes.

VICTOR: She wrote one, sealed the envelope, wrote another and *didn't* open the first to put them together, no! Posted them separately! Do you think there's something wrong in her blood also?

SONIA: What am I doing marrying a man who hates me, I thought to myself? You were so silent, so angry. But afterwards – well – I didn't ever say but I used never to be able to take my eyes off you.

VICTOR [*complaining*]: When can *I* remember?

SONIA: No one had ever been so tender *and* certain.

VICTOR: I can't remember things.

SONIA: And you used to sing.

VICTOR: She *used* to laugh a lot.

SONIA: Once a visitor came from abroad –

VICTOR: In the early days.

SONIA: I can't remember where, France . . . I think . . . and he said to me 'Good God, there's someone who can still sing.'

VICTOR: In the early days she used to laugh a great deal. At predicaments!

SONIA: Our son sang also.

VICTOR: When an innocent bystander was caught up in someone else's confusion – that! That amused her.

SONIA: I remember we'd wake and find him standing up in his cot looking down on us, not crying, not murmuring, nor nothing, just patiently waiting for us to wake up. And when we did he was the first thing we looked at and he knew it and waited for it and then gave us a slow smile and started to hum. Nearly every morning was like that.

VICTOR: Once, when she was learning to drive, she came out of a side-turning too quickly and another car, coming across our path and with the right of way to pass straight in front of us, was forced to turn right into the street opposite us, which he did and went straight on. God knows why he didn't stop and tell her off. And she laughed! She laughed till she ached. 'He didn't want to go down that street', she kept saying. 'Poor man! He was on his way to one place and now he's got to go somewhere else!'

SONIA: You were daft about our son.

VICTOR: That *did* amuse her that did. Laughed till tears came. And she looked beautiful with it.

SONIA: Wanted him to be a composer.

VICTOR: I remember. Radiant.

SONIA: You used to play classical records in the bedroom while he was asleep. 'It's best it sinks into him unconsciously', you said. Weird theories you had. You wouldn't ever *tell* him to think of music as a career, that would put him off, but if it went in . . . if it went in . . . [SONIA *leaves off writing and reaches for the Shorter Oxford Dictionary*] . . . now what was that word he used? Began with an S. [*flicks pages*] P, Q, R, S. S! 'S' what? 'S' 'i'? 'Siderite' – a steel coloured stone. Well it wasn't that. 'Sibilate' – to hiss. It wasn't that either. What a lot of lovely words. 'Solatium' – a sum of money paid for injured feelings. 'Solazzi' – a stick of liquorice. Liquorice? I always thought the word was lickerish. I'm sure it was. [*Looking back to the 'l's*] 'Lichen, lichgate, licit, lick, lickpenny', ah! 'Lickerish! To be good like a cook at preparing dainties, stopped using in 1600, used likerous instead.' Did they, now! And what else have I been missing all these years I wonder. Huh! [*Flicks back to 'S's*] Ah ha! Subliminal! That was it! Subliminally! [*Turns back to letter*] That would put him off. But if it went in subliminally . . .

[*She continues writing a few seconds in silence, tongue out, then we hear voice over*]

There! See what writing to you does for me?

[SONIA *puts sheets between pages of the dictionary. Moves to kitchen where she continues with polishing the brass.* LIGHTS UP *on kitchen during which we hear her voice over continuing*]

SONIA'S VOICE: Where was I? Music! There was one day, my God don't I remember that day, the children must've been about nine and eleven and you took us up a climb on the Peaks. Dangerous old route you took us. *You* were scared too. You won't remember it but you got us on to a tricky part where you had to go back and forwards across a gap four times in order to help me and the children, and you were sweating. The children thought it was great fun. They would. You would never let them be frightened of anything. Not always a good thing I thought. Still, I remember

that trip for three reasons. The dangerous climb was one. The other
was you letting out by accident that you'd had a girl-friend before
me who'd climbed with you on that same walk. You blushed when
you realized it'd been let out. In fact I wasn't sure if you were talking about a girl-friend before me or *after* me ... And the third
thing was the song we sang at the top when we got there.

[*Voices singing – the family, adults and children, forming a background
to –*]

We ate sandwiches and there was a big wind and you cried out like
a madman 'we must sing against the wind. Good for the lungs and
the spirit.' So you taught us a round. The words were:

> By the waters, the waters of Babylon
> We lay down and wept and wept
> For these I am.
> Thee remember thee remember thee remember
> These I am.

[SONIA *carries the brass objects – candlesticks, trays, ashtrays, horse-
brasses etc. – to the lounge where a shaft of light catches her thoughtfully
and lovingly laying them out. Possibly in a new order.*]

What did it mean? I never knew what it meant. Not all this time.
'We wept for these I am.' What *are* 'these I am'? Do you think
you got it wrong? We all used to get songs wrong as children.
I used to think it was 'Good King Wences last looked out,' instead
of 'Good King Wenceslas looked out'. Perhaps it should have been
'thee Zion'. Perhaps we should have wept 'for thee Zion'. Or
no –

[*She catches sight of her reflection in a brass tray, holds it up and sadly
looks at herself as if in a mirror.*]

– now I come to think of it, you were probably right after all and
we wept because I am these things, we are these things, all are these
things.

[*Singing finishes.* LIGHTS OUT *on lounge.* UP *in bedroom*]

VICTOR: I could only remember the hair-raising climb. Nothing
else.

MAURICE: They're getting better. Each one more fluent than the
last. It's obviously giving her great pleasure to write them.

VICTOR: More fluent and madder. In this one she wants us to go on holiday to visit the children.

MAURICE: So?

VICTOR: So? So? All the way up to the Orkneys to see Graeme doing research on God-knows what? Thank you! Here, help me make the bed, please.

[*Both men do it very expertly and neatly, both having been in the forces, stripping it completely and putting it together with corner folds*] And we don't even know where Hilda and her husband are, some archaeological dig somewhere. [*Reading from letter*] 'What's the good of all those savings to us when we're too old to use it that's what I say and *you* should say it too.' She's mad! We've got no savings. A few hundred pounds! Travel! Ha!

MAURICE: She's not simply talking about travel, she's talking about plans to do things and it seems to me that on this hope of a new drug ...

VICTOR [*angry despair*]: *What* new drug? It's not been tried yet. It might be 'that old drug'. And *what* plans? I've *got* plans. I want to write this book. What should I want to travel for? Haven't I done enough of that sort of thing? I'm tired now. Stupid woman! [*Pause*] She hated me being a trade union leader you know. Hated it. Man as a political or social animal she could never understand. Men were good or bad, selfish or generous, sensible or idiots, never victims. Discussion, debate, the consideration of political principles – a foreign language! And it used to make her so angry that I was tied up in it all, she deliberately crept into the background. The years from forty to fifty were the worst. Like strangers we were. Hardly spoke. Terrible time, that. At least for us. But not – funny, this – not for *her*. She seemed to grow. In confidence, cockiness, independence – some bloody thing or other. Grow, mature, take over. Aye, that was it, she took over, all but me General Secretaryship, became another woman, formidable, a huge presence. [*Pause*] Here, a few more notes for that bloody book. They're no good and it's a waste of everybody's time but could you keep the illusion going for me and have them typed, please?

[MAURICE *flicks through notes*]

MAURICE: Escher? The Dutch Artist? You're poking about in the obscure corners of the art world. Taken a liking to him?

VICTOR [*wearily*]: No, I haven't taken a liking to him, and he's no longer an obscure artist. In fact there's quite a cult growing up around him. Unhealthy it seems to me. Read it. Or don't read it. Whatever you like.

MAURICE [*reading*]: 'Escher delights in the cheatability of perspective.' 'Cheatability'?

VICTOR [*mischievously grinning*]: Why not?

MAURICE [*continuing reading*]: 'He seems unmoved by what moves man to contort his body or arrange the bones in his face. There's no face weeping, no eyes laughing, no body leaping, no figure suffering. Only the sterile, geometric shapes of life seem to obsess him, not life itself.' [*Pause*] You're a very remarkable man, Victor, Ruskin would have been proud of you. Wasted on union matters.

VICTOR: Wasted? You think so? You're charitable. But the men had to be protected. You should have seen some of the employers I had to protect them from. Wished they hadn't needed protection, looked after their own bloody selves. But there it is. Done now.

[*Sound of Janacek Sinfonietta.*

   LIGHTS UP *on lounge.* SONIA *has the radio on. She turns it up loudly, it's near the end, the most vibrant part, a passage full of tall mountains and echoes*]

MAURICE: What's that?

VICTOR: My mad wife. Whenever she hears a bit of music she likes she turns it up loudly so's I can hear it also.

[*They listen a moment.*]

MAURICE: Janacek.

VICTOR: Who?

MAURICE: Czeck composer.

VICTOR: Oh.

[MAURICE *prepares to leave.*]

VICTOR: Don't neglect me, Maurice, don't forget your old friend.

[MAURICE *reassuringly squeezes his friend's shoulder, and leaves.*

   *He pauses at a point between a rapt* SONIA *listening to the music in the lounge and a dejected* VICTOR, *slouched, utterly miserable, in his bedroom*]

MAURICE [*closing his eyes*]: It's not me, not me! Thank God it's not me, thank God it's not me.

[*Then ashamed and depressed he covers his face with his hands. The music rises to a crescendo as a rear flat rises and a platform glides forward carrying a hospital bed on it, moving in like the crematorium box moves out.* VICTOR *rises to meet it, as to meet death, gets into bed. Lights and music fade.*

LIGHTS UP *on a hospital bed. No glaring white cushions here, starched crisp with love and protection. A metallic thing, of cleanliness only.*

VICTOR *sitting up in bed.* MAURICE *standing by, opening a brief-case*]

VICTOR: It's going to be a long bloody job. Longer'n I thought. Longer'n they told me, in fact.

MAURICE [*handing him a folder*]: Your notes, typed.

VICTOR [*sitting up to look at them*]: Oh, aye.

[*He reaches for his glasses. They're of no use. Then his enormous magnifying glass*]

No good. It's no good. I'm going blind. Oh bloody Christ! Maurice!

MAURICE: They're good notes, Victor. Fine. Some things I don't agree with, you'd expect that, but it has the makings of a unique little book on art, I promise you.

[*Pause*]

VICTOR: *You* don't believe in God, do you, professor?

MAURICE: I don't really think I can.

VICTOR: Right! You can't. Nor can't I. But the ceasing forever of all this [*Knocks angrily on his skull*] . . . *that* doesn't make sense either. [*Pause*] Of course there are *some* people to whom it makes ecstatic sense, but they're a type, the put-downers I call them. Any bloody opportunity they get, they enjoy putting men down. They have a special tone of voice, the kind of voice that rubs its hands together. 'Look at the ocean' they cry, 'see what a little thing is man in all that sea!' And when space-rockets came they had a real ball. 'Look at all those stars. How insignificant is man now!' Instead of marvelling that man could make it to the bloody moon they found it another opportunity to put him down. And now there's those stupid computers. Oh how they do love putting men down because they can't store up facts mechanically. But a computer's a poor thing compared to a brain isn't it? I mean, bloody hell! I'm no scientist but even *I* know that. Can't store a shred of what the brain can. But on they go. The putdowners! Of which I mercifully have never been one. So it doesn't make sense. It just doesn't make sense. I *know* it's going to happen and nothing's ever stopped it happening, but it just doesn't make sense. It's so – so unjust. No reason for it. I mean what've I done to have all those bloody marvellous things taken away from me? What? What, what, what for Christ's sake? [*Pause*] Daft bugger, me!

[MAURICE *finds the outburst almost unbearable. An unhappy* VICTOR *gives him a letter on blue paper to read, then turns away.*

LIGHTS DOWN *on hospital bed.* UP *on kitchen.* SONIA *is preparing a jar of fresh fruit slices for* VICTOR. *The operation is made up of precise movements* (*see note at end of play*) *which she deftly and lovingly carries out, compelling attention, during which –*]

SONIA'S VOICE: You took me and you shaped me and you gave me form. Not a form I couldn't be but the form I was meant to be. You needed only to be in the house and I felt my life and the lives of the children I cherished could never go wrong. It was so. They never did go wrong. They have confidence and pity and daring in them. And in me there are flowers. Blossoming all the time. Explosions of colour and energy. You see it, surely? Surely you see it? Or feel it? There's nothing I couldn't do. In me is you. All you've given me. I've been a white sheet, a large white canvas and you've drawn the world upon me, given outline to what was mysterious and frightening in me. Do you *know* how proud I've been of you? Do you know I've felt myself beautiful only because *you* chose me? Do you know that I've shuddered with pleasure to think you love me? You are my rock my hero my love. I feel such strength. Do you know these things?

[LIGHTS DOWN *on kitchen.* UP *on hospital bed.* VICTOR *now has a blood-drip attached to his arm, he's very much weaker.* MAURICE *sits beside him.*]

VICTOR: Have to renew it every three hours. Stop the flow and I die. Look at it! A bottle of someone else's blood, just that red stuff in there to keep me able to see you and talk and think ... and remember and reason. [*He shifts a little*] Bloody bed-sores. I've got a rubber ring under my backside but it makes no odds. Lying horizontal still stops the blood circulating! [*Pause*] This is it, Maurice, isn't it? Oh, don't protest, lad. I don't think I mind now all that much. Like your mother. I understand her. In fact, I've got back me curiosity. [*Pause*] You know what helped? I woke up the other day and suddenly out of the blue, no connection with anything, I thought: Leonardo Da Vinci is dead. And that seemed reassuring. So I went on: Mozart is dead. Socrates is dead, Shakespeare, Buddha, Jesus, Gandhi, Marx, Keir Hardie – they're all dead. And one day Sonia will die. And my son, Graeme, he'll be dead, and my daughter Hilda, and their son, Jake, and so will all the grand-children ... And there seemed a great unity to it all. A great simplicity. Comforting.

[*He pauses.* MAURICE *is greatly distressed and* VICTOR *can see it. He offers a reassuring smile*]

VICTOR: Poor Maurice. Here.

[*Hands him a letter on blue paper*]

SONIA'S VOICE: Oh my beloved, my dearest dearest one. I have *adored* you. Do you know that? That I am full of you – do you? Know it? Know it? That I feel you there as I've felt my children in me, your blood in my blood, rivers of you, do you know it? Do you? Do you?

[LIGHTS DOWN *on hospital bed,* UP *in bedroom. A lost, lonely* SONIA *is in the middle of the room, looking around for what to do. She moves slowly to turn back a corner of the bedcover, as though preparing the bed for the return of its occupant. Achingly she moves from one pointless tidying action to the next during which –*]

The sound of your voice, your judgements, your praise, your love, your pity – all in me, do you know it? My darling, Oh my darling. Nothing has been wrong for me and nothing will be. I will give you my everything, cut from me my everything – all my body's everything. To flow in you ... What nonsense do I write instead of just I love you and I always have loved you? But I must catch up on too much silence. So this nonsense, this silliness, this too-much-writing-and-talking-and-shouting is all for you because I can trust it all and anything to you. Don't you know now what I feel? Can't you feel what I feel, mad old woman that I am now? Can't you understand I'd rip myself apart for you, Oh my beloved, Oh my sweet sweet sweetest one. Why am I so clumsy, never graceful as you deserved. Wretched body, wretched heart, dull old mind. not any part of me good enough for you I know but Oh I love you love you love you Oh my Victor Victor, love you, Victor, love you, Oh my Victor my heart.

[*She has stopped by the framed Ruskin. She has been holding back too long. Now she weeps.*

FADE LIGHTS. LIGHTS UP *on hospital bed.* VICTOR *lies still, he seems to be staring into space.* MAURICE *sits in a chair at his side, leaning forward wretchedly, head in hands, elbows on knees. It's as though he's imagined* VICTOR *was asleep and is waiting for him to wake up. This image, of friend in attendance to dear friend, is held for many seconds, until –*]

SONIA'S VOICE: There will be, my darling one, I know it, a blinding light –

[*At which* MAURICE *starts up and stands at once to look at* VICTOR. *He touches his face. He is dead.*

MAURICE *takes his friend's hand, slowly sits, and presses it to his lips.*

*As he sits down the* LIGHTS GO UP *slowly on* SONIA *who is putting on a black coat. She then ties a black silk scarf over her head, picks up a holdall and moves to the hospital bed.*

MAURICE *rises to her. Both look down on her husband. Then she begins to gather together his belongings, folding each item very carefully. Shirt, trousers, jacket, cardigan, tie, socks, shoes . . . and places them in the holdall.*

*Then, having kissed him, she closes his eyes. During which –*]
– a painful light when suddenly the lie will fall away from truth. Everything will make its own and lovely sense, trust me, trust me. It won't be logical or happy, this sense, but clear. Everything will become clear. Trust me. Contradictions won't cease to be contradictions, I don't say that, but nor will they any longer confuse. I'm not promising all will seem to have been good, but evil won't bewilder you as it once did. Trust me, I adore you. And with this

blinding light will come an ending to all pain. The body's pain the heart's pain the pain in your soul. All in a second. Less than a second. Less than less than a second. I'm sure of it. That's how it will be for us all, I've always known it. No matter how it happens to us. Accident, torture ... suddenly at the top of our energies, quietly in bed. There will come this flash, this light of a colour we've never seen before. It's a glorious moment beloved. Even for the simpleton, even for him, his foolishness falls away just as from the madman his madness falls away. In the instant they know death so they know truth. In the blinding light of truth they know death. One and the same. I promise you, trust me, love O my love O my Victor O my heart.

**FADE OUT**

# CUTTING THE FRUIT

A board, a large very sharp knife, a bowl, and large oranges.

The fruit is laid on its side, topped, swivelled round, the other end topped. Then it's stood on its end and the knife is run in a curve from the top to the bottom, judging the cut to slice off both the peel and the inner skin. After the first slice it's easy to see where the next cut should come. When all the peel is off then the ribbing between which each segment of fruit sits can be seen. The fruit is lifted into one hand on its side and the knife used to cut down alongside each rib of inner skin so that each segment comes cleanly away into the bowl, leaving the skeleton of the skin. Squeeze the remaining juice into the bowl.

Practice will make perfect. The actions must be swift from expertise. Confident. The knife must be sharp. The oranges must be large. Some oranges are better for this operation than others. To make the scene compelling it is worth looking for the right orange.

## NOTES ON THE LETTERS

Here are my reasons for conceiving the letters as voice-over and not spoken by the actress.

Sonia's letters are unexpected. They must surprise us. It must not seem possible that such a woman could be writing them. This dichotomy is central to the play and should be emphasized. Sonia should be engrossed in the details of keeping the house functioning while her other persona emerges through the letters. The character and the first letter are like strangers. As the play evolves, they move closer together to become, magnificently, one and the same.

There are two other reasons for the actress not speaking the letters: to look for actions to be silently carried out, to fill the stage with a mute but living presence is a greater challenge for both actress and director.

Besides, an element of the absurd occurs if the actress has to deliver the last three letters live, especially the final one which would end being addressed to her husband who lies dead before her.

A word about their rendering. A rough guide is that we are hearing the letters as though she had written them and was now reading them back to herself aloud. Therefore they are more radio than theatre. They come through with more simplicity than theatricality. Punctuation should be carefully followed to achieve the rhythm of their construction.

This is not to say they must be delivered blandly but more for their narrative than their emotion. Emotion, as we know, follows from meaning. The exceptions are the last three letters which take off and possess a greater degree of intensity. But even then only one of them, the penultimate one, moves into pure emotion. In this one, and this one only, Sonia loses control. Not that she weeps her way through the entire letter – she weeps only at the end – but the words flow very swiftly, tumbling out. It is the one time that the 'center does not hold.'

So, the last three letters could be described thus: first – calm but urgent; the second – spinning out of control; the last – strength returned, magnificent, regal.

# FOR THE BEST IN PAPERBACKS, LOOK FOR THE 🐧

In every corner of the world, on every subject under the sun, Penguin represents quality and variety – the very best in publishing today.

For complete information about books available from Penguin – including Puffins, Penguin Classics and Arkana – and how to order them, write to us at the appropriate address below. Please note that for copyright reasons the selection of books varies from country to country.

---

**In the United Kingdom:** Please write to *Dept E.P., Penguin Books Ltd, Harmondsworth, Middlesex, UB7 0DA.*

If you have any difficulty in obtaining a title, please send your order with the correct money, plus ten per cent for postage and packaging, to *PO Box No 11, West Drayton, Middlesex*

**In the United States:** Please write to *Dept BA, Penguin, 299 Murray Hill Parkway, East Rutherford, New Jersey 07073*

**In Canada:** Please write to *Penguin Books Canada Ltd, 2801 John Street, Markham, Ontario L3R 1B4*

**In Australia:** Please write to the *Marketing Department, Penguin Books Australia Ltd, P.O. Box 257, Ringwood, Victoria 3134*

**In New Zealand:** Please write to the *Marketing Department, Penguin Books (NZ) Ltd, Private Bag, Takapuna, Auckland 9*

**In India:** Please write to *Penguin Overseas Ltd, 706 Eros Apartments, 56 Nehru Place, New Delhi, 110019*

**In the Netherlands:** Please write to *Penguin Books Netherlands B.V., Postbus 195, NL–1380AD Weesp*

**In West Germany:** Please write to *Penguin Books Ltd, Friedrichstrasse 10–12, D–6000 Frankfurt Main 1*

**In Spain:** Please write to *Longman Penguin España, Calle San Nicolas 15, E–28013 Madrid*

**In Italy:** Please write to *Penguin Italia s.r.l., Via Como 4, I-20096 Pioltello (Milano)*

**In France:** Please write to *Penguin Books Ltd, 39 Rue de Montmorency, F-75003 Paris*

**In Japan:** Please write to *Longman Penguin Japan Co Ltd, Yamaguchi Building, 2–12–9 Kanda Jimbocho, Chiyoda-Ku, Tokyo 101*

**Volume 1: The Wesker Trilogy**
Chicken Soup with Barley/Roots/I'm Talking About
Jerusalem

'A trilogy which will act as a monument to its era' – Robert
Muller in the *Daily Mail*

'The passion of Mrs Wesker's themes is matched by the
living fire in his writing . . . its quality is undiminished by
the passing years' – Bernard Levin

'Magnificently indestructible' – Francis King in the *Sunday
Telegraph*

'This remarkable experiment . . . is very funny, very personal, very touching, very bright, very lively, very human
and very beautifully written' – *Daily Express*

*Over 350,000 copies sold.*

**Volume 4: Shylock and Other Plays**
The Journalists/The Wedding Feasts/Shylock

THE JOURNALISTS
'There's no denying the play's originality of form or richness of content' – Michael Billington in the *Guardian*

THE WEDDING FEAST
'One of the most devastating developments I have experienced in the theatre' – Gerard Dempsy in the *Daily Express*

SHYLOCK
'A thoroughly original work, with Shakespeare's words surfacing only briefly, and adroitly, among the elegant speeches that are typical of Mr Wesker . . . a play that works as an ingenious theatrical puzzle . . . a passionate document' – Ned Chaillet in *The Times*

'Perhaps Wesker's finest play' – Clive Barnes in *The Times*

*also published or forthcoming*
**Volume Two: The Kitchen/The Four Seasons/Their Very Own and Golden City**

**Volume Five: One Woman Plays**
Yardsdale/Whatever Happened to Betty Lemon?/Four Portraits of Mothers/The Mistress/Annie Wobbler

**Volume Six: Lady Othello/One More Ride on the Merry Go Round/Caritas/When God Wanted a Son**